The Five Phases of Project Management

The following lists the tasks completed in the five phases of project management and the rules you should keep in mind to get things done on time and within budget.

Phase 1. Initiating
- ➤ Recognizing that a project is worth doing
- ➤ Determining what the project should accomplish
- ➤ Defining the overall project goal
- ➤ Defining general expectations of customers, management, or other stakeholders as appropriate
- ➤ Defining the general project scope
- ➤ Selecting initial members of the project team

Phase 2. Planning
- ➤ Refining the project scope, which includes identifying the balance required among results, time, and resources
- ➤ Listing tasks and activities that will lead to achieving the project goals
- ➤ Sequencing activities in the most efficient manner possible
- ➤ Developing a workable schedule and budget for assigning resources to the activities required to complete the project
- ➤ Getting the plan approved by the appropriate stakeholders

Phase 3. Executing
- ➤ Leading the team
- ➤ Meeting with team members
- ➤ Communicating with stakeholders
- ➤ Fire fighting (also known as conflict resolution) to resolve problems that always arise during a project
- ➤ Securing necessary resources (money, people, equipment) to carry out the project plan

Phase 4. Controlling
- ➤ Monitoring deviation from the plan
- ➤ Taking corrective action to match progress with the plan
- ➤ Receiving and evaluating project changes requested from stakeholders and team members
- ➤ Rescheduling the project as necessary
- ➤ Adapting resource levels as necessary
- ➤ Changing (usually cutting) the project scope
- ➤ Returning to the planning stage to make adjustments to the project goals and get them approved by the stakeholders

Phase 5. Closing
- ➤ Shutting down the operations and disbanding the team
- ➤ Learning from the project experience
- ➤ Reviewing the project process and outcomes with team members and stakeholders
- ➤ Writing a final project report

The 12 Golden Rules of Project Management Success

1. Thou Shalt Gain Consensus on Project Outcomes.
2. Thou Shalt Build the Best Team You Can.
3. Thou Shalt Develop a Comprehensive, Viable Plan and Keep It Up-to-Date.
4. Thou Shalt Determine How Much Stuff You Really Need to Get Things Done.
5. Thou Shalt Have a Realistic Schedule.
6. Thou Shalt Not Try to Do More than Can Be Done.
7. Thou Shalt Remember that People Count.
8. Thou Shalt Gain the Formal and Ongoing Support of Management and Stakeholders.
9. Thou Shalt be Willing to Change.
10. Thou Shalt Keep People Informed of What You're Up To.
11. Thou Shalt Be Willing to Try New Things.
12. Thou Shalt Become a Leader as Well as a Manager.

Conventions for a Network Diagram

21

12		
This is a Task		A rectangular box indicates a task. The number in the top right is the duration of the task. The number at the left is the task number, used for tracking.

This is a Milestone

A box with rounded corners is a milestone. Milestones do not have a duration like a task because they represent the completion of a series of tasks.

Precedence is indicated by the sequence of tasks joined with a line and an arrow.

Concurrent tasks are shown in the same vertical plane and are not connected by lines and arrows.

Two tasks that must be completed before a third task can begin look like this.

CONVENTIONS FOR A NETWORK DIAGRAM

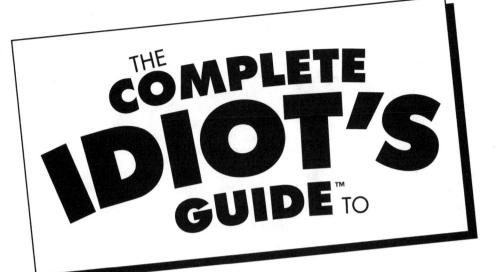

THE COMPLETE IDIOT'S GUIDE™ TO

Project Management

by Sunny and Kim Baker

alpha books

A Division of Macmillan General Reference
A Simon and Schuster Macmillan Company
1633 Broadway
New York, NY 10019-6785

Macmillan Publishing books may be purchased for business or sales promotional use. For information please write: Special Markets Department, Macmillan Publishing USA, 1633 Broadway, New York, NY 10019.

THE COMPLETE IDIOT'S GUIDE name and design are trademarks of Macmillan, Inc.

International Standard Book Number: 0-02-861745-2
Library of Congress Catalog Card Number: 97-071187

00 99 98   8 7 6 5 4 3

Interpretation of the printing code: the rightmost number of the first series of numbers is the year of the book's printing; the rightmost number of the second series of numbers is the number of the book's printing. For example, a printing code of 98-1 shows that the first printing occurred in 1998.

Printed in the United States of America

Brand Manager
Kathy Nebenhaus

Director of Editorial Services
Brian Phair

Executive Editor
Gary M. Krebs

Managing Editor
Bob Shuman

Senior Editor
Nancy Mikhail

Development Editor
Jennifer Perillo

Editorial Assistant
Maureen Horn

Editor
Matthew X. Kiernan

Production Editor
Mark Enochs

Copy Editors
Susan Aufheimer, Theresa Mathias, Lynn Northrup

Cartoonist
Judd Winick

Book Designer
Glenn Larsen

Cover Designer
Michael Freeland

Indexer
Nadia Ibrahim

Production Team
Kim Cofer, Tricia Flodder, Mary Hunt

Contents at a Glance

Contents

Part 3: The Project Planning Phase   71

9 The Breakdown of Tasks: What Really Needs to Be Done?   73

10 The Network Diagram: A Map for Your Project   85

Foreword

Project management isn't just for construction engineers and military logistics experts any more.

Consider the case known in my circle as "The Wedding from Hell." Two of my friends—a pair of the most organized managers I've ever met—once catered an out-of-town, afternoon wedding for a colleague. They spent days consulting with the bride and her mother, hiring bartenders and waiters, lining up transportation, and buying and preparing the food, all in addition to handling their busy jobs at a major arts institution. Then, at noon on Friday, the day before the big event, they received a phone call from another colleague. "I have some bad news about the wedding," he said. "It's *today*."

The wedding still took place, with dinner only an hour late. Not bad, considering that when they arrived at what had been promised was a fully stocked kitchen, there wasn't a pot or pan to be found anywhere, and they had to cook the vegetables in coffee percolators. But the moonlighting caterers paid a high price for their failure to manage the project properly. The mistake cost them their friendship with the bride, not to mention their fee. And they had to spend a fortune to dry clean their business suits. (Try making ceviche while driving 70 miles an hour up Interstate 95.)

"The Wedding from Hell" makes a good argument for project management. Like my friends the caterers, you may be taking on a project as a way to launch your own small business. Perhaps you have to organize a conference for your company's hundred biggest clients. Or your company asked you to open its new store on Madison Avenue or its regional sales office in Sioux Falls. You may even have been charged with reconfiguring your company's whole information system or developing a new product or service.

Top executives like to talk about how their strategy depends on their company's vision, mission and values. But when pressed, they admit that what really matters is their ability to execute—to get the job done flawlessly, under budget and on time. Without that ability, strategy is just wishful thinking. And great project management skills are essential to anyone who wants to put their strategy into action.

This book will teach you the nuts and bolts of project management, from setting priorities to controlling schedules and expenses to reporting on the results. Using plenty of humor and plain-spoken good sense, Kim and Sunny Baker tell you how to plan a project, set up and lead a team, monitor progress, and bring your project to a satisfying close. Along the way, you'll learn techniques for communicating with team members and anyone else with a stake in the project, resolving the inevitable conflicts, and handling any changes that come your way. Finally, you'll find out how to choose the right computer software to make project management easier.

Don't let all the planning, charting and reporting, that good project management demands scare you off. Even if you don't know a Gantt from a gnu, the tools this book offers will help you succeed in running any project.

You may still end up having to cope with the unexpected, but at least you won't end up with raw seafood all over your suit.

Miriam Leuchter
Editor
The Journal of Business Strategy

Miriam Leuchter is the editor of the *Journal of Business Strategy,* the bimonthly magazine for the corporate strategist, published by Faulkner & Gray in New York City. Before taking the helm at JBS, she served as its consulting editor, while running *Forecast,* the magazine of demographics and market strategy. She has also covered the banking industry and economic development for *Crain's New York Business,* and she has reported on personal finance, investing, taxes, and economic issues for *Money* magazine.

Introduction

Is rubbing the Magic 8 Ball your best shot at coming up with a project schedule? Does the word "budget" send chills up your spine? When your boss asks for a project status report, do you call the Psychic Network first? Do your project team meetings remind you of clown practice at Barnum and Bailey? Even worse, do you keep a copy of the "Help Wanted" ads in your "Action" file fearing that someone might find out what's really going on with the project? Well, you don't need to resort to psychics, magic, or wizardry to manage projects. And you don't need a genius IQ, or even an MBA, to succeed. What you need is this book, *The Complete Idiot's Guide to Project Management*!

It doesn't take a magician, a soothsayer, or a genius to manage a project, but it does take special skills to bring projects in on time and within budget. Yes, there's some planning and charting involved in getting projects from start to finish, but this book takes the complexity out of the process and puts you in control. The road to successful project management is mapped in the following pages.

The book explains in easy-to-understand language how the power of time-proven project management methods can help your mission-critical projects blast off to bring you and your company to new heights. You'll learn how project teams, in spite of politics and personalities, can be pointed in the same direction; and how changes, no matter how frequent, can be guided to keep projects on track. You'll learn that it's skill, not luck, that makes the difference in reaching your project destination.

How to Use This Book

The book has seven parts, which we recommend you read from beginning to end. To-gether, the parts demystify the steps and tools behind successful project management and offer practical advice that can be adapted to the needs of today's fast-moving, ever-changing organizations.

Part 1, "Project Management Power," explains how to identify projects that need better management. You'll be introduced to steps that can be used to bring any project to a successful conclusion, on time and within budget, and to the three secrets to success behind any project: the project manager, the team, and the plan.

Part 2, "The Project Initiation Phase," presents techniques to start a project off on the right foot with clear goals and a motivated project team. This part is especially important because the way a project starts off usually defines the way it will end up.

Part 3, "The Project Planning Phase," explains the basic planning processes central to successful project management. You'll observe how tasks are defined, scheduled, and budgeted using powerful charting and analysis tools that can help you scope out projects of all sorts and sizes. This is the most technical part of the book, so you might want to read it twice. Mastering the tools in this part is important because no project is ever better than the plan used to manage the effort.

Part 4, "The Executing Phase," presents proven techniques to transform the plan into action focused toward meeting the project objectives. This is key to successful project management. The end result of a project is always related to the way the plan is translated into actual work in the real world.

Part 5, "The Controlling Phase," talks about ways to monitor, track, and adjust each project so that you can keep everything on schedule and within budget. You'll also find easy-to-follow guidelines for dealing with the most common project problems and for minimizing the impact of the changes and conflicts that are part of almost every project. Using the techniques in this section, you can put even a totally derailed project back on track.

In Part 6, "The Closing Phase," you discover how to finish your project and reap the rewards of a job well done.

In Part 7, "The Final Chapter," you learn how project management software tools help you automate the process of planning and managing projects of all sizes.

Some Extras to Help You Out

Because successful project management depends on keeping track of lots of details, we've provided friendly, easy-to-read tips throughout the chapters to make key concepts easier to find. Look for the shaded boxes to discover important concepts, expert advice, and practical suggestions for managing your projects.

> **Project Lingo**
> These boxes define the most important concepts in project management. These are the words you should use in meetings to impress your boss and your co-workers.

> **Time Is Money**
> Use the suggestions in these boxes to keep your schedule up-to-date and your budget under control. Hopefully the advice will spare you the embarrassment of running out of money before the project is completed. You'll also pick up on a variety of tips used by veteran project managers to run projects of all sizes and kinds.

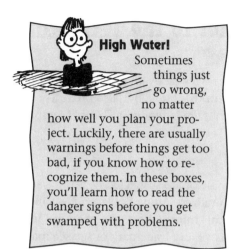

High Water!
Sometimes things just go wrong, no matter how well you plan your project. Luckily, there are usually warnings before things get too bad, if you know how to recognize them. In these boxes, you'll learn how to read the danger signs before you get swamped with problems.

Words from the Wise
These quotes and tips include observations from our experience and other experts that may help inspire you to greater achievements, or simply help keep you motivated to do your best, even when the project seems impossible.

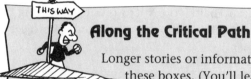

Along the Critical Path
Longer stories or information tangentially related to the text appear as these boxes. (You'll learn about critical path—an actual project management term—in Chapters 10 and 11.)

Acknowledgments

Over the years and through countless projects of all sizes, people too numerous to mention have offered advice, shared techniques, and provided examples (good and bad) that have helped us hone our skills as project managers. All of these people deserve our thanks, as they've taught us the ropes and provided us with models to copy (and avoid) as we bring our own projects from idea to fruition.

Regarding this project, the book, all of the people at Macmillan—editorial paragons, production wizards, and marketing gurus—deserve our special thanks for their professionalism, skill, and good ideas. We appreciate the opportunity to work with such a class act. We also want to express our gratitude to our agent, Mike Snell, who is always smart enough to see an opportunity that makes sense.

Most important, we want to thank you, the reader, for considering the tools and techniques we lay out in these pages. We understand the importance of your projects, and appreciate that you are taking time to consider our ideas for getting them done better, faster, and cheaper.

Special Thanks from the Publisher to the Technical Editor

The Complete Idiot's Guide to Project Management was reviewed by an expert who not only checked the technical accuracy of what you'll learn in this book, but also provided invaluable insight and suggestions. Our special thanks are extended to James MacIntyre.

Trademarks

All terms mentioned in this book that are known to be or are suspected of being trademarks or service marks have been appropriately capitalized. Alpha Books and Macmillan General Reference cannot attest to the accuracy of this information. Use of a term in this book should not be regarded as affecting the validity of any trademark or service mark.

The product examples in this chapter were produced in Microsoft® Project 4.1 for Windows® 95, courtesy of Microsoft Corporation. Thank you, Microsoft, for providing the software to create this chapter. The names of other companies that produce project management software are provided in Appendix B.

Part 1
Project Management Power

Meeting the demands of the fast-changing environment of modern business requires a focus on priorities, better management techniques, and effective structures for communication. For these reasons, people like you are turning to project management techniques to meet their goals. The process and methods of project management provide the structure, focus, flexibility, and control to help guide teams to outstanding results, on time and within budget.

In this section, you'll be introduced to the phases of the project management process and the success secrets of experienced project managers. You'll also learn how to differentiate among important projects and just plain work, the first step in consistently bringing your projects in on time and within budget. And if you can do that, you'll be quite a hero in your organization. That's the power of project management.

Projects, Projects Everywhere

The 21st century is here, along with tighter budgets, less time, and fewer resources. Sure, tele-transportation and faster-than-light travel are still *Star Trek* fantasies, but rapid change, expanding technologies, and global marketing are real in this, the new millennium.

To compete in the new century, you'll need to do more with less. Competition will continue to pressure you to come up with better ideas. You won't have time to waste on stale methods or wimpy techniques. To captain your business in the future, you'll need to build things faster, cheaper, and better. And you'll need to get things done right the first time.

But before you can use any of the advice in this book, you need to distinguish the projects in your business from the ordinary work. In this chapter, you'll not only learn how to recognize the projects in your business, but you also will see why projects need a special kind of management to get them done right. This will be the first step in taking your projects into the 21st century.

Project-Oriented Outlook

are responsible for ordinary work and projects. You
the difference. You just think you have too much to do.

too much to do. But people often fail at managing
lve too much work, but because the difference between
clear.

end for a moment that you're a salesperson at Spacely
ckets. You're already working full-time, day in and day
. Then your boss asks you to open the new sales office in
mond. Every day you respond to customer requests,
make sales presentations, and write trip reports after your
client visits. It's pretty easy to figure out that setting up a
new sales office is different than your day-to-day sales
activities. But what exactly is it that makes the job of
opening the sales office a project and the work with your
customers just plain work?

Both the project to build a sales office and the every day
work of contacting customers may involve similar activities,
such as making phone calls, writing reports, and going to
meetings, but projects have different goals than ongoing,
day-to-day job activities. You do a project only once and
when the project gets done, something exists that never
existed before. In this case, you'll have a new sales office.

techniques to
control a project
may seem like an
additional burden, but it saves
time and money in the long
term. Properly applied, PM
techniques allow you to hold
the project in the palm of
your hand rather than having
it swirling around like a
tempest in your brain as you
contemplate all the elements
involved.

All Projects Are Work, but Not All Work Is a Project

Here's another example. As the administrative assistant to the CEO, you might be responsible for coordinating the company's annual United Way fund-raising drive, but you'd
still be responsible for day-to-day activities, including writing minutes of board meetings,
scheduling appointments, screening mail, and a myriad of other recurring tasks. The
fund-raising drive is a project because it only gets done once a year and has a clear end
result—the deposit of a large sum of donations in the United Way fund account. The
ordinary calls, reports, and letters of your job just keep getting done, over and over, every
day. There is no end to the process.

To look at assignments as projects as opposed to just plain work, you need to change your
perspective. The goals and deadlines of the business routine are general. Routine work is
defined within the scope of a department or functional job description. For example, you
probably open your incoming mail every morning and respond to letters. You also might
read reports, schedule appointments, attend meetings, screen phone calls, draft letters, or
perform numerous other tasks. All this has to be coordinated and completed every day. As

much effort as this involves, none of these tasks are projects. They're all just ordinary work.

Most ordinary work is repetitive, process-oriented, and, yes, often boring. Projects usually are defined as specific end-results outside the routine job functions. Projects have a life of their own and, even though the successful completion and coordination of projects is critical to the success of an organization, projects generally operate outside the normal routine of business life.

It may not always seem fair, but you have to get your projects done in addition to your ordinary work. That's why you need some special tools to make it easier. Projects add excitement to an otherwise work-a-day business. They turn office/factory doldrums into new experiences.

Project Lingo
A *project* is a sequence of tasks with a beginning and an end that are bounded by time, resources, and desired results. This means that a project has a specific, desired outcome; a deadline or target date when the project must be done; and a budget that limits the amount of people, supplies, and money that can be used to complete the project.

Above and Beyond the Ordinary Work

To better understand the differences between ordinary work and projects, consider the lists that compare the two in the following table, which compares ordinary work and projects. Note that the projects all have definable goals. They also have a beginning and an end. Most ordinary work must be done over and over again. Most projects are done only once (if they're done right the first time).

Ordinary Work	Projects
Responding to a customer's request for information	Producing a monthly customer newsletter
Making coffee for the office	Catering the inaugural ceremonies for the President
Writing a letter to a prospect	Writing and publishing a book
Hooking up a printer to your computer	Implementing a company-wide computer network
Meeting with an employee to discuss a new procedure	Hiring a sales team for the new office in Madison
Attending a conference	Promoting your product in a two-week program across the country
Ordering office supplies	Opening a new sales office
Writing a progress update memo to your boss	Producing the corporate annual report

If It's Not a Project, It's Just Plain Work

As you examine the lists in the preceding table that show differences between ordinary work and projects, you'll see that projects have five important features that make them different than most ordinary work:

➤ A project has a defined beginning and end. Getting from the beginning to the end of a project typically involves a definable sequence of steps or activities.

Project Lingo
Resources are the time, people, money, equipment and facilities used to complete a project. When you read this word, unless one element, such as money, is specifically mentioned, you can assume that the reference is to all four of these elements.

➤ Projects use resources (people, time, money) that have been specifically allocated to the work of the project, as opposed to the general operation of the business.

➤ The end results of a project have specific goals of quality and performance. Remember: When a project gets done, something new exists that didn't exist before.

➤ Projects (hopefully) follow a planned, organized approach to meet their objectives.

➤ A project usually involves a team of people to get it done.

A Balance Among Time, Resources, and Results

In addition to the five features that differentiate projects from ordinary work, as you learn more about projects you'll learn that the success of all projects is a result of the proper balance among three things: time, resources, and results. And, when a project is completed for a customer or client (and most projects in business have something to do with customers directly or indirectly), a fourth success factor comes into play—customer satisfaction.

This pyramid demonstrates the balance among time, resources, results, and customer satisfaction required to bring a project to a successful conclusion.

How Can You Tell a Project When You See One?

To test whether an activity in your life is a project or just plain work, ask yourself whether the work in question meets the five features discussed earlier. As you examine your goals based on these five criteria, you'll see that all the things you do, even most of your entertainment activities, can be divided into these two categories: the ordinary, repetitive stuff and the projects.

Remember, ordinary activities get done as necessary. (Well, most of the time. Filing isn't high on our list either). Your goal in completing ordinary activities is probably just to keep things going. The goals of most projects involve getting things done on time, within budget, and to specifications.

Yes, it may be hard to believe that a project for transporting astronauts to Mars has much in common with opening a new sales office in Richmond, but check it out and you'll see that both of these undertakings meet the criteria to be called projects.

Regardless of their size, both projects share the five features of projects, and their success is measured in terms of time, resources, and results. Both projects will be deemed successful if they get done on time, use only the resources that have been budgeted or planned, and deliver the results that were agreed upon in advance.

Project Lingo
Program is another name for a recurring project. Programs happen over and over again. Good examples are: producing the monthly customer newsletter, publishing the annual report, and coordinating the Rose Bowl parade. Recurring projects happen predictably, but each cycle involves a new plan and a unique end product. The plan, resources, and results are what make programs different from other repetitive tasks, such as filing.

Because all projects share similar features and require a balance among time, resources, and results, similar management techniques can be used to help bring them to successful conclusions. These techniques are what you're going to learn about in the rest of the book.

Whether it's training a team of new employees, creating an ad campaign, or reorganizing the corporation—the techniques of project management can be used to improve productivity and assure timely completion. Project management tools also can be used to correct mid-course problems that would otherwise go undetected and undermine the success of the project. Most of the project management techniques best used in business are the same ones applied by engineers to manage complex projects, but in this book they are presented so non-engineering managers can easily apply them to everyday projects.

They're Not Always Created Equal

Of course, in spite of their similarities, all projects are unique. Projects involve different goals, employ different people with unique personalities, take place over varying time frames, and produce different results.

No two projects, even recurring projects with the same general objectives, are ever identical in implementation. Thankfully, project management offers techniques for identifying and managing the unique attributes as well as the similar aspects of projects. You will learn about these techniques later in the book.

People who manage projects successfully learn to become managers of exceptions, because there are always plenty of surprises, even in small projects. So, the project for opening a sales office and the project to build a spaceship to fly to Mars depend on different project management tools, even though all the tools come from the same toolbox.

How Many Projects Are You Responsible For?

As you start reviewing the activities in your business, you'll see that the endeavors in business that meet the project criteria are endless, varying from small to large, and from simple to complex. If you try listing all the projects in your area of responsibility, you may discover a lot more on the list than you anticipated.

All Projects Great and Small

It's usually easy to identify the most complex projects in business, such as developing a new model automobile, designing a new data processing system, or building an overseas manufacturing facility. But smaller and more mundane business endeavors are projects, even though they may not be called projects.

Now consider the job of hiring a new marketing manager for your company. Most experienced managers wouldn't consider this a project because they know how to plan and schedule all the steps in their head. You simply put an ad in the paper, interview some people, and make a choice. But hiring a new marketing manager involves deadlines, people, money, and time—and hopefully you only have to do it once. You'll probably use a team of people to interview the candidates as well. And when you're done with the project you'll also have something you didn't have before—a new marketing manager.

When viewed this way, hiring a marketing manager is a project and deserves to be treated with the respect of a project. Good project management will help you hire the right marketing manager in the shortest period of time—and that could make a big difference to your company.

Sure, it won't take as long to plan the project to hire a marketing manager as it will to plan how to build a new bridge across the Potomac. You probably won't have to use a computer program to create the schedule or manage the budget either (although you might). But using good project management techniques from this book is still important because the choice of the marketing manager is important to your business.

You can't afford to treat even a small project, such as hiring a new employee, like ordinary work. Now would be a good time to identify two small but important projects, one from your work and one personal project, that you have been postponing. For practice, you can apply on them the techniques you learn in this book.

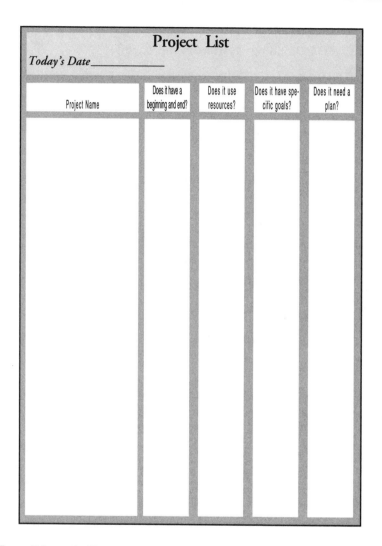

Project Name	Does it have a beginning and end?	Does it use resources?	Does it have specific goals?	Does it need a plan?

Project List

Today's Date_____

Use this form to list all the projects in your business.

The Next Step

Now that you have identified the projects in your business, you'll be able to manage them better with the techniques in this book.

In the following pages, you'll be taken step-by-step through the fundamentals of planning, scheduling, tracking, and controlling the costs and resources of any project. The practical techniques are applicable to the projects that people in sales, marketing, human resources, finance, and general management positions

Words from the Wise
No project is too small to not be taken seriously.

—An Intel project manager

are responsible for—yet they are based on the same general, accepted methods employed by engineering project managers in building skyscrapers and satellites.

After learning about project management techniques, you'll be able answer questions like these:

➤ How can I best define the work that needs to be done to make the project a success?

➤ How long should the project really take to get done, and how much should it cost?

➤ Who should I put on my project team?

➤ How much work can be expected of each person on the project?

➤ How can I control cost overruns?

➤ Where is the project in danger of failure?

➤ What can be done to make sure things are completed on time?

➤ Is my budget on track?

➤ How can I keep everybody happy and motivated to get things done?

➤ How do I know if we're really on schedule?

If you can answer all those questions, who knows? Maybe with good project management you really could build that tele-transporter.

Beam me up, Scotty! We're ready to go.

The Least You Need to Know

➤ Projects differ from ordinary work and thus need special management techniques to make them successful.

➤ The factors of time, resources, results, and customer satisfaction are interrelated. If you change one of these, you must change the others to keep things in balance.

➤ Projects can be managed with similar techniques because they share many of the same attributes.

➤ Even though projects share attributes, they are still unique because of their different contexts and their particular use of resources, time, and results.

Chapter 2

The Process That Works

In This Chapter

➤ Why modern businesses need project management tools

➤ The benefits of learning about project management

➤ Why the project management process works

➤ The five phases of the project management process

The pressure is on. Like most people in business, you have more projects to manage than ever before. Whether you're responsible for major projects, such as bringing new products to market, or smaller projects, such as producing a customer newsletter, you need to get them done on time and within budget. And you don't have just one or two projects to do, you've got a list of projects a mile long and you need to get them all done now! Even worse, you're expected to get your work done faster, better, cheaper, and with fewer resources.

Don't panic. You're not doomed—yet. You just need a new method and the right tools to sort things out. The new method is called the project management process, and the tools are the procedures, strategies, and tips that can be used during this process to keep things focused on the project objectives. Together, the project management tools you'll learn about in this book can help you bring sanity to the chaos of managing multiple projects, diverse personalities, and constant change associated with modern business.

Why Do You Need to Learn About Project Management?

The cost reduction programs and management approaches of the past are not enough to meet today's corporate challenges. Meeting the demands of the fast-changing environment of modern business requires a focus on priorities, better tracking techniques, and effective structures for communication. Companies need to streamline operations, reduce risks, and improve overall productivity. Project management techniques are one part of a solution to adapt and prosper.

Project management is simply a combination of steps and techniques for keeping the ol' budget and schedule in line. Project management tools offer a way to avoid the frustration of missed deadlines, unclear expectations, and budget overruns. By clearly defining responsibilities for the activities, focusing resources on specific objectives, and providing a structure for communicating within and across organizational boundaries, the project management process can help anyone meet project goals better and with less frustration.

Time Is Money
Good project management saves money. And providing effective control of expensive resources (people, money, equipment) involved in projects helps not only the bottom line but also delivers the "goods" when they need to be delivered.

Project Lingo
Project Management is the process of combining systems, techniques, and people to complete a project within established goals of time, budget, and quality.

What Is Project Management All About?

The project management toolbox for business includes manual and computerized processes that are directly applicable to improving performance and efficiency in today's organizations. Project management techniques offer proven methods for working with project teams formed across traditional, functional, and organizational boundaries.

Putting You in Charge

In a project-driven business, work is managed and controlled by the people doing the work—not by an executive two or three levels removed from the tasks. People in project groups are able to assume responsibility for and derive satisfaction from their own objectives, while continuing to contribute to the larger objectives of the organization as a whole.

Okay, but Does It Really Work?

At this point, you're probably thinking that project management tools may be useful for engineers who need to structure and focus their efforts for building bridges and dams, but why are the techniques relevant to my needs and those of my modern business?

Along the Critical Path

The first modern application of project management is often attributed to the building of the first nuclear submarine in the 1950s. Adm. Hyman Rickover was the project manager for this undertaking. The admiral was faced with coordinating hundreds of contractors who kept asking for more resources. Everything had to be done by hand, and there were few methods available for coordinating all the complexity. Out of this need came the technique now known as Program Evaluation and Review Technique (PERT) and the critical path method. (You'll learn a version of these methods later in the book.) Over the years, the techniques continued to be used on large-scale aerospace, military, and construction projects. Project management really took off in the 1960s when computer programs for project management were made commercially available (the programs cost hundreds of thousands of dollars and ran on computers the size of a house).

As a skeptic, you may ask how such massive projects as the Pyramids in Egypt or even /the Great Wall of China were completed without the aid of project management tools. And, given that projects obviously got done long before anyone came up with project management techniques, why should you bother learning how to plan, schedule, track, and control your projects with anything more than you have in the past. After all, most of *your* work gets done, eventually—and it doesn't go over budget too often.

Sure, just like the engineers in Egypt with thousands of slaves and unlimited resources at their disposal, it is still possible to get projects done today without using proven project management techniques. But why work harder than you have to? Project management can help you reduce risk and make it easier to get more done with less effort. If you don't believe us, try it out. You'll see that the project management process will really help you achieve more predictable results.

High Water!
Beware that project management may be called something else in your organization. For example, project management is often called "program management" in the U.S. Department of Defense, "construction management" in the construction industry, and "product management" in consumer-oriented industries. With only minor adjustments, the concepts and processes in this book apply to all of these flavors of project management.

It's Not Perfect, but It Sure Helps

That's not to say that project management techniques will make managing projects a perfect science. Projects always involve people, and getting people to work together to accomplish defined goals is always complex. The techniques and discipline of project management just make it easier to coordinate things and help you secure more predictable results. The techniques also help in getting you out of trouble when things go wrong.

Tools for Modern Times

The project management process offers you clear steps and powerful tools that can be employed to get projects done on time and within budget—that's something every business and every worker can benefit from. The tools of modern project management were originally developed by scientists and engineers, but because the tools can be adapted to any project that meets the criteria described in the last chapter, any project can benefit from the techniques.

Some organizations have already introduced project management processes into their everyday operations. For this reason, some tools may already be familiar to you, including teams, charted schedules, matrixed management, zero-based budgeting, and streamlined reports.

All Projects Mundane and Marvelous

If you're still thinking that your projects are too small or too ordinary to benefit from project management, think again. The project management process is for people to use with all sorts of projects, whether they are one-time endeavors, or recurring projects (often called programs), or product-oriented. The project management process supplies the necessary structure, organization, focus, and control to drive any project from concept to successful completion.

Can Project Management Help You?

To decide if you or your organization would benefit from the project management process, even for your small projects, take a few minutes to answer the questions on the following worksheet like most people, you can probably do better at getting things done on time and within budget—and the project management process can help.

The Five Phases of the Project Management Process

Project Lingo

PMI is an acronym for the Project Management Institute, a professional organization that studies and promotes project management techniques. If you want to join PMI to learn more about project management, contact information is provided at the back of this book.

It's important to remember that the project management process works for projects of all kinds because of the project similarities discussed in Chapter 1. Like living beings, all projects have predictable stages that start with an idea to do something and end (hopefully) with the delivery of a complete project that meets its goals for quality or performance.

In total, there are five phases in every project: initiation, planning, executing, controlling, and closing. These five phases outline the project management process as defined in the Project Management Institute (PMI) Project Management Body of Knowledge (PMBOK). The PMBOK is PMI's reference document describing core project management techniques.

Are you managing your projects effectively?

	Yes	No	I Don't Know	

To determine if you can benefit from the use of project management techniques, answer **Yes**, **No**, or **I Don't Know** to the following questions:

I have identified and named all the current projects in my area of responsibility.

All of the projects are prioritized.

All the projects have clear, agreed upon goals and initiatives.

All the projects are scheduled in writing.

All the projects have approved budgets.

All of the projects have adequate resources for completion.

All the people and vendors involved with the projects are appropriately skilled and adequately trained to complete the project work.

Potential conflicts with other projects are easily identified because of clear project plans and open communications.

The potential problems in my projects are easily identified in advance and actions are consistently taken to eliminate or minimize them.

All the people working with me on projects are enthusiastic and committed to work.

Other project participants willingly respond to requests related to the projects I am coordinating.

When project disagreements and conflicts arise, effective agreements are reached quickly and with minimum disruption to the work flow.

I am always clear on the current status of the projects I am involved with.

Project changes are clearly communicated on a regular basis and always understood by project participants.

My projects are consistently completed on time, within budget, and to specification.

Total

Total your score. "No" and "I don't know," get no points. Give yourself one point for each Yes answer. If you scored 13 to 15 points, congratulations—you are already an excellent project manager, though you may discover some useful techniques to become even better using this book. If you scored 9 to 12 points, you are doing okay, but there are definite areas that could be improved. If you scored below 9, you are perceptive and honest about the state of project management in your company. If you follow the guidelines in the book, you'll be able to complete your projects more easily and with less anxiety.

Complete this worksheet to determine whether you and your enterprise could benefit from employing the power of the project management process in your projects.

A Rose by Any Other Name

Be aware that other project management books may refer to project stages with different names or may break the phases into more levels. Even so, all project management experts agree on the same basic project cycle. For example, some project management experts break projects into phases of conceptualization, feasibility, preliminary planning, detail planning, execution, testing, and termination. These phases can still be equated to the five phases of initiation, planning, executing, controlling, and closing. The number of phases you identify for a project depends on its size, complexity, and the preferred terminology in your organization; ultimately everything boils down to the same general phases and employs the techniques described here.

Getting Familiar with the Phases

In each of the five phases there are different tasks, behaviors, and skills necessary to be successful. You'll learn about these in subsequent chapters. For now, take a look at the five phases to understand how the project management process proceeds from beginning to end.

The five phases of the project management process can be used to manage any project to a successful conclusion.

The Five Phases of the Project Management Process

Project Phase 1: Initiating

The initiating phase stresses the development of a vision for a project and establishment of goals. In this phase, some key individuals will be brought together to form a core project team and start the planning process (Phase 2). The general steps in the initiating phase include:

➤ Recognizing that a project should be done

➤ Determining what the project should accomplish

➤ Defining the overall project goal

➤ Defining general expectations of customers, management, or other stakeholders as appropriate

➤ Defining the general project scope

➤ Selecting initial members of the project team

Project Phase 2: Planning

The planning phase involves defining resources required to complete the project, devising a schedule, and developing a budget for the project. Planning also involves identifying objectives for stakeholders and team members involved in the project, and establishes the means to achieve those objectives. Some of the typical activities involved in the planning phase include:

➤ Refining the project scope, which includes identifying the balance required among results, time, and resources

➤ Listing tasks and activities that will lead to achieving the project goals

➤ Sequencing activities in the most efficient manner possible

➤ Developing a workable schedule and budget for assigning resources to the activities required to complete the project

➤ Getting the plan approved by the appropriate stakeholders

Project Phase 3: Executing

The executing phase involves coordinating and guiding project team members to get the work done as laid out in the approved project plan. This phase also stresses keeping resources and people focused on the work. Some of the tasks in the executing phase include:

➤ Leading the team

➤ Meeting with team members

➤ Communicating with stakeholders

➤ Fire-fighting (also know as conflict resolution) to resolve problems that always arise during a project

Project Lingo
Scope is the size of the project. The scope determines how many resources, how much time, and how large the final product is. For example, the scope of a written procedure for inventory control is much smaller than that of a computer-based inventory control system.

Project Lingo
Stakeholders are people who have a personal or entrepreneurial interest in the end results of a project. Not all stakeholders are involved in completing the actual work on a project. Common stakeholders include customers, managers, corporate executives, and representatives of government agencies.

➤ Securing necessary resources (money, people, equipment, time) to carry out the project plan

Project Phase 4: Controlling

The controlling phase is about watching over the project. This involves measuring progress toward the objectives and taking action to assure that deviations from the plan do not adversely affect the end results of the project. The controlling phase stresses your understanding of unexpected delays, cost overruns, or changes in scope. During this phase, the project manager must decide among alternatives for solving problems. Activities in the controlling phase may include:

➤ Monitoring deviation from the plan

➤ Taking corrective action to match actual progress with the plan

➤ Receiving and evaluating project changes requested from stakeholders and team members

➤ Rescheduling the project as necessary

➤ Adapting resource levels as necessary

➤ Changing (usually cutting) the project scope

➤ Returning to the planning stage to make adjustments to the project goals and getting them approved by the stakeholders

Project Phase 5: Closing

The final phase of the project, the closing phase, is a time both for celebration and reflection. This phase involves keeping people involved in closing the project, even when their thoughts may be moving on to new enterprises. The closing phase stresses gaining acceptance of the end-product and bringing the project to an orderly conclusion. The activities at this phase may include:

➤ Acknowledging achievement and results

➤ Shutting down the operations and disbanding the team

➤ Learning from the project experience

➤ Reviewing the project process and outcomes with team members and stakeholders

➤ Writing a final project report

How the Project Phases Work Together

As you study the diagram of the five stages of the project management process, note that phases 2 through 4 (planning, executing, and controlling) are in a circle. This is because these three phases are interdependent and cyclical throughout the project. For example, plans may need to be revised due to things learned in the execution and controlling phases. Execution changes because the plans change, and controlling is important throughout the project to keep things on track.

Not Just the Same Old Routine

Overall, the five phases of the project management process may seem pretty ordinary—but they're not. Yes, many management methods used in business today follow a similar pattern based on planning the work and developing schedules and budgets; implementing the work with teams of people and other resources; and controlling the work through tracking and monitoring progress against a plan. The reason so many methods use the same process is simple: the process works.

The Least You Need to Know

➤ The constraints of time, resources, results, and customer satisfaction are interrelated. If you change one of these, the others must change to keep things in balance.

➤ The five phases of the project management process include initiating, planning, executing, controlling, and closing.

➤ Different skills, steps, and techniques are applicable to managing each phase of the project effectively.

➤ As things change on a project, the phases of planning, executing, and controlling may need to be repeated again and again.

Chapter 3

The Rules of the Project Game

In This Chapter

➤ Standard reasons for project failure (and how to avoid them most of the time)

➤ 12 golden rules of project management success

➤ Simple ways to help you follow the rules for success

We know you're just champing at the bit to get started managing your projects. In the rest of the book, you're going to learn about the processes, plans, charts, and techniques to guide your projects through the five phases of the project management process, from initiation to closing, that you learned about in Chapter 2. But before you become convinced that project management is more about process than substance, you need to know that all the ingredients that make up the project management recipe for success boil down to only 12 rules you need to follow.

These 12 golden rules have been honed from years of experience by all kinds of project managers responsible for all types of projects in diverse managerial and political environments. So, whether your projects involve building spaceships or building ships in bottles, you'll get better results by paying attention to these rules from the initiation phase to the closing phase of every project.

Project Failure—The Reasons Are Simple

For almost all projects, success is defined as meeting the goals of the project within a specific time frame and budget that has been agreed upon by the project team and the project stakeholders. Thus, there are really only four reasons why an otherwise viable project can fail:

➤ Not enough resources are available to complete the project

➤ Not enough time is approved to complete the project

➤ Unclear project expectations lead to inappropriate or incomplete results

➤ Disagreement among stakeholders regarding the expectations for the project leads to dissatisfaction with the end results

Words from the Wise
He enunciated no rules for success, but offered a sure formula for failure: *Just try to please everyone.*

—E.J. Kahn Jr.

People don't start a project hoping it will fail. Yet projects fail all too often because project managers disregard the 12 basic project management rules that can help avoid the four reasons for failure.

12 Golden Rules of Project Management Success

The 12 basic rules of project management define the focus needed to get things done on time, within budget, and to the expectations of the stakeholders. As you read on in the book, you'll see how project management techniques are designed to help project managers put the 12 golden rules into action over and over again.

In the sections that follow, you'll be guided to the chapters of the book that offer specific advice related to the rule being discussed. Of course, if you consistently break or ignore the rules of project management, regardless of your diligent use of charts, plans, and reports recommended in the rest of this book, you'll probably doom your project to failure or at least cause a lot of problems that otherwise could be avoided.

Rule 1: Thou Shalt Gain Consensus on Project Outcomes

If you don't know what you intend to accomplish, it's not likely you'll accomplish anything of value. A project without clear expectations is really just a bunch of work without a purpose. To be considered a success, a project must have clearly defined goals that specify what the project looks like when its done.

But it's not enough for *you* to know exactly what you want to do. You also have to reach consensus with the stakeholders and team members in the project that the goals and expectations are the right ones. In Chapter 6, you'll learn how to set clear project goals and expectations, and you'll get tips for gaining the consensus required to assure the project you finally finish is the project people wanted to get done.

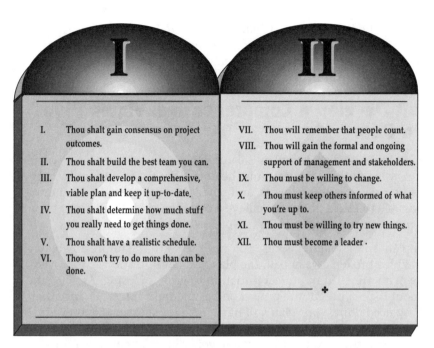

You'll be wise to keep this list of rules in front of you throughout your projects.

I. Thou shalt gain consensus on project outcomes.

II. Thou shalt build the best team you can.

III. Thou shalt develop a comprehensive, viable plan and keep it up-to-date.

IV. Thou shalt determine how much stuff you really need to get things done.

V. Thou shalt have a realistic schedule.

VI. Thou won't try to do more than can be done.

VII. Thou will remember that people count.

VIII. Thou will gain the formal and ongoing support of management and stakeholders.

IX. Thou must be willing to change.

X. Thou must keep others informed of what you're up to.

XI. Thou must be willing to try new things.

XII. Thou must become a leader .

The 12 Rules of Project Management

Rule 2: Thou Shalt Build the Best Team You Can

A willing, skilled, appropriately organized project team is the key to success. This is a group of people you'll have to develop, because the perfect team almost never starts out that way. A good team starts with good choices on your part; however, sometimes the people you pick may turn out to be total dummies or uncooperative blockheads.

It's your challenge to make sure the project team gets smart really quick and stays ambitious in spite of inadequate experience and training, family problems, or conflicting priorities. If people must be trained to get things done right, that's one of your responsibilities as project manager. Of course, the people must also be willing to work on the project and learn the new skills. That means you'll have to use your best management skills and motivational tactics to guide them in the right direction (that's the direction *you* want them to go).

Time Is Money

Review the 12 golden rules at least once a week, and you'll have a much better chance of getting things done the *right* way, on time, within budget, and to the specifications agreed upon by customers or management or other stakeholders. Of course, the schedule and budget may change over time, but as long as people agree on the changes, you're still getting things done the right way. A review of the rules will remind you of that.

Concentrate on mastering the techniques in Chapters 4 and 16 if you're a bit weak in the people skills and leadership areas. Also, because your project staff must ultimately be organized in a way that encourages teamwork and quality end results, you'll need some team building skills. Chapter 16 can help you out in that regard as well.

Rule 3: Thou Shalt Develop a Comprehensive, Viable Plan and Keep It Up-to-Date

A complete, appropriately detailed project plan is central to successful completion of any project. The plan helps you guide the project. It is the document that communicates the overall intentions, tasks, resource requirements, and schedule for the project. Without a plan, its almost impossible to lead a group to achieve a common goal. You'll learn about creating the various parts of the project plan in Chapters 9 through 15.

Of course, creating a plan isn't enough. Because you can't see into the future any better than a fortune teller with a broken crystal ball, the plan you develop and get approved will probably change many times from project initiation to project closing. As you gain more information about the realities of the project and as the stakeholders change their minds about what they need done, your plan will have to be reevaluated. Be forewarned (you'll hear about this again in Chapter 23), if you don't update the project plan—and negotiate these changes with the stakeholders—you're going to be responsible for the budget and schedule of the original plan.

THIS WAY

Along the Critical Path

Think about all the really smart people who use project management techniques and develop detailed plans and still seem to fail in getting projects done on time and within budget—like the engineers and rocket scientists at NASA who designed the space shuttle. According to the news media, that project was out of control and over budget. But, if you think about it, even the space shuttle got off the ground eventually. If you remember that the space shuttle was a high-risk project with lots of speculative technologies, it's unlikely that the original budget or schedule could have ever been met with certainty. From the perspective of the original plan, the space shuttle might seem a failure. But from another perspective, the space shuttle flights ultimately succeeded on many levels. In spite of the accomplishments, the news media and the taxpayers still held NASA to the original (and highly speculative) plans. Don't let this happen to you. Make sure the changes in the plan get communicated to everyone as they are made—even to the news media.

Rule 4: Thou Shalt Determine How Much Stuff You Really Need to Get Things Done

No matter what your boss says, you can't squeeze blood from a turnip. Without adequate people, capital, and equipment to complete a project, there is no way you can make it happen. You must get sufficient resources allocated to the project or you must renegotiate what is going to be done so fewer resources are required (refer to Rule 1). Getting sufficient resources (including equipment, people, and supplies) for a project is an ongoing problem in most companies—and one of the most important responsibilities for all project managers. In Chapter 11, you'll learn how to scope out what you really need to get a project done, and in Chapter 24 you'll find some techniques for negotiating when you don't get everything you need the first time around.

Rule 5: Thou Shalt Have a Realistic Schedule

Without a realistic schedule, you'll never succeed—you'll run out of time before you get to try again. You can get more people and buy more supplies, but you can't produce more time no matter what you do. (Of course, if your last name is Wells and your initials are H. G., you might be *the* exception.)

There's no faster way to lose credibility as a project manager than to change the schedule without a really good reason. Then again, if you follow Rules 1 and 8 you can get more time for yourself by getting a new schedule approved. In Chapters 11 and 12, you'll learn how to develop a schedule you can meet (and how to change it when necessary).

> **Words from the Wise**
>
> Time waits for no one and nowhere is that more true than when managing a project.
>
> —Project manager and PM teacher Jim MacIntyre

Rule 6: Thou Shalt Not Try to Do More than Can Be Done

You must have an appropriate scope for the project. The scope of the project involves more than goals. For example, the goal could be to build a two-story building on the location of the back parking lot by next December. But the scope of the project could range from putting up a pre-fabricated metal building with a cement floor to building a miniature Taj Mahal for the chairman of the board. While the first scope is feasible, the second is not. Make sure the objectives *and* the scope of the project are clear to everyone if you want to be considered a success when the project is done.

Rule 7: Thou Shalt Remember that People Count

Sometimes in focusing on the process of project management you may forget that projects are mostly about people. Project success depends on people, not reports or charts or even computers. To be a successful project manager, you must accommodate people's

Time Is Money
Learning to work with people takes a lifetime—and at the end you'll still be wondering how people really work. Even with all the good advice in this book, people will surprise you in mysterious and wonderful ways. That's what keeps project management interesting.

needs and priorities. People manage the project. People do most of the work. People enjoy (or curse) the end results. Projects also put stresses on these people, because projects almost always involve new group structures, deadlines, and extra work. If a project's end results don't serve people, then the project has failed.

Projects almost always incorporate built-in priority conflicts between ordinary work and project work. The bad news is that you must eventually satisfy people's needs, priorities, and conflicts for the project to come to a happy ending. The good news is that in Chapter 22 you'll learn some techniques to help you deal with the inevitable conflicts among the people and the priorities in your projects.

Rule 8: Thou Shalt Gain the Formal and Ongoing Support of Management and Stakeholders

It's obvious (or at least it should be) that you must have approval from management and the key stakeholders before you initiate a project. This will involve not only communication skills, but also negotiation skills. This rule is a lot like Rule 1, except that it means you must add a formal approval stage to the general consensus you gained in keeping Rule 1. You will need to get all the people who have to contribute resources (time or money) or those who may be impacted by a project (if it will change their job or life) to formally endorse your project and to agree that the project is worth doing. For many of these stakeholders, support requires their signed approval, but it doesn't stop with a signature. Keeping this rule also demands that you assure the stakeholders' ongoing interest in your project. If you start a project for your boss, and your boss has no real interest in the project even after he's signed on the dotted line, it's unlikely you'll get any praise for finishing the feat. Remember to read Chapters 22 and 23 whenever support wanes for your projects.

Rule 9: Thou Shalt Be Willing to Change

This rule goes along with Rule 3. You must be willing to adapt the project plan and implementation to guide the project where it needs to go. Sometimes things change for justifiable reasons, such as a rain storm that stops the work on a construction project. Sometimes things change because you get new information, like the time that researchers in Utah discovered cold fusion in a test tube, which changed the whole perspective about building fusion reactors and stopped projects worldwide (for a while a least—the whole experiment was found to be erroneous and unscientific). As one researcher put it, "It was like we were trying to invent the biplane and someone shows us up with a 747." Sometimes changes are simply the result of peoples' whims, like the advertising agency's customer who now wants a videotape instead of a brochure to promote a new product—even though the brochure is almost ready to go to the printer.

You'll also learn in Chapter 23 that change is an important part of controlling a project—and thus good project managers need to identify when changes are needed, learn how to introduce changes, and know how to measure the impact of change.

Rule 10: Thou Must Keep People Informed of What You're Up To

You must keep all the relevant stakeholders informed of progress, problems, and changes. The way to obey this rule is simple: communicate, communicate, communicate. As things change on the project (and they always do), you'll find through your communications that the stakeholders may want or need to introduce their own changes into the project. You'll have to frequently refer to Rule 9 while adhering to Rule 10.

> **Words from the Wise**
> Graham's Law: If they know nothing of what you are doing, they suspect you are doing nothing.
> —Robert J. Graham in *Understanding Project Management*

Rule 11: Thou Must Be Willing to Try New Things

Because every project is different, with different people, goals, and challenges involved, it would simply be inappropriate to use the exact same methods, software, charts, graphs, or other aids on every project. The standard methods and tools can be used with all projects, but not all projects involve the same risk or complexity. Thus, not all the techniques in this book should be used on all of your projects.

Large, complex projects will likely use more methods or tools than smaller projects. Both too many methods and too few tools can doom a project. You must adapt the processes, technologies, tools, and techniques to the needs of the project at hand. For example, you obviously need to put more detail into the network diagram (read Chapter 10) for building a new corporate headquarters from scratch than you would have to for setting up a new sales office in a rented building. And some recurring projects, such as managing the monthly production of a newsletter, might not need a network diagram at all.

Rule 12: Thou Must Become a Leader

Leadership is an art that comes naturally to some, but the rest of us have to work at it. Chances are, you have to work on your leadership role, too. Reading management books won't be enough to bring your projects in on time and within budget. As a project manager, you must put what you read into action. You need to become a leader as well as a team member. You must not only plan, track, and control the project, but you must also be a source of wisdom and motivation for the team members and the stakeholders. Without leadership, even a well coordinated project can fail to meet its goals—the people in the project won't feel they have the support or guidance they need to make things happen. That's your job as the project manager. In Chapter 4, you'll learn a lot more about being a good project manager.

You Can Do It!

It may seem difficult to follow all the rules all the time. But with knowledge of the steps in the project management process and the right project management tools in your toolbox, you have a good shot at celebrating a project's success instead of bemoaning its failure. Just in trying to keep the rules, you can attain good results—at least most of the time.

Keep Your Eyes on the Prize

Projects help further personal goals as well as those of companies and organizations. If you keep the 12 golden rules of project management in front of you throughout the project phases, project failures can be minimized, if not eliminated.

Yes, there will be times when fate plays a role and you can't do everything to everyone's satisfaction. But if you remember the 12 golden rules throughout the five phases of the project management process, you'll succeed more times than you fail. Keep working at it. The prize for your effort will be projects done on time, within budget, and with less stress on mind and body.

The Least You Need to Know

➤ Follow the 12 golden rules of project management to help guide projects of all sizes and complexity to more successful conclusions.

➤ Your first loyalty is to your project even though you may be pressured from all sides for change.

➤ Keep a list of the 12 golden rules of project management on your desk or, better yet, put the list on your wall to keep you focused on the success factors during the tough times of a project.

➤ Remember that the success of a project always depends more on people than on process, but some processes and structures (like the ones you'll learn about in this book) are important in helping people stay on track.

Chapter 4

You? A Project Manager?

In This Chapter

➤ The skillful project manager

➤ The skills possessed by effective project managers

➤ The art of becoming a skillful project manager

➤ Your roles as "PM"

➤ Six traits of effective project managers

Your business card may not say manager or executive or even supervisor, but when you are responsible for any project, large or small, you *are* a project manager—albeit an accidental one. In this chapter, you'll learn what it takes to be a good project manager, because project success depends on good project managers.

The Accidental Project Manager

Pretend for a moment that you work at NASA. You are responsible for developing a new space shuttle that will transport astronauts to Mars and back. To succeed, you must schedule all the tasks for building the vehicle, as well as hire and coordinate the best people and right suppliers for each job. Throughout the five phases of the project, you will manage complex interrelationships among staff, vendors, and the government. You must also track the budget and control costs.

Words from the Wise

Be not afraid of greatness: some are born great, some achieve greatness, and some have greatness thrust upon them.

—William Shakespeare, *Twelfth Night*

Project Lingo

The *project manager* is any person who takes overall responsibility for coordinating a project, regardless of size, to make sure the desired end result comes in on time and within budget.

High Water!

If your boss or someone else asks you to add projects to an already overloaded work schedule, you'll need to politely employ the most important word in the project manager's vocabulary. That word is "No!" You can cloak it in friendlier terms, but you must stand your ground. Agreeing to do the impossible still leaves whatever you agreed to, well, impossible! Negotiate later.

You need special project management skills for planning, executing, and controlling a project of this scope, which involves hundreds of people, tons of supplies, thousands of tasks, and millions of dollars. As the capable person responsible for this complex mission, you deserve a special title, and you have one. You are the *project manager*.

In many product- and program-oriented companies, there are people with primary responsibility for managing large projects. These people, like the project managers at NASA, have titles and authority to match their project responsibilities. But in most enterprises, people like you are project managers by accident, not by design. And you are part-time project managers with other jobs to do.

Dealing with Dual Responsibilities

In some ways, full-time project managers have it a lot easier than the accidental ones. Full-time project managers, like the person at NASA responsible for the Mars shuttle, have only one major responsibility: the project. The majority of the job involves managing the project and other priorities rarely interfere with this work. Thus, everything the full-time project manager at NASA does revolves around the planning, coordination, and monitoring of the Mars shuttle. But most people in business have responsibilities outside their project goals—and these responsibilities may conflict with project priorities.

People in business must competently finish their ordinary work *and* their projects. In this chapter, you'll learn what it takes to be a good project manager, despite the fact that you may have been thrust into the role by accident, and in addition to the other work you have to do.

As a project manager (accidental or otherwise), you are the one person assigned to lead the project management process, and you alone are ultimately responsible for the project's success. Even if you have other work to do, you need to make sure the project gets done as specified.

The responsibility of being a project manager can be a heavy load, even for the superheroes among us. As an accidental project manager, your dual responsibility for projects and ordinary work makes the skillful use of project management techniques vital to the success of your projects (and your career, we might add). Through effective scheduling and prioritization of tasks, the project management process can make it easier to maintain control of projects while continuing to meet the priorities of everyday life.

What Do You Need to Do?

Bringing a project to fruition is a creative process with a focus on the "management" of the process. To be effective, whether you're a full-time or accidental project manager, you need to employ technologies, charting techniques, and budgeting tools to define the project. But to be truly successful, you must first establish yourself as a competent manager.

Learn to Plan and Act

Project management as a discipline evolved because of a need to coordinate resources and technology to secure predictable results. The common project management tasks include establishing objectives, breaking work into well-defined tasks, charting the work sequences, scheduling, budgeting, coordinating a team, reporting, and on-going communication. These tasks involve two general types of activities: planning and definition activities, and implementation and control activities.

Time Is Money
According to the Project Management Institute (PMI), project managers must coordinate nine areas of expertise: cost, time, scope, quality, communications, human resources, contracts, supplies, and risk management. Whew! That's a lot of stuff to handle. No wonder project management was invented.

Because of these two types of activities, people who manage projects effectively, no matter what the size, must know how to plan effectively and act efficiently. In fact, balancing the interplay between planning and acting may be the most important skill a person must learn to be effective at managing projects. Planning benefits from tools, charts, and techniques—the ability to take action requires the skills of a leader.

You Must Be a Manager and a Leader

Good project managers command both the authority and the responsibility to guide the project. Management of the project and leadership go hand in hand. As a leader, your team will expect you to be honest, competent, and inspirational, as well as competent in the use of project management techniques.

It is possible to complete the management part of the project—the meetings, assignments, audits, reports, and other communications—and not attain the status

Words from the Wise
The most important quality in a leader is that of being acknowledged as such.

—André Maurois, *The Art of Living*

and influence of a leader. But to be a successful project manager, you must be both a manager and a leader. You must gain the trust and respect of the project team, so people feel comfortable taking your direction. You must also develop administrative procedures for ensuring that work is getting done on time and within budget.

Focus on the Project's End

In the 1970s, a popular management fad was to look through tasks of all sorts as though they were already complete. Only the work in the middle remained. For example, a salesperson, instead of focusing on the unlikelihood of a sale, would look through to the close as though it was already in hand. Although this fad largely died (fortunately), you should use part of it in managing projects. Instead of looking at a project as 50 tasks, always keep the end in mind. That way, the project is less likely to stall mid-stream. It also makes you a stronger project leader. Like General Patton, you have your goal firmly set in your mind and nothing can deter your success in reaching it!

The Leadership Roles of the Project Manager

You'll need to develop your people skills to become regarded as a leader. As part of your responsibility for leading the five phases of the project, you'll need to assume a variety of roles with other people, including interpersonal, informational, and decisional roles. Accomplished leaders move effortlessly among these roles as required.

THIS WAY

Along the Critical Path

After a seminar on project management, one of the attendees, a wag obviously, ran up to us and told us that after listening to our presentation, she had finally figured out how to be a perfect project manager. "All you have to do is have the intelligence of Einstein, the patience of Job, the integrity of a Supreme Court judge, the negotiating skills of a Mongolian horse trader, the savvy of James Bond, the appeal of Marilyn Monroe, the charisma of Sir Ralph Richardson, the communication skills of Tom Peters, the ideas of Stephen King, the planning skills of Colin Powell, the personal drive of Bill Gates, the skin of an armadillo, and the ego of Mother Teresa." Maybe she's right. Maybe we should shorten our seminars to give attendees less time to think up stuff like this...

Interpersonal Roles

To be perceived as a leader, you must be regarded as honest, capable, and dependable—as well as personable. In your interpersonal roles, you'll need to do these kinds of things:

➤ Deal effectively with people from various professional backgrounds and create team unity

➤ Solve team disputes

➤ Focus and motivate team members to achieve milestones on the way to achieving the project goal

➤ Build positive relationships with project stakeholders

Informational Roles

You need to assume informational roles to keep people up-to-date and on track. When you do so, you'll need to accomplish these sorts of tasks:

➤ Arrange and lead team meetings

➤ Create and maintain work schedules for other people

➤ Communicate project vision to upper management

➤ Provide feedback regarding results, quality, and project deliverables

Decisional Roles

To move forward, projects demand countless decisions to be made, ranging from trivial to critical, at every phase of the project. When a decisional role is required, you'll need the expertise to do the following without alienating the people who may be affected by your choices:

➤ Distinguish between features and benefits

➤ Appropriately allocate resources if a project falls behind schedule

➤ Strike a balance between cost, time, and results

➤ Prevent scope "creep" (when the project keeps getting bigger and more complex) and budget "slippage" (when the money starts running out)

Time Is Money
A project manager who views the responsibility for managing a project as one of guiding, facilitating, negotiating, and coordinating will do better than will one who views the project management responsibility as one of ordering, dictating, and coercing.

The Six Traits of Good Project Managers

In addition to having knowledge of project management processes and an understanding of your various roles as a project manager and leader, research and experience point to six additional traits that can help you become a successful project manager. These six success traits are shown in the following figure, and we will discuss each one of them in turn.

As project managers gain experience, the successful ones develop these traits to make their work easier and more satisfying.

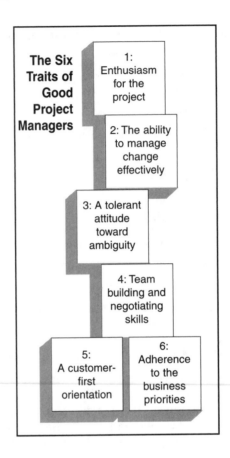

The Six Traits of Good Project Managers

1: Enthusiasm for the project

2: The ability to manage change effectively

3: A tolerant attitude toward ambiguity

4: Team building and negotiating skills

5: A customer-first orientation

6: Adherence to the business priorities

Trait 1: Enthusiasm for the Project

Good project managers *want* to do a good job. Your enthusiasm for the project permeates to other people on the team, making it easier to keep people motivated and involved.

Trait 2: The Ability to Manage Change Effectively

Change is inevitable in projects. Customers change their minds about the end results. Managers decide to make changes to the scope of the project. Team members need to change their schedules. People who manage projects successfully learn to become managers of exceptions, because there are always plenty of surprises, even in small projects.

Trait 3: A Tolerant Attitude Toward Ambiguity

Project managers often have ambiguous authority. This means that people may have other bosses to report to during the project, and may not consider you a manager (unless you earn their respect as a leader). In fact, many of the roles in large projects are not clear cut.

Some of the team members may make more money or have more senior jobs than the project manager; customers may get involved as team members; other departments may have a stake in the project. A good project manager must feel comfortable with these ambiguous roles and expectations, and learn how to manage them to see the project to a successful conclusion. If you need clear authority and an absolute plan, your project management days are numbered.

Trait 4: Team Building and Negotiating Skills

A project manager needs to build coalitions among the various stakeholders in a project: management, customers, the project team, and suppliers. Power is only granted to a project manager who builds these relationships. Project managers must negotiate authority to move the project forward, so the success of any project depends on the project manager's ability to build a strong team among internal and external players.

Time Is Money
Talk to any experienced project manager. They'll tell you (if they admit it) that at least one of their first projects was a dismal failure. If this happens to you, don't kick yourself. Instead, pick up the pieces and move on.

Trait 5: A Customer-First Orientation

In those projects that involve customers or clients (and most do), a good project manager keeps the customer first and understands the customer's perspective regarding the project. After all, the ultimate measure of the project's success is the customer's satisfaction with the results. In a partnership with a customer or client, a skilled project manager crafts a vision for the project that can be communicated to the rest of the project team. Through alliances and team building and empathy with the customer or client, the project manager is ultimately able to turn changing expectations into satisfaction with the completed project.

Trait 6: Adherence to the Priorities of Business

Even though projects often focus on people, project managers need to keep the business aspects of the work in mind. Because most projects need to turn a profit, the project manager also needs to keep the larger organizational and profit-making goals in focus when making decisions about the project. Even when projects don't involve a specific profit goal, successful project managers must control the cost, time, and quality constraints of their projects, and that's a business orientation no matter how you look at it.

Be the Best You Can Be

Of course, there are other traits that project managers would be wise to develop, such as written and verbal communication skills, computer literacy, and above all dependability.

Words from the Wise
Every man is the son of his own works.
—Miguel de Cervantes

If you aren't dependable, you can't expect the rest of the team to be dependable.

If you work at being all of the things talked about in this chapter, you'll reap the rewards of your labor with the help of project teams that respect your efforts as a leader. As a result, your projects will meet their goals more often than not.

The Least You Need to Know

➤ You need to coordinate and prioritize your ordinary work along with your projects, so both get done effectively.

➤ To be successful as a project manager, your team must perceive you as a leader.

➤ You need people skills, communication skills, and technical skills to be an effective project manager.

➤ As a project manager, you'll need to assume interpersonal, informational, and decisional roles, depending on the phase and needs of the project.

➤ Being a good project manager takes ongoing, enthusiastic effort.

Part 2
The Project Initiation Phase

You may think it's easy to get a project started. But starting a project off right takes some hard thinking and involves some tough decisions.

One of your initial tough choices is deciding which project to do first. After that you need to define the specific goals for your project and identify all the risks and constraints that may cause problems for the project after it is started. Then you need to choose (or meet) the team members for the project who will help you get things done. Only then will you be ready to start the project plan (which you'll learn to produce in Part 3).

Okay—this seems like a lot to do just to get to the planning phase. But that's what you need to do to start your projects off on the right foot—and that's what this part is going help you do.

Identifying Projects That Are Worth Doing

Some projects simply shouldn't be started. They might not have enough priority when compared with other work, or they might suffer from fatal flaws that are not evident when the idea first pops into your head. It may sound silly to say, but in most cases, the most important projects should be started first. So, it isn't enough just to identify the projects in your business. You also need to prioritize them before you start them. Why waste your time managing projects that don't really need to be done?

Sometimes, as the project manager, you might be brought in after the project prioritization step. For example, you might be assigned a project by your boss or you might be chosen as the project manager after other people have been considered. For other projects, you will be responsible for project selections on your own or as part of a project team. Whether your project is selected by management or you are asked to evaluate a project, you need to carry out the steps in this chapter to ensure you're not taking on an unachievable project.

The First Step in Project Initiation: Deciding What to Do

Project prioritization and selection is the first of many decisions in the initiation phase. In this chapter, you will learn how to prioritize the projects in your area of responsibility into those that need to be done now, those that should be started later, and those that simply should be scratched off the list and forgotten.

The selection and prioritization of projects is the first step in the project initiation phase of the management process. Remember the phases of the project management process in Chapter 2? To remind you what they are, keep the reference card provided at the front of the book handy as you read through the book. You're going to have a lot to keep ordered in your mind; the reference card will help to keep your memory fresh.

First Things First: Learning to Prioritize Projects

In Chapter 1, you learned how to tell the difference between projects and ordinary work. Simply knowing this difference is an important first step in taking advantage of the power of the project management process you learned about in Chapter 2.

Now it's time to list all of the current and pending projects in your life. On the first column in the following form, list all the projects you need to complete, including those you have started and those you just want to do.

Not Every Project Is Worth Doing

Okay. The next point is pretty obvious, but we're going to focus on it for a while because too many businesses spend time on the wrong projects. Just because a project is on your list doesn't mean it's worth doing.

Telling Good from Bad

Words from the Wise

A job not worth doing is not worth doing well.

—Jerry Pournelle, Pournelle's Fifth Law

All projects start as ideas or concepts. There are always more ideas in a business than there are time and resources to implement them. And we all know that not all ideas are good ideas. Some ideas turn out to be inappropriate or unfeasible; others don't have enough importance to take up your valuable time or the company's resources. Still others are better shelved for completion at a later date, when the timing is more appropriate.

Project Priority Worksheet			
Your Name _____ Today's Date _____			
List Projects by Name In Order of Priority	Risk: High, medium, or low?	Current Status	Primary Objective
1.			
2.			
3.			
4.			
5.			
6.			
7.			
8.			
9.			
10.			

Use this worksheet to identify and prioritize the projects in your enterprise.

Eight Steps to Determine the Most Important Projects

Whether prioritizing projects for a major corporation or as an individual, there are eight basic steps that can help you choose the most important projects to work on. They are:

1. List all current projects and project ideas in your area of responsibility.

2. Determine the need or opportunity for each project.

3. Establish rough delivery dates and budgets for each project. These can be very rough at this point; you're just determining the relative cost and time required to complete one project compared to another.

4. Judge the overall feasibility of each project. This may take some guesswork. For example, if one of the projects on your list is to discover a cure for cancer, you have to make some (hopefully) educated guesses about your team's ability to bring the prize home at the end of the day.

5. Establish the risk (possibility of failure) associated with each project. This step goes hand in hand with step 4. High feasibility means relatively low risk in most cases. But there can be a high feasibility and high risk when lots of money is involved.

6. Review the project list, objectives, feasibilities, and risks with your manager or boss (and the customer, if appropriate) and other members of the potential project team to gain consensus on the projects. The more complex the projects, the more important it is to get the opinion of other people before you prioritize the work.

7. Eliminate from the list projects that are inappropriate or unfeasible, and prioritize the rest. If the decision about prioritizing a project is not yours alone, this process may take a few meetings with your boss or customer or other members of the project team. Read Chapter 24 on negotiation and Chapter 22 on conflict resolution before you come up with the final priorities.

Reasons for eliminating projects from your priority list include:

➤ Lack of money, people, skills, time, or other resources that are required to make the project successful.

➤ Goals that are in conflict with the long-term organization or enterprise goals.

➤ Outcomes that will violate existing policies or laws, or otherwise negatively affect the position or public image of an organization. Even government or corporate officials have pet projects, and your evaluation techniques can help them to see the bottom-line effect of their projects. If they insist on going ahead anyway, find your way out as diplomatically as possible.

➤ Inability to act quickly enough, even if the project is otherwise feasible. Who wants to be the second man on the moon?

➤ Conflict with other projects that are in progress or are planned that have a higher priority and are grabbing key resources.

Some projects that ultimately need to be done may be rejected because of low priority or bad timing. These projects should be considered again in the next project selection review. Their priority may change as other projects get done.

8. Select the most important projects and act on these now. Get going (as soon as you read the rest of the book, that is).

Try out these eight steps on your own project list, using the Project Priority Worksheet we provided in the beginning of this chapter.

The high priority projects on your list should be the most important projects in your area of responsibility. The priority projects should also be the first ones you manage with the tools and techniques described in the rest of this book. If you do this, you'll have a much better chance of getting them done on time, within budget, and to everybody's satisfaction.

> **High Water!**
> If you're managing your first project, select one of limited scope, limited time, and limited impact to try out the process. For example, choose a project of less than 6 weeks; a team size of less than 4; and a project with a positive impact if it succeeds—but something that won't kill the business if it does not.

So, How Will It All Get Done?

You've identified the projects you're going to be working on, but how are you going to coordinate all this with all the other work you have to do? Without some tricks up your sleeve, it's pretty tough to schedule, budget, and coordinate a project while still getting the ordinary work done—and getting everything completed to everyone's satisfaction. It may sound like an impossible challenge, but the project management tools and techniques you'll learn about in the upcoming chapters can help you sort things out.

The special methods of project management can help you get projects done while you continue to do your ordinary work. Special guidelines and tools can help you schedule a project and control the budget and team. Together, these methods, guidelines, and tools are called the project management process.

Don't panic if it seems like more than you can handle. The project management process isn't that hard to master. The responsibility that goes along with managing projects doesn't need to be stressful because the project management toolbox offers a structured approach for handling projects that makes them easy to control. Project management reduces the surprises and makes it possible to bring work in on time and within budget, even when large numbers of people and strict deadlines are involved. The project management process includes both manual and computerized techniques that can help improve performance and efficiency in today's fast-paced, objective-driven businesses.

The project management process has proven value in getting things done on time and within budget in any organization. These proven tools and techniques are commonly used by engineers and scientists in complex projects with huge budgets, thousands of tasks, and hundreds of people; but the power of project management is not limited to large-scale scientific, engineering, and construction applications. The techniques and advantages of project management concepts can be applied to any project in any business—if you know how to recognize a project when you see one (you should have a pretty good handle on that by now).

The Least You Need to Know

➤ Most people have to complete ordinary work as well as projects.

➤ Projects differ from ordinary work and thus need special management techniques to bring them to successful conclusions.

➤ Projects should be prioritized so the most important projects get done first.

➤ The success of all projects depends on the appropriate balance of time and resources to meet specific objectives.

➤ The project management process can help you get things done on time and within budget.

Scoping Out the Goals for a Project

Even a good idea can be a bad idea if the goals and scope of a project are not clearly defined before major resources are committed to it. Fuzzy goals can be interpreted differently; thus people may never agree whether you're done or if you succeeded or failed.

In this chapter, you'll learn why you need to get very specific about what you expect to accomplish on your projects. You'll also learn how to set goals for your project that no one can argue with.

Why Bother with the Goals? I Know What I Want to Do!

Okay. Okay. Patience is not always a project manager's best virtue, and lots of projects get started without clear goals. Please don't let that happen to you. Slow down. Don't rush into the next phase of planning until you have consensus on the goals. The time you spend on setting goals will help ensure that the project you deliver is really something worth crowing about.

The fate of the people-mover project that a major American city invested in years ago may help you understand the importance of setting clear goals. The project seemed like a good idea at the time. Just like the Jetsons, people would be transported to where they wanted to go within the downtown area. The city council that approved the project wanted to be progressive and modern, and maybe they thought the project would help solve downtown congestion—or maybe they had watched too many cartoons.

You see, the goal of the project was to move people around the downtown area in carts on a conveyor belt. The approach worked at Disneyland, so they figured it must be viable for a real city. No one asked the critical questions about the project before it got started: How many people would need to be moved around? Would people pay to take a people mover? How long would it take to use the people mover as opposed to walking to and from the same place? What about all the health conscious types who prefer to walk anyway? And most important of all, did anyone really need or want a people mover?

Millions of dollars were spent on studies, on property for building the ramps, and on engineering the people-mover components. Then, about the same time researchers determined that most people wouldn't pay to take the people mover, the engineers discovered that it would take as much time to get on and off the moving ramp as it would take to walk the distance between locations. The project was killed. Sadly, more useful projects for solving the problems of downtown congestion would have to wait because of the funds wasted on the people-mover fiasco. Perhaps a new version of the people moving idea could be viable today—with a new design and a justifiable goal—but the project as conceived should never have been started. Rushing ahead with a good idea isn't always the same as reaching consensus on the viability of a good idea. Consensus takes more time.

Words from the Wise
A project is different from usual work. It has a single focus... It is a child in the midst of a family of adolescent and adult tasks.

—Bennet Lientz and Kathryn Rea in *Project Management for the 20th Century*

The lesson to be learned here is that you want to be clear on some things before you commit to a project: the goals, including measurable benefits to the stakeholders and users; the scope; the time to carry out the project; and a rough estimate of resources and costs. Doing this work up front gives your project more credibility and manageability.

Clear Project Goals Make Sense to Everyone

In the most simple view, goals are the specification of what you hope to achieve at the end of the project. But the people-mover story illustrated some important concepts to know about setting appropriate goals for your projects:

➤ Any project you undertake must make sense in terms of an overall goal that benefits people in some way. If a project doesn't have a benefit for someone, why bother? Another way to look at this is to make sure the goals for the project specify how completing the project will make things better than they would be without the project. You should be able to clearly describe the outcomes, deliverables, and benefits to stakeholders and end users.

➤ Project goals must be carefully thought out; even the most obvious questions should be considered to make sure the idea is really as good as people think it is.

➤ Project goals should provide the criteria you need to evaluate your success in completing a project. These criteria include measures of the time, costs, and resources required to achieve your desired outcomes.

➤ The project goals need to be reviewed with the core team and consensus must be reached before you move into the next phase of the project.

Of course, you can use project management techniques on projects with inappropriate goals and accomplish something, but you may still fail to do anything useful. For example, if your goal is simply to build a bridge over the River Kwai, as the project manager you might feel quite proud when the bridge joins the two banks of the river. But if that same bridge collapses under the weight of rush hour traffic, your project isn't really a success. Or, what if your goal is to build a better mousetrap to rid your city of rats—but after you build it, no one comes rushing to your door to buy it. Has the project succeeded? Not really. Even if the rat trap works, people have to want to use it to get rid of the vermin.

Six Criteria for Setting Great Goals

Goals are the heart, the mission, and the purpose for initiating a project. The goals are usually set by the people responsible for approving a project. (This is often the core team you'll learn about in Chapter 8.) As a project manager, you will usually be part of this initial team and part of the goal setting process.

As you and the key project stakeholders begin setting goals, you should be aware that there are six general criteria that adequate project goals should meet to ensure that the project will accomplish something of perceived value.

Write goals for your projects that always meet these six criteria and you'll be working on projects with a purpose.

The Six Criteria for Good Project Goals

High Water!
Taking over someone else's goals can be difficult. If you aren't in on the goal-setting process, carefully review the goals before you assume the project. Make sure the goals are complete and well formed. If they are off base, ask to review and revise them with the key stakeholders. If you're not given that opportunity, consider looking elsewhere. It's better to decline the offer to be responsible for an ill-defined project than to be blamed for it later.

Criterion 1: Goals Must Be Specific

Your goals are adequately clear if another, equally competent manager can take over your responsibilities and guide the project to completion. If your goals meet this criteria, you're pointed in the right direction. Ask coworkers to read your goals and determine what has been stated and what the project will look like when it's done. Confused, surprising, or conflicting responses mean more refinement is required.

Criterion 2: Goals Must Be Realistic

Your goals must be possible or at least be within the realm of the possible. For example, if you have a project to build a house on land that costs $1 million and you only have $100,000 available in cash and credit, you obviously have little chance of getting the house done. In this case, perhaps you should consider a preliminary project to build up your cash reserves before you draw up plans for the house.

Criterion 3: Goals Must Have a Time Component

Projects must have a definite finish date or they never are completed. Projects with no terminus never terminate, so to speak. Projects with unrealistically short dates blow up like an overloaded fuse.

Criterion 4: Goals Must Be Measurable

You must be able to measure your success at meeting your goals, be it with a powerful computer or a chart full of colored push-pins tacked up on the wall. These results are called deliverables—the results of the project. Quality is a vital part of this criterion.

Projects can have interim deliverables that don't reflect the final product. For example, a part might need to be machined early in the project cycle so more work can be completed downstream. The part required is a deliverable.

Deliverables, like projects, are not only evaluated by the fact that something is produced but by their quality as well. A perfect example is the more than 1,000 pairs of shoes that were delivered on time by a work group in the former Soviet Union. As required in the plan, the shoes were stitched all the way down to the mounting for the soles; however, no one specified soles in the plans. The shoes were delivered but the results weren't too useful. The shoes lacked that subtle edge of quality most buyers would prefer for the demands of the Soviet winter.

Project Lingo
What's a *deliverable?* Deliverables are the clearly defined results, goods, or services produced during the project or at its outcome.

High Water!
Goals and estimates you agree to during this goal-setting phase tend to get "cast in concrete" in the minds of other project participants. Part of your responsibility as a project manager is to get consensus by the core team and stakeholders that they may be expected to review, approve, and revise plans and schedules (and even budgets) as the project progresses and conditions (and goals) change. This tells your team members you intend to keep them in the loop so surprises won't happen, and it increases your credibility as a manager of the project process.

Criterion 5: Goals Must Be Agreed Upon

At the onset of a project, you as the project manager and the other initiators of the project (your boss, for example, or the customer or the city council in the case of a city project) must agree on the goals before you take any further steps toward planning the project. If you don't reach consensus, there's no point in beginning the project; it's doomed from the start because the stakeholders can't agree about the outcomes that will make the project a success. In a large project that crosses many departments or other organizations, gaining consensus can be a long and thankless process. (Refer to "Seeing Eye to Eye" later in this chapter.)

Eventually, all the team members as well as the stakeholders must buy into the project goals if you're going to manage the project effectively. Without consensus on the goals, the project faces a bumpy road to completion. Projects started with misunderstood goals often have team members working at cross purposes or occasionally duplicating each other's efforts.

Criterion 6: Responsibility for Achieving the Goals Must Be Identified

While you, the project manager, bear the brunt of responsibility for the overall success of the project, others may be responsible for pieces of the goals. Like agreeing on the goals, the people responsible for the goals must be identified and be willing to accept responsibility before the project proceeds further.

If you can identify all the major players who will be making decisions and contributing major pieces to the project, it is best to get their sign-off up front. For example, if your project is to choose and implement a new piece of software to allow field personnel to input customer requests from the field, you need to get an agreement from your hardware and software groups that the communications hardware and extended computing power will be there to support the software.

Establishing Goals Step-by-Step

It's easy to establish goals for your project. In fact, it's so easy that you'll find yourself with more goals than you can handle. The trick is to limit goals to those of priority to the project. Here's what to do:

1. Make a list of the project's goals. At this point don't rule anything out. Just make a list and check it twice.

2. Study the list and zap anything that has no direct bearing on the project.

3. Eliminate anything that is really a step in meeting the goals, but not a goal for the end result of the project.

   You should now have a "pure" list of project goals. It's now time for the final step in goal setting.

4. Study the list again. Check that all the goals meet the six criteria. Now, determine if all these goals are doable within one project. Look for goals that really belong to a separate project or are not directly germane to the project at hand. Cross them out. They may be really important and should not be forgotten, however, so don't forget to consider them again when planning another project. But leaving them in your current project confuses team members and eats resources *you* need for *this* project to succeed.

If the items you yanked from the list are important, then you should consider alerting your management of them so they can decide what, if any, action to take. This may require explanation on your part as to why you can't take on the extra work and how each item deserves a project world of its own.

Successful projects must meet their goals with a minimum of changes and without disturbing the main work flow of the organization. If a project derails for one reason or another, additional resources may be used in an attempt to meet dates. This causes serious organizational problems as other important work is put aside to accommodate the problem project. Your task is to run the project as smoothly as possible with no requirement for additional time or bodies or money that interferes with other projects or day-to-day operations.

The best goals are spelled out in writing. Written goals are a powerful consensus builder, especially in a large, complex, or multi-layered project. When you and other decision makers need to make changes to a project, the goals help you decide whether the change fits the confines of the goals. If it doesn't, then the change may be unnecessary or detrimental to the project. It may indicate that a problem needs further research, which could require the approval from other team's managers and possibly senior management or whomever is paying the bill.

The goals document becomes the vehicle for discussion and consensus, and in its agreed form, gives you the authority to proceed with the project.

Seeing Eye to Eye

Consensus has been mentioned several times in this book. It is the process of getting honest buy-in from those involved that all phases of the project plan are workable, that those chosen for the roles will accept them eagerly, and that the goals are realistic.

Objectives and Your Project

Unlike goals, you can have as many objectives as your project demands (and you can afford). The establishment of objectives takes time to ensure that you aren't, well, biting off more than you can chew.

> **Words from the Wise**
> The best preparation for good work tomorrow is to do good work today.
> —Elbert Hubbard

> **High Water!**
> Goals and objectives must be established and agreed upon by other team members and managers before project execution. You can't expect team members to hit invisible targets, although the more loyal or uninformed ones may make a go of it.

> **High Water!**
> Too many objectives are like too many cooks in the kitchen—they spoil the broth. When considering a project, look for tasks or sets of tasks that should really remain as separate projects. Split them off as such. A word of warning: Management may attempt to add objectives to your project that they know don't belong there just to save money.

Project Scope

No, it's not a mouthwash development project. The *scope* is the size of the project. When looking at any project, you always look at its scope. Some project managers specialize solely in projects of a certain scope, considering small ones too petty for their talents and massive ones too long-lived or problematic to get involved.

As scope "width" increases, the project has fewer tasks. As it decreases, more projects may spin off. Where the lines meet in this simple model is the ideal point—a balance of complexity versus simplicity.

Complexity versus Scope

Project Lingo

Scope is project management lingo for project size. As you would rightly assume, the project scope for assembling a marketing plan for a minor new product is much smaller than for building an attack jet. As a project manager might explain, "it's a small-scope project."

Project scope can include one or more of the following considerations:

➤ How much is to be achieved in the project

➤ The length of the project window (when it must be completed)

➤ Obligation of resources (the usual: money, people, supplies, equipment)

With the exception of the simplest projects, squeezing the scope often spins off additional subprojects. Making it too broad adds a complexity because too many disparate elements must be managed simultaneously.

The Least You Need to Know

➤ Project goal number 1: Completing the project on time.

➤ Project goal number 2: Completing the project within budget and available resources.

➤ Project goal number 3: Completing the project by achieving the desired quality in the final result.

➤ Objectives consist of specific aims. Building a house is an objective.

➤ Objectives require clear, concise writing so project participants understand each one.

➤ When planning a project, its size (scope) must be considered.

WELL, WE COULD'VE DONE THIS BETTER...

Chapter 7

Understanding Risks and Constraints

In This Chapter

➤ Risky business

➤ Constraints that bind you

➤ Trouble with a capital T right here in River City

➤ Managing risks and constraints

Those new to project management often create project goals that have more in common with fairy tales than business objectives. The project goals are visions of an implementation in a perfect world. Well, quit dreaming and get real. Even the smallest projects are constrained by reality. As projects get larger, more risks come into play that can change your vision of utopia into a nightmare in hell.

A good project manager measures risks in advance. Even with clear goals, you need to establish the feasibility of what you have set out to do. On a small project, this step may only take a moment to ponder, but on larger projects, risk assessment can be a complete project in its own right. The goal of the risk and constraint analysis is to establish the feasibility of the project within the constraints of economy, politics, laws, and organizational structure that limit your business. This risk and constraint analysis establishes whether the goals of the project you just defined in Chapter 6 are really feasible.

To continue beyond the initiation phase, a project should meet the criteria for feasibility that are appropriate for the organization. A project that moves beyond initiation without taking into account risks and constraints, including the organizational and business environment for a project, becomes much like a silver ball in a pinball machine: it bounces with abandon from bumper to bumper by elements beyond its control. Bad weather? A delay. Your main supplier goes bankrupt? A delay. A strike? A delay. Waffling among senior management? A delay, and maybe even project termination! Maybe even your job...well, we won't say it. You get the idea.

A risk involves something that's anticipated that can go wrong. Many risks can be planned for in advance. The likelihood of some risks is unknown, but by identifying potential risks in advance, their impact is often reduced. As a good project manager, your job is to make decisions that reduce the risks associated with your project while keeping focused on the goals.

Constraints, unlike risks, are known in advance. If you have only $10,000 to buy a car, that's a constraint. No matter how much you want that new Mercedes, $10,000 won't buy it for you. Constraints are the real world limits on the possibilities for your projects. Violate the constraints in defining your project, and the project will fail in some way. Your job as project manager is to make sure you understand the constraints of your project and work within their limits.

Look at the Upside and the Downside

Instead of looking at everything you can/should do, look at everything that will get in your way or become a potential roadblock. While motivational speakers may convince you otherwise, looking at the downside of a project is the best way to anticipate events that might slow down or even kill the project. Because you, as project manager, are directly responsible for the success or failure of your project, you must look at both the positive and negative sides of the equation before making a commitment to the project. It could be a relatively risk-free venture, or you could be handed the task of captaining the equivalent of the maiden voyage of the *Titanic*.

Risky Business

A project is anthropomorphic: like a life-form, it has a life cycle and body parts. The various parts of a project must function in harmony to produce a successful result. When people discuss it, they talk about The Project as if it were a person. People don't remember the vendor who was late installing the carpet who held up the opening of the new sales office. They only know "The Project is behind schedule," and not, "They're opening the research lab late because the carpet is still being laid."

As project manager, you're responsible for all aspects of the project, including those that, while a part of the project, are largely out of your control. Projects may involve risks in any one of a hundred areas beyond your direct control; but as project manager, the finger of responsibility will point directly at you.

Identifying risks and constraints beforehand provides you time to mitigate those that can be fixed or to notify the stakeholders (both verbally *and* in writing) that the project may be in jeopardy even before it begins. A critical analysis of the project is crucial to get it off to an acceptable and workable start. It is not unheard of for a would-be project manager to be handed a project that has languished for a period of time because no one in their right mind would touch it. This is especially typical of a new employee handed an obvious boondoggle. While the people delegating

Words from the Wise

There is much to be said of failure. It is more interesting than success.

—Max Beerbohm

the job congratulate her on getting off to a good start with an important piece of work, once the poor soul has left the room, they sigh with relief, all pleased with themselves.

Going into a project with a "we can do anything" attitude may support team spirit at the onset, but when things come unglued and reality sets in, your team will become frustrated, management will complain, and you will kick yourself for not fixing the up-front problems up front. Plus, budget and schedule problems will blow any possibility of getting things done within the constraints of the original plan, which means asking for more time and more money. You need to learn to communicate and negotiate change (read Chapters 23 and 24).

If you're lucky, you'll get a new lease on life and resources to revive and revise the project. If you're not, you'll have to read Chapter 27 to learn how to bring such a project quickly to its termination—not the most pleasant process in project management, although we must admit that we've been forced to that stage once or twice through the years.

Break It Apart to Make It Doable

If your project goals seem too big or too risky, you might consider breaking your project into smaller projects, each with more feasibility. The approach of using levels of projects is commonly employed in large-scale, engineering and scientific research projects.

For example, when a new airplane idea is proffered by one of Boeing's customers, a design feasibility project is usually the first form of the project. If the design feasibility project meets its goals, then a project to build a prototype might follow. The project changes from a project with design goals to one with engineering goals. If the design is successful, the Boeing folks would evaluate the goals for a production airplane, and if everything still seemed appropriate, they would plan that project.

This would require another shift in project orientation—from just building something to also making it profitable to do so. Thus, the risky venture of bringing a new plane to market is broken into three smaller, more feasible projects. If any of the interim projects fails, Boeing's losses are minimized. As each of the subprojects is completed, the risks at the next level are reduced.

Constraints

Project constraints are a major factor when establishing the project plan and when the project is underway. You may want to add a third tower to New York's twin trade towers, but be constrained to assembling little more than a tin-roofed shack with tar-paper windows. The constraints that bring a high flying project to earth include:

Words from the Wise
Laws and regulations can be constraints, sometimes acting in strange ways. For example, a project might be planned to implement a new accounting procedure to meet new laws or regulations. In that case, the constraint is that, if the project is not completed by that date, the organization might be breaking some law. So perhaps the scope might be pared back in other ways: for example, deciding to implement a manual procedure first, and then later integrate it into computerized systems.

—James MacIntyre, project management expert

➤ How much money is really available and when?

➤ By when must the project be completed?

➤ What inside resources are required?

➤ What outside resources are required and can you afford them?

➤ Can you get consensus among project members, executives, and stakeholders that the project is important and deserves your time and effort?

➤ What are you willing to settle for that will still meet your needs?

➤ Is there a way to do it using less expensive or fewer resources? (If there is, then your problem may be solved.)

The process of answering these questions permanently grounds some projects as the real world intrudes on what's really little more than an energetic pipe dream. Constraints are a modicum of reality. Use them as a tool to fine tune a project as well as to brush off grandiose suggestions.

Project constraints are quite broad. Similar to the restrictions every manager faces when confronted with any task, constraints must be identified beforehand or an expensive project may hit the skids (along with its manager) after bogging down in an avoidable quagmire.

There are three kinds of project constraints:

1. *Those that can be anticipated.* If you know that down the road something is likely to occur that will affect your project (bad weather, work issues, or the departure of a key project member), you can build this into the schedule.

2. *Those that pop up mid-project.* Experienced project managers build in slip time for contingencies and react proactively when the unexpected occurs. Any range of disasters is possible on a project; from acts of God (your development lab gets washed into the sea in a hurricane) to a key employee who turned in a misrepresentative resume and knows nothing about the project at hand.

3. *Projects that stem from poor plans or lack of support.*
   Any enterprise that begins a project must have a
   commitment to complete it. Sadly, some projects
   never reach completion, and you may become
   the scapegoat for a failure for which you are not
   wholly responsible. Examples include:

Project Lingo
The *Statement of Work* (SOW—nice acronym, huh?) is an integrated set of goal descriptions, conflicts, and assumptions that accompany the evolving master project plan during its development.

   ➤ Impossible projects, such as assembling a
     huge computer database to supervise a
     company with 10,000 employees, sales
     orders, inventory, and manage the phone
     system, and so on.

   ➤ Projects already in the works or with an assigned team. Re-interview the team
     to ensure you aren't being handed a loaf of day-old bread.

   ➤ Projects with no staff and no budget to hire a staff.

   ➤ Projects that have been underway for more than six months with no percep-
     tible progress.

   ➤ Projects that assume you will bring in the money to keep the project rolling.
     Common among modern corporations and a long time standard among not-
     for-profit organizations, you become a fundraiser *and* a project manager. No
     one person can do both roles and it's unfair of the organization to demand
     that you bring in $1,000,000 in capital to fund your $55,000 salary.

   ➤ Projects in which a senior manager is fighting with others in upper manage-
     ment to cancel or significantly modify the project.

   ➤ Projects with multiple and/or unfocused goals (more common than you would
     think). "Develop a cure for the HIV virus while using the same team to build a
     suspension bridge like San Francisco's Golden Gate Bridge capable of linking
     England's south coast to that of Calais, France."

Constraint 1: The Budget

Most projects suck up money faster than you may realize. Whether you're opening a new
sales office or developing a new product, the budget will constrain your efforts. Most
organizations will also charge your project budget for the employees you borrow and any
company-provided services you may require. Depending on the charge-back service, you
may find it less expensive to bring in outsiders because you can choose exactly the skill
set you require without the corporate baggage that comes with insiders within some
organizations. You should be aware of the danger of agreeing to a budget in order to
please the boss, management, or the customer when you know in advance the funds will
be inadequate. See Chapter 13 for more information on project budgeting.

Constraint 2: The Schedule

Time waits for no one, especially not the manager of a faltering project built around impossible dates. The schedule is always a constraint, even if a project's due date is not that critical. If it rambles on after the predicted end date, the budget will expand and team members may be pulled off to handle other responsibilities. Missing an end date may cause serious marketing consequences. A new, but late-to-market product may arrive at the market window, only to find it closed and firmly locked.

Constraint 3: The People

Time Is Money
A project that has more than one manager controlling it is likely to be unsuccessful no matter how hard you work. Pass on such opportunities unless you can (politely) demand that you have only one boss running you and the project. On the other hand, many projects require the approval of managers in more than one department. Your skill as a project manager may also be measured by your ability to form a schedule and budget that they agree on. Just make sure you're the one to control things after consensus is achieved.

We'll explain how to build a team in Chapter 8 and deal with people conflicts in Chapter 22. For now, keep in mind that people conflicts are always a project manager's most pressing concern. You can argue for more money and time, but it's the people who really make the project. If the right ones are not available or are unaffordable, then you will have to make do with the team that's available—no matter how inexperienced.

Constraint 4: The Real World

Once a project is underway, reality has an ugly habit of settling in. Inadequate budgets, impossible schedules, and team members with more spirit than skills make for a project that's late, underfunded, and difficult to complete. Getting a project underway is like breaking in a new car. It takes time to get all the parts accustomed to working with each other. On a project, this synchronization may require fine tuning. Some may not get along with their supervisors, or a brilliant engineer may quit and join a competitive company. Communication is the best vehicle for keeping the watch fine-tuned. The first milestone, positioned at about 10 percent of the project (five percent on large projects), is the time to review relationships, progress, and the effects that the actual project is having on your workforce, the project budget, and the schedule.

Constraint 5: Facilities and Equipment

Every project assumes that equipment required will be available within the project's time. Be it a 20-ton grader, an electron microscope, or a simple freight elevator, the right tools must be available for their period in the spotlight. Just like people, equipment resources are key to completion. If a project slips its dates, that slush drink machine you ordered for the big party may be tied up at another get-together.

Constraint 6: Acts of God

As humans, we can do little to avoid acts of God affecting projects, but we can take steps to avoid the most likely. Don't build precision models in San Francisco under concrete freeway ramps, and avoid vibration-sensitive experiments near the runways of Dallas-Fort Worth airport.

Otherwise, with this in mind, your project should be insured. It's the best, well, insurance against hurricanes, floods, earthquakes, and other unpredictable acts of God. (Check the policy to verify that such events are covered and not exclusively prohibited, as is common in most commercial policies.)

As you might assume, the nature of constraints varies with the project. Team members fail at their tasks, sunspots blow away your satellite uplink in the middle of an important transmission, and the concrete rebar used in your new corporate headquarters turns to rust about one month after installation. *You can't predict everything!*

Managing Risks and Constraints

Going into a project with the risks and constraints clearly documented is the best tool for handling senior management. Assuming they actually read your concerns, when something jumps the tracks, it's a risk that was clearly documented up front (not that they'll love you for it anyway).

If the best offense is a good defense, then when problems are encountered, having a contingency plan in place is vital to ensure continued success of the project. You can document plans to alleviate known constraints, but planning for a risk is more difficult because you might not be aware that the risk even exists. For constraints, you work around them, even if it slows the project and/or requires extra money. For risks, rub a lucky rabbit's foot and be prepared to go head to head with management for a bail-out—more money, more time, a less ambitious project—whatever it takes.

A well-crafted presentation is the best tool, but if it's a finger-in-the-dike-time emergency, then the sooner you get what you need to fix the problem, the better. Projects that pose significant safety risks or a stock price meltdown the next morning justify 3 a.m. phone calls to senior decision makers. Just hope you never need to take such drastic action!

The Least You Need to Know

> ➤ Project risks and constraints are known roadblocks that should be accounted for before the project is underway.

> ➤ Some projects should simply be avoided. Be especially careful of "inherited" problem projects.

> ➤ The impossible remains impossible no matter how enthused your team.

> ➤ Rome wasn't built in a day, and project management won't let you do it either.

GET IN THERE AND
WIN! WIN! WIN! WIN!
GET 'EM ON THE RUN
AND KEEP 'EM ON—

Chapter 8

Building a Project Team

In This Chapter

➤ Identifying what you need and what you want in a team

➤ The core team members—who are they?

➤ Matching skills to talent

➤ Choosing team members who fit the mold

➤ Team players versus individual contributors

A single person doesn't win a basketball game—a team does. The same is true of projects. Thus, as in sports, project success depends largely on the team members selected. In fact, choosing the core team could be the single most important decision you make as a project manager. Strong team leaders effectively combined with knowledgeable experts (where necessary) build the momentum required for successful project completion.

The ideal project team completes the work on time and within budget with little micro-management on your part. A weak or misaligned team requires substantial management on your part to limp past the finish line days, weeks, or, for a major project, even years late. San Francisco's BART (Bay Area Rapid Transit) project and Los Angeles' unfortunate subway are prime examples of projects gone awry in part due to bumbling project teams as well as the ill winds of fate.

In this chapter, you'll learn how to build the best team you can.

The Project Team: Diversity and Skills

A project team is made up of people with differing personalities, skills, ability, knowledge, and temperament. Your mission is to evaluate the project prior to choosing personnel, and to build a team that takes advantage of each team member's skills without taxing their weaknesses.

With a form like the example shown here, you can list the actual skills you'll have available to complete your project.

Use this worksheet to detail the skills of your project team.

Skill Requirements Worksheet

Project Name _____ Today's Date _____

Your Name _____

Task	Skills Required	People or Vendor Possibilities

➤ What skills are required to complete each task of the project? Does a team member require specific skills for a task or will general skills suffice? Are strong interpersonal skills or the ability to communicate verbally and in writing vital prerequisites?

➤ If you could choose anyone you wanted for your team, who would these people be and why? (Hint: Your answers should involve both skills and personality for each person you choose.)

➤ Given the team that you actually get to work with, what levels of supervision will be required? You must be brutally honest here, especially if you're evaluating the skills of people who also happen to be friends or colleagues. Regardless of the talent involved, there's no sense pretending that your team members will be self-sufficient. Some people simply need more direction than others—and these people will need some of your time.

> **Words from the Wise**
> There is no substitute for talent. Industry and all the virtues are of no avail.
>
> —Aldous Huxley, *Point Counter Point* (1928)

➤ Where will the people come from? Do you have the talent in your own department (assuming these people have the time to be assigned to your project) or must you hire outsiders or raid another department for talent?

Answering these questions will allow you to compare the talent required for the project to the people actually available. Are the people you need ready, willing, and able? If so, are they affordable? Will your project demand that already overburdened coworkers take on yet another responsibility? How much will outside resources, such as consultants, experts, and grunt labor, *really* cost?

> **High Water!**
> When taking over an on-going project and its staff, check out the team before you accept the job. Make sure you have the authority to make changes to the team as necessary. There might be good reasons why there's an opening for a project manager. Forced inheritance of a poor team could make you the project scapegoat instead of its savior.

Once you complete this outline of job responsibilities, you will have a document that will help you choose the best team members for your project.

The Core Team Members—Who Are They?

The core project team usually consists of the most important players, who will be associated with the project from start to finish. On small projects, the core team might be the only members of the team.

Rank is not always a consideration in forming the core project team for a larger project—sometimes skill or experience are more important factors. The core members work on the project from start to finish while other workers come and go as their tasks are completed. Your core team will consist of:

➤ You

➤ Managers, coordinators, and supervisory personnel

➤ Key players, such as engineers, design specialists, scientists, advisors, and other experts who have important roles in the project

The core team is directly responsible for the overall success of the project, assuring it finishes on time and within budget. The core team may shift, as mentioned, as segments of the project are completed and new ones open up. Your core team should consist of your most trusted employees and central advisors. You might get stuck with people who are less than loyal and experienced, depending on your project's structure and who provides the team members.

THIS WAY

Along the Critical Path

Free help! If your project is in any way civic minded, you can get volunteers to assist in the day-to-day operations and not pay them anything! Amazing as it may seem, there are a lot of people with time on their hands who will assist in any worthy cause. You might have to throw in lunch and a plaque or two, but many complex projects have been completed entirely with volunteer help. How can you find these people? Most large newspapers will run your plea for assistance at no cost or a reduced charge. Treat these people well and you can have a helpful, dedicated staff on tap with a payroll close to nothing.

The Other Team Members—Who Are They?

In addition to your core team, you might need outside consultants and specialists. Generally, these people perform a role during one part of a project and then are phased out once their work is completed. In addition to these players, administrators and staff play a role in most projects, but because their roles are generic and they are replaceable, they are not considered to be core team members.

Where Will the People Come From?

Manning (or womaning) a project can be difficult because coworkers are already buried in their own work and hiring outsiders is expensive. Typically, your options are limited by manpower availability and the cost of hiring staff. But an organization that wants or needs to complete a project must make staff available, even if it means pulling people off other projects or bringing in outside help. Staffing options include bringing into the project:

➤ Your own staff and other people from your department

➤ Staff from other departments

➤ Contracting with consultants, outside vendors, or temporary agencies

➤ Hiring and training new staff

> **Time Is Money**
> It's common to use people for projects on segmented time. That means that they may work on other projects part-time or have dedicated duties, such as unstructured management or administrative ones, while they help you out.

Like business options, each of these choices has an up side and a down side. Just working with unfamiliar faces can mean a few surprises. You might have to adjust the project to accommodate each personality and productivity level while keeping a weather eye on the project dollars and timing.

Your Own Staff and Other People from Your Department

If staff with appropriate skills exist in your department and aren't already (fully) committed to other projects, then you have the easiest alternative. You have easy access to these people, you have a working knowledge of their strengths and weaknesses, and, depending on your rank, you may have control over them.

On the downside, if your project requires outside expertise, you'll have to get it elsewhere, either inside or outside your organization, which will require time and money. Projects with high visibility can be problematic politically, too. If other departments see you utilizing vast amounts of resources on a single project, you may have to justify your resource use as other projects slip. Further, you may be considered hard to work with because you use only people from your group when more experienced talent is known to exist elsewhere in the company or organization.

Staff from Other Departments

Working with others in your organization makes for good communication and camaraderie among those involved. In a large organization, this might get you the technical or specialized staff you need or it might allow you to bring in a competent project manager whom you watch with awe as he keeps the gears oiled. For example, you might need a financial wizard from the finance department to track your budget and streamline purchase orders.

On the downside, the main difficulty you will encounter is one of convincing someone's manager to allow him or her to join your project. Down the line, you also might discover that your outside staff member is late on his tasks because his boss agreed to let him join your project without reducing his current workload.

Contracting with Consultants, Outside Vendors, or Temporary Agencies

Outsiders are always available—for a price. With careful selection, you can fully man a project with exactly the right mix of people. Hire them when you need them and let them go when they're done. This is a flexible arrangement in that you have no responsibility (other than paying the bill) for keeping them on or even providing office space because all but some temp agency employees will already have space of their own.

High Water!
When accepting someone else's employee, watch both the internal charges (if any) and the quality of the hire. If the project is long, you may be accepting someone else's failed hire. Or, they may be known as hardworking, but difficult to manage; or, they may plainly lack the skills you require.

One the downside, outsiders can be expensive. The key to using outside consultants is to schedule their work carefully. The cost for a highly trained welder priced at $100 per hour by his agency is mitigated if, with careful scheduling, he comes in, welds using his own equipment, and leaves in five hours. But, should the work fall behind and he spends three weeks cooling his heals while the clock is running, he'll become an expensive liability, regardless of his admirable skills.

Along the Critical Path

Be careful of using the "headcount" word when you talk about additions to your project team. Headcount is the term used to describe the fixed number of internal employees approved to work in an organization or on a project. Hiring a new person "increases headcount." In many projects, using an outside consultant or other temporary worker only increases costs. Sometimes its easier to increase costs than to raise headcount because headcount enlargement shifts the permanent overhead costs. Expenses for office space, furniture, tools, benefits, and even additional management time must be accounted for. Thus, if you need a person for a project and you don't have a job for that person after the project is done, it's usually easier to propose an outside team member than to propose additional headcount.

Hiring and Training New Staff

If the project is a long-term commitment or is ongoing with a finish date far enough out, then you might find that adding to the headcount is the most expedient method for bringing in the manpower and expertise required. Of course, you noted the word *training* in the title of this section. You must be fully prepared with time and money to train your new bodies in everything from their task requirements to the culture of your organization. But, adding new workers often brings a fresh point of view, takes some pressure off other staff members, and is an easy way to add a much needed skill set not available elsewhere in the company.

Words from the Wise

Groups of two or more people are political entities.

—Kim Baker, explaining graphic design realities at an Apple Computer-sponsored seminar in 1991

On the downside (yes, you've heard those words before), headcount increases are enormously difficult to justify in most organizations, especially those furloughing long-time employees while you are looking to add. You may be told "no way" in so many words or asked to take on an employee otherwise slated for a one-way trip out the back door. The latter could force you to choose someone with no appropriate skills for the task at hand. Avoid this potential nightmare by being very specific in your description of the job. If no one with a pink slip exactly fills the bill, you'll have an opportunity to choose from fresh stock.

Individual Contributors Versus Team Players

Not everyone you hire will like being a part of the team or will be good at playing the role of a team player. Team players function like members of a football team: they work together and build on each other's strengths and accomplishments. They make for great project supervisors, and you'll see them having a beer with other team members after work on Fridays. But there are also the invaluable individual contributors in many projects.

Those with specialized creative skills, such as engineers, designers, writers, and (for lack of a better phrase) project visionaries, may appear to you and other team members as downright hostile. That's okay if their expertise is a must-have for the project. Although you should avoid mercurial personalities with no people skills whatsoever, a genius with a compelling vision might make the difference between a mediocre project and great one. Just keep them out of supervisory roles wherever possible.

The Team Players

You must structure the project team to work like a clock. Appropriate matches of worker to coworker, manager to worker, and manager to manager are crucial. Assuming you are the team leader, you must also be comfortable working with the parties you have direct interaction with.

In a long project, this team assembly becomes more important. Someone who gets along with a colleague for a five week project may grate on their nerves during a project spanning a longer period of time. Conflicts are inevitable, but you can do your best to assemble a team who's structure minimizes their likelihood.

> **Time Is Money**
> There is no perfect team. Looking to build one is futile. Instead, build the best team from those available and work with each player to ensure smooth operation and to eliminate personality conflicts. Fewer conflicts result in less expensive projects.

Building the Best Team with What You Have Available

As you would assume, staffing a small, closely held project is less complicated than building the personnel list for a major one. A really large project involves more risk and goes through large sums of money quickly. To help you make your choices better then the luck of the draw, a skills inventory is required.

For most projects, the skills inventory involves two steps. First, based on the general project goals completed earlier, list the overall skills required to complete the main objectives of the project, grouping like skills together into a "job description."

Second, describe the characteristics of the individual who should fill the shoes of the person you described in each job description. These descriptions should be brief, to the point, and realistic. (If one of the job descriptions requires the skills of a Supreme Being, then you need to revisit Chapter 6 and work on the project's goals and scope prior to this step.)

Next, attempt to put names of available personnel next to each job description. Work in pencil! You might find that you can handle the project with people already on staff with no problem; or, you might find that expensive (or maybe even cheap) outside resources are required because

> **Words from the Wise**
> In order that people may be happy in their work, these three things are needed: they must be fit for it: they must not do too much of it: and they must have a sense of success in it—not a doubtful sense, such as needs some testimony of others for its confirmation, but a sure sense, or rather knowledge, that so much work has been done well, and fruitfully done, whatever the world may say or think about it.
> —W. H. Auden

the time available simply won't allow you to train existing staff to do the job. At this point, it's a "we can do it!" or "it's too expensive" decision. This chart will help you make the decision. The chart points out the degree of resource drain and quantifies the use of people not available on staff or in other departments.

Choose Me!

After you identify the tasks and pencil in the names, you must move people around for the best fit. If there are too many question marks instead of names next to the job descriptions, you might need to take a longer look at the project and its scope. Maybe the project really isn't viable after all; or maybe you're trying to do something too ambitious with your existing talent pool.

If, after matching people to jobs, it still looks like you have the right talent available for the project, it's time to study the political ramifications of your choice of project team members. If the people are under your direct management, it's no problem. Simply have a meeting and explain the project to your staff. If you need to put a team together with resources from other departments, then you need to answer these questions before you go further:

> ➤ Who will you have to deal with in other parts of the organization to get approval for a prospective team member's participation? Is this politically workable?

> ➤ How much will outside services cost? Plop the *Yellow Pages* on your desk and make calls to get quotes. Would it be easier to use outside resources than to get approval to use the inside people?

> ➤ How much training is required for each team member? Is it worth it?

> ➤ Will team members come willingly or are you imposing your agenda on workers who would prefer to have no part in the project?

> ➤ Is another manager offering you a team member because they want to get rid of him or her? (Beware!)

Words from the Wise

Work expands so as to fill the time available for its completion.

—Cyril Northcote Parkinson, *Parkinson's Law* (1957)

Time Is Money

As part of your choice of supervisors and managers, look for people who can work within an ordered system of checks and balances. Prima donnas may seem to perform admirably on the surface, but if they impose their own agendas on your project, you could lose control. If you have a choice in the matter, choose someone who will accept your role as manager without resentment or hostility.

Putting Your Best Foot Forward

Because there is no perfect project team, what do you do with the intangibly less-than-perfect set of players? First, try to avoid the imposed team whenever possible. Always negotiate for the right team members, even when your choices must be approved and/or paid for by the stakeholders and managers who approve your project budget. Suggest alternatives and justify why your recommendations make economic sense. "Well sir, Jenkins is an accomplished microprocessor designer, but I'd rather see Biggles take the job. He can do it in half the time, according to the research I've done, and that saves the company money..."

Second, whether the team is imposed or not, you should interview each possible team member as if he or she were taking a new job (they are, unless the project is ongoing—and even then, if you are interviewing them, they're getting a new boss). In the interview, try to get a reading on their enthusiasm for the project and ask for a resume before the interview, if you hadn't already done so. This gives you basic details on their backgrounds and interests so you can ask probing questions about specific skills.

Finally, when you find that you really are stuck with certain team members, training is almost always an alternative. Pair your novice team member with an experienced one. Working together to learn new skills has long been a standard educational practice. It usually works (unless the two team members kill each other in the process). If you match the two players appropriately, you might have the joy of watching an immature team member graduate to the status of important contributor once he sees how the "pros" do it.

What About Next Time?

It's rare in a project-oriented workplace that the same exact group of people works over and over again on the same kinds of projects. Projects usually bring a unique group of people together—groups of people from different departments or companies or points of view. Thus, it's important that you don't get married to your favorite project members. You need to be willing to work with new people and be willing to take on different roles in other projects. It's all part of the project management style.

The Least You Need to Know

➤ The choice of the team is critical to project success, but sometimes you have to do the best you can with who you have available or who you're forced to use.

➤ Disparate personalities are standard in most projects; disparity must be accommodated as much as possible.

➤ The assignment of internal staff from other departments must be handled carefully to avoid political problems.

➤ A comparison of project needs and people skills can help you match the right people to the right jobs on your project.

➤ Outsiders are an expensive but often necessary addition to project teams.

Part 3
The Project Planning Phase

Congratulations! You've made it through the initiation phase, selected the right project to work on, and identified a core team to work with you. Now you can start planning the work, schedule, and budget for your project.

The plan is a template for your project that helps you guide the work from start to finish. It not only details the work that will be done, but it also serves as a tool for communicating with stakeholders and the project team.

In addition to the goals and objectives for your project, the risks and constraints, and the core project team which you established in the initiation phase, there are three standard components in most project plans: the task list or work breakdown structure (WBS)—which may or may not be put into a network diagram or other charting format—the schedule, and the budget. Even a plan for the simplest project should contain these three parts. In this section, you'll learn how to put them together for projects both large and small.

Chapter 9

The Breakdown of Tasks: What Really Needs to Be Done?

In This Chapter

➤ Why breaking a project into tasks is a good idea

➤ Defining tasks

➤ Subprojects as milestones and milestones as groups of tasks

➤ Understanding the work breakdown structure (WBS)

➤ The right WBS levels for your project

Okay, you've earned it—a complete breakdown—a work breakdown that is. And, you're ready for it! With the goals and objectives agreed upon, risks understood, and core team members in place, you need to figure out the specific work required to achieve the project's objectives. You need to break the project into manageable tasks that can be assigned, scheduled, tracked, and organized. This isn't always an easy chore, but someone has to do it—and as project manager, you're the most likely candidate.

Of course, you can call on the individual expertise of your core team to help you break the work into manageable, trackable segments, but as project manager you ultimately are the person who will put all these segments together into a workable plan of action.

The All-Important Task

Why break your project into tasks? A good question. There are five reasons for organizing your project into smaller work packages, called tasks:

➤ When breaking work into tasks, you can put the work in your project in the most logical sequence for completion. This can help you determine the best schedule for your project. By wrapping up related elements into units called tasks, it's much easier to see how things fit together in a project, how work overlaps, and how one task may interfere with another if its not done on time.

➤ Tasks are a way of modularizing the project into manageable segments. Thus, tracking progress on tasks is a way to assess and control the work done on a project.

➤ By breaking work into tasks, you can determine the skills you need to complete the work on a project and you can quantify how many people will be required to do the work.

➤ Tasks allow you to communicate the work that needs to be done to other team members without getting into too much detail. A task list also can be used to negotiate necessary changes to the work sequences during the project.

➤ Breaking the work into tasks ensures that all the work sequences are identified and understood.

The bottom line is this: Tasks help you organize the hundreds of small work elements that go into completing a project. Without tasks, the amount of work to track would make your head spin. You would have no way of keeping track of things or prioritizing work.

Tasks: What Exactly Are They?

Each task represents some related package of work completed toward getting the project done. Tasks are also called *activities* by some project managers, but in this book, we call them tasks. Tasks can be combined to become subprojects or milestones.

Project Lingo
A *task* is a cohesive unit of work on a project—one that's not too big or too small to be tracked.

As you'll see on the following pages, building a task list for a complex project takes time. Tasks are listed so the overall amount of work can be assessed and the work can be sequenced in the most logical fashion. A list of tasks can be short and simple or long and detailed, depending on the size and goals of the project. Don't try to sequence the tasks or estimate time and budget during task definition. Those steps come later (Chapters 10-14).

The task list makes communication among core project team members easier. And, as mentioned (nay, harped on throughout the book), forgetting to list an important task can have a very negative effect on the project's bottom line *and* its schedule. Therefore, it's a good idea to have someone else, or maybe even a few people, review the task list before you complete the rest of the project plan—or before you start working on the project, for that matter.

A Tisket, a Task...

Developing task-sense (something like horse-sense) takes time. "Do I lump all these procedures into one task, or are they actually two, five, or nine separate ones?" Correctly defining the level of tasks in a project provides an easier way to control the project and keep it in the groove.

High Water!
To make things really confusing, some project management books and software programs call milestones "activities" and describe tasks as "events."

Given that you're only going to write a sentence or two about each task, here are some hints for helping you define the right level of tasks within your projects:

➤ A task should be unambiguous. The "design the button layout on the handheld remote control" task is much clearer than the "design the TV control system" task, which is really five to ten separate tasks. The latter is so unclear that you can't schedule it because there are too many elements; team members won't know where the "task" starts or stops. ("Do we complete the remote control and the TV's receiver side of the system as well as the power controls, or just the remote control?") But the "design the TV control system" task could be a milestone—one that includes tasks for the remote control, primary power system, and television receiver.

➤ All work within the same task should occur within a sequential or parallel time frame, without gaps for possible other tasks in between. Thus, "framing and plumbing the bathroom," is not a well-formed task in your bathroom remodeling project, because plumbing the bathroom is not necessarily related to framing the bathroom—and other tasks, such as adding insulation, also could come after the framing task. It's better to define the tasks as separate units, "framing" and "plumbing," in the project plan rather than to risk confusion about the sequence or priority of events. Also, don't confuse tasks with milestones, which are a logical combination of tasks or a subproject.

➤ A task should only include related work elements. In the washing the car example, the task "get soapy water" wouldn't fit with "polish the car" because there's no relationship between the procedures and they occur at different times in the project cycle. (At least they do when I wash *my* car!) Therefore, a task called "get soapy water and polish the car" is not a well formed task because it involves unlike steps.

➤ Most (but not necessarily all) steps in a task should use the same team members. Within a complex task, this improves communication and makes scheduling easier. Should something go wrong somewhere, the responsibility for the task will also be clear, which makes fixing the problem easier as well.

➤ While not always possible, a task that involves multiple people goes smoothly if all the people working on the task work at the same site or within walking proximity of each other.

As an example of a task list for a small project, we've provided a list of tasks to produce a customer newsletter. Note the active aspect of each task description. Do this, do that. Tasks are also known as activities for good reason! Dates are eventually assigned to each of these tasks to further clarify the work plan. Thus each task must be something that can be scheduled and measured. On a larger project, the scheduling step may not occur until after the network diagram is assembled (which you'll learn how to do in the next chapter). In a small project, however, the schedule can be put right next to the tasks, as shown in the illustration of the newsletter project.

Also note that some tasks on the list are more complex than others. For example, the task called "complete focus research" is really a small subproject that involves designing the focus research, finding subjects for the research, initiating the focus sessions, and summarizing the results. Tasks that involve a plan of their own are often called "subprojects" or "milestones."

Milestones or subprojects should get a task list of their own within the larger project plan. On a small project, we usually note the milestones with an asterisk or a different typeface. On a larger project, each milestone will get its own plan of tasks—called a work breakdown structure (WBS). (We'll talk more about that later in this chapter.)

Over and Over Again

If you manage projects in which many of the same kinds of tasks are duplicated over and over again, you may want to create a "standard task unit" for these common tasks. This technique is used often in construction and engineering, where the time to complete a standard operation has been established and proven over time. It is important to remember that standard task units may change over time. Building a suburb with four house models used to build 100 homes? Standardization is a great (maybe the only) alternative to individual house plans. You wouldn't want to plan each house from scratch because you'll be building at least 24 others exactly like it.

Task List and Schedule

Project Name <u>Customer Newsletter</u>   Date <u>January 4</u>

Scheduled Start <u>Jan 3</u>   Scheduled Finish <u>February 4</u>

Prepared by <u>Gail</u>   Date <u>Dec 28</u>

Approved by <u>M. Baxter</u>   Date <u>Dec 31</u>

Task	Duration	Responsible	Target Start	Target Start	Target Start	Target Start
1. Focus group to establish audience needs	5	Gail	Jan 4	Jan 8		
2. Meeting to identify stories and editorial for the first issue	1	Department Staff	Jan 11	Jan 11		
3. 1st draft of stories	5	Gail	Jan 11	Jan 15		
4. Stories reviewed	1	Dept. Staff & Mr. Baxter	Jan 18	Jan 18		
5. Final draft of stories	2	Gail	Jan19	Jan 21		
6. Final draft approved	4	Mr. Baxter	Jan 22	Jan 25		
7. Layout stories with computer	3	Gail	Jan 25	Jan 27		
8. Layout approved	1	Mr. Baxter	Jan 27	Jan 27		
9. Final changes and proofreading	1	Gail & Dept. Staff	Jan 28	Jan 28		
10. Final sign-off	1	Ms. Smith	Jan 28	Jan 28		
11. Type output on Linotronic typesetter	1	Gail	Jan 28	Jan 28		
12. Camera-ready film to printer	1	Gail	Jan 29	Jan 27		
13. Review "blueline" proof at printer's shop and approve	1	Printer, Gail	Feb 1	Feb 1		
14. Finished newsletter delivered to office	1	Printer	Feb 3	Feb 3		
15. Distribution of newsletter	1	Gail	Feb 4	Feb 4		

Standardized task units should be measured and evaluated on a regular basis. As technology and culture evolve, a standard task unit that took two days back in 1979 might take less time today because of new tools and techniques. And it's always possible that the standard task unit was established based on faulty information. If in actual practice the task takes longer or shorter than the standard task unit you'll waste time (money) or add a crimp to your schedule when a supposed two-day task really takes a week. Thus, you need to track actual task times and adjust the standard task units as necessary over time.

Also, be careful not to assign a standard task unit to a task that sounds similar, but in practice, is really quite different. In language study, words that sound the same in English as they do in another language may mean something very different in the foreign tongue. The same is true in project management. Producing a marketing report for X division may be a much shorter document than that required by Y division. But when planning, the tasks of "writing the marketing plan" sound identical. Make sure you research the requirements for an ordinary sounding task before you assign a schedule or budget to it.

Some kinds of tasks are not easily standardized. You may perform the function once on a unique project and never use anything like it again. That's not to say that you can't keep a library of tasks and timetables on a computer and modify them as needed, but sometimes changing the tasks is more work that figuring the work out from scratch. Only standardize tasks that are really repeated on a regular basis in multiple projects.

The Work Plan and Your Project

Project Lingo
A *standard task unit* is an agreed-upon description of a common task performed in multiple projects and the amount of effort used for that task.

The work plan is the document that organizes and summarizes the tasks necessary to complete the project. Every work plan starts with a summary of project tasks and milestones. A work plan can be as simple as the sequential list of tasks, like the one shown earlier for the newsletter project. For most larger projects, however, the tasks you list for a project should be organized into some kind of hierarchy (which you'll learn about here) and then translated into a network diagram (explained in Chapter 10). The complete work plan ultimately will include a schedule (see Chapters 12 and 13) and a list of resources required to complete each task (see Chapter 11).

The work plan you create should be able to help you do all of these things:

➤ Identify the major tasks in the project so all the work that needs to be done is clearly indicated.

➤ Organize tasks in the most logical sequence so the tasks can be efficiently scheduled.

➤ Identify tasks that need to be assigned to various team members.

➤ Identify the resources necessary to complete each task so a budget can be developed.

➤ Communicate the work to be done in an unambiguous way so team members understand their assigned jobs and responsibilities for completing the project.

➤ Organize related tasks into logical milestones.

Task organization is crucial in the work plan. In a large project, related tasks should be organized into milestones or subprojects. This makes it easier to visualize the overall project without getting into the details.

Your work plan is the underpinning of a successful project because the need for resources and the schedule fall out of your task list and work sequences. On larger projects, the task list will likely undergo several revisions before you get it right. If you are new to project management, you should have the core team members or other key stakeholders review your task lists and sequences until you include all the work necessary to get things done.

Five Steps to the Work Plan

There are five steps you must complete to develop a work plan that meets all of its goals.

1. Define the work as independent tasks that can be sequenced, assigned, scheduled, and monitored.

2. Define the tasks at a level of detail appropriate for the length and complexity of the project.

3. Integrate the tasks into a total system with a beginning and an end. This may involve combining tasks into milestones (also called subprojects).

4. Present the sequence of tasks in a form that can be easily communicated to people involved in the project.

5. Verify that the completion of the tasks will result in the attainment of all of the project goals and objectives.

For most large projects, assembling and organizing a work plan takes time, but a carefully assembled tasks list goes a long way towards streamlining a project after the work begins.

The WBS

One standard way of organizing tasks for a project is called the work breakdown structure. The WBS is a sort of organizational chart for a project. We've provided some examples of WBS charts to give you an idea of the different ways the same project can be organized.

High Water!
When you believe you have a credible draft of a work plan, put it away for a week and then revisit it. This gives you a chance to get an objective view of the various elements. You might see something you forgot to consider or you might notice a better way to organize the tasks.

Project Lingo
A *work breakdown structure* (WBS) is a hierarchical chart used to organize the tasks of a project into related areas. It often is completed as a tree diagram or as an outline. In the WBS, milestones and tasks are clearly defined. The completed WBS can be used for budgeting and personnel selection purposes, as well as scheduling and network diagramming.

The WBS can be used to assign project task responsibilities, build the budget, and look for money "sinks" (tasks that require excessive amounts of capital). You also can use it to rough out the schedule and time required, but scheduling for large projects is more accurate when a network diagram is used, as explained in Chapter 10.

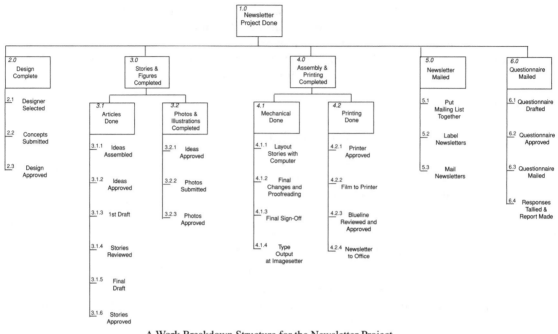

A Work Breakdown Structure for the Newsletter Project

Levels and the WBS

The idea behind the WBS is to break larger tasks (or milestones) into their individual components. In the newsletter example, you want to separate disparate functions, such as writing stories and shooting photos, from printing and production.

Once the milestone structure of the project is created, the real work breakdown begins as shown. You can have as many task levels as befit your needs. In a complex project, such as building a new ride for Disney World, the first level in the master work breakdown is actually a list of smaller projects that are themselves projects within projects. Without this type of organization, large projects are simply too complex to manage.

Some projects may need as few as three layers in a WBS. Others require 10 or more layers, or require a WBS for each subproject or milestone within the WBS. You might set three levels for the comparatively simple newsletter project versus seven or more for creating a new division in a corporation or 10 or more for building a 600-unit apartment complex. Here is a list of the steps in breaking down the work in a project of any size:

1. The total project
2. Subprojects or milestones
3. Major tasks
4. Subtasks
5. Minor tasks or work elements

```
Outline of the WBS for the Newsletter Project

1.0 NEWSLETTER PROJECT DONE
    2.0 Masthead and Design Complete
        2.1 Designer Selected
        2.2 Concepts Submitted
        2.3 Design Approved
    3.0 Stories and Photos Complete
        2.1 Articles Done
            2.1.1 Ideas Assembled
            2.1.2 Ideas Approved
            2.1.3 First Draft of Articles
            2.1.4 Stories Reviewed
            2.1.5 Final Draft
            2.1.6 Stories Approved
        2.2 Photos and Illustrations Completed
            2.2.1 Ideas Approved
```

An outline-style WBS: If the tree method doesn't appeal to you or doesn't work for your project, you can accomplish a similar result using the outline method shown here. This method works best for projects with too many layers to conveniently lay out in tree format.

You can choose to focus on whatever level of the project is germane to your current management needs. Remember, the smallest unit in your WBS should be the smallest unit of work you must track in your project.

As a project manager, the levels in your project plan will help you control work at each level. Consider these two different questions asked during the newsletter project:

➤ Level two (high level) question: "Should we assign printing to AAA Printers or to Acme Brothers?"

➤ Level three (lower level) question: "I need someone to get approvals for the photos for the newsletter. Jenkins, can you take care of this?"

An appropriately organized task list or WBS can help identify the right time to ask and answer each of these questions.

The lowest level in your WBS should not reach the level of absurdity—but you should track everything that could affect something else in the plan. While doing this, you must remember that not everything in life can be planned down to the minute; if it could, nothing would ever go wrong. Unless you're omniscient or equipped with a time machine, you'll need to make your best guess about the detail and sequence of most project tasks.

Always remember that planning is a tradeoff. The cost of planning and tracking at too low a level may far exceed the benefit, add tons of paperwork, and alienate your team to the point that they question not only your plan, but your leadership and judgment as well. Practice will help. Seek guidance from your manager or another experienced person before you present your task list to the world to ridicule.

Plumbing the Depths

To judge the lowest level task you should accommodate in your WBS, budget or time can be used. The lowest level task should require at least .5 to two percent of the total budget or project time. You also can use segments, such as half or full days, to define the smallest task levels. These approaches may appear initially imprecise, but they establish a general guideline for the lowest level tasks in your project.

Including too many elements in the WBS amounts to micromanaging at the extreme. Again, this may miff your staff; they might think you're attempting to manage their lives as well as the project—an impossible and thankless task.

Dividing the WBS

There's no magic formula for organizing a WBS. Like washing the car, in the newsletter example, the WBS is based on the category of tasks. Alternately, you could base it on any of the following (and I'm sure you can think of other ways, too):

➤ *Functional or technological disciplines.* What is required in each phase of the project? Schedule the machine tool operators separately from the marketing specialists.

➤ *Organizational structure.* In a clearly divided organization or cooperating set of separate organizations, choose to establish the WBS according to reporting structure. If outside vendors are involved, they can be included in this kind of planning.

➤ *Physical location.* Working with separate facilities? Build the WBS based on the geographical locations instead of the people.

➤ *Systems and subsystems.* If there is clear demarcation between several aspects of a project, then the WBS can be assembled to reflect this.

Project Lingo
Deliverables are the clearly defined results, goods, or services produced during the project or at its outcome. Deliverables and goals are often synonymous. Deliverables, like goals, may include organizational attributes, reports and plans, as well as physical products or objects.

You can use the *"wrap-up"* approach as well. In a wrap-up, you start at the bottom, listing each element, and work up. Each layer as you move up contains a wrap-up of all the elements of the layer underneath it. The detailed newsletter WBS example works like that, although you may want to draw lines across the chart to ensure that all applicable levels are addressed for each level in the chart.

There are a few other suggestions for creating a WBS that you might want to consider. These are especially important for assembling a complex WBS and include:

➤ Each element of work should be assigned to only one level of effort. Never repeat an element in another part of the tree.

➤ Narrative must accompany the WBS. You may want to label each box with a number that references a page in an overview narrative document to provide more detail than "Get CEO approval for expansion plan."

➤ Related tasks should be clearly identified in the WBS. A color printer can help with this.

➤ At all levels, the WBS should provide measurable deliverables for each aspect of the project. At a low level, the selection of the masthead designer for the newsletter is a deliverable. At a high level, on the same project, the completion and approval of the masthead is also a deliverable.

➤ Assemble the WBS in a format that allows changes if and when the project shifts slightly in direction. Computers are ideal, but a carefully protected whiteboard (wrap it loosely with plastic wrap) can fill the bill for a simple project. And lots of sticky notes can be used, as well, so things are easy to move around as you make changes.

THIS WAY

Along the Critical Path

When maintaining a WBS for a large project, you need *version control* in place. That means that each version, no matter how preliminary or final, should be date- and time-stamped. That way, older plans can be relegated to the file and everyone works only with the most current document. Even if you work on a computer and don't print all versions of the WBS, each iteration should be saved separately by date so you can be sure you're using the latest and greatest plan. Also, the older versions should be saved so they can be used to track project history and serve as a learning tool to evaluate what (if anything) went wrong.

So that's a wrap! Now you know how the work breaks down in your project. But that's just one important step in planning. Now, take a look at organizing the work in a network diagram.

The Least You Need to Know

➤ A single task is a cohesive package of work that can be monitored and tracked.

➤ The work on a project must be broken into tasks to make things easier to schedule and control.

➤ A work breakdown structure (WBS) organizes the tasks of a project into hierarchies and milestones.

➤ The WBS can be assembled in many ways. You need to choose the one that's right for your project and style of leadership.

➤ A milestone is a point in the plan that indicates when a group of related tasks have been completed.

➤ Milestones divide the project into logical, measurable segments. When all the milestones are completed, the project should be done.

➤ When a complete task list and WBS are done, then the schedule and resources for the project can be planned.

The Network Diagram: A Map for Your Project

You may think this is the cool chapter where you get to use networks and computers to plan and control your project from the depths of cyberspace. Forget it. This is a book about project management—and even though you could put information about your project plans and status on the Net or the Web to keep team members up to date, when most project managers talk about the network, they're not talking about an information superhighway or even a slow road.

The network in project management terms is a tried and proven way to organize and sequence the tasks of a project. Anything but the simplest project should have a network diagram. Yes, the network diagram is a roadmap of sorts, but you won't find mondo sites on weird cults by following the links like you would on the Web—you'll just get your project done a lot easier. In fact, you don't even need a computer to create a network diagram (but it sure helps on big projects).

In this chapter, you'll learn how to create a network diagram by hand, with pencil and paper, although we mention how computers can help throughout the text. In Chapter 28, we talk a lot more about the computer tools you can use to do the same thing (a lot faster). It's important that you understand how to create your own network diagram before you start letting the computer do your thinking for you. For small projects, doing it by hand is often easier and faster. (Don't tell our friends at Microsoft and Intel about this heresy—they think everything is better and faster with a computer.)

What's a Network Diagram?

The network diagram shows the path of the project, starting and completion dates, and names the responsible party for each task. For those not already familiar with your project, such as management and new team members, the network diagram explains at a glance (well, it might take more than a glance) how the work on the project goes together.

A network diagram, if properly sequenced, will accomplish the following:

➤ Show the sequences and relationships among tasks necessary to complete a project

➤ Identify relationships of milestones in the project that can be used for monitoring progress and completion

➤ Show the interrelationships of tasks in different parts of the task list and work breakdown structure (WBS) hierarchy

➤ Establish a vehicle for scheduling tasks (covered in Chapters 12 and 13)

➤ Help reduce uncertainty in the project by breaking it into many small phases that have been analyzed and sequenced in advance of starting the work

If you put the network diagram on a wall where the whole project team can see it (especially your boss) and then use a bright color to mark of the tasks as they are completed, the network diagram can be a powerful way to communicate what has been done on the project, and what remains to be accomplished. Of course, if the project gets stalled and the tasks don't get done, it also can be a sure way of letting people know you're in trouble. (Hopefully this won't happen to you.)

Why Do I Need a Network Diagram?

For simple projects of fewer than 30 tasks, the list of tasks is often all you need to schedule a project. If you're the only person working on a small project, you'll likely complete the work one task after the other until the project gets done. If that's the case, simply list the tasks in your project in the proper order and you can move on to Chapters 12 and 13 right now to learn about project scheduling.

Before you start scheduling, be aware that if your project involves more than one person or more than a handful of tasks, the sequence of tasks is probably not a simple matter of working on one task after another. Project work also happens in parallel because people may be working on different tasks at the same time. To make things more complicated, the tasks may be related to other tasks that depend on them. All these relationships and interdependencies can be tough to figure out in your head—and impossible to understand from a list of tasks.

That's why you need a network diagram: to help understand how the work should really go together. Only then can you develop a somewhat reliable schedule for your project.

The WBS and the Network Diagram

Detailed task lists and a WBS are a great first step in identifying the work packages or tasks in a project. However, WBS representations don't graphically display the sequencing relationships between various parts of the project. A WBS only shows hierarchical relationships—you can't schedule a hierarchy as easily as a sequence. Therefore, it cannot be used to create a schedule or to coordinate work done by different people or resources unless all of the tasks in a project are sequential (and they rarely are).

Project Lingo
A *network diagram* is the logical representation of tasks that defines the sequence of work in a project. A network for a simple project might consist of one or two pages. On a large project, several network diagrams might exist: one for the overall project based on the project milestones and one for each subproject that leads to the completion of a milestone.

Network diagrams reveal the workflow, not just the work. Networks are usually drawn from left to right, with lines drawn between tasks to indicate the precedences among tasks. Arrowheads are placed on the lines to indicate the direction of the workflow through time. Though it is possible to create a network diagram for a small project without first developing a WBS, there are some limitations to network diagramming that make this undesirable. Network diagrams simply sequence the work tasks and identify their relationships in time. Networks are not as good as a WBS in demonstrating hierarchical relationships (milestones) in a project, but they can be used to demonstrate the sequence of tasks and relationships among tasks in different milestones in the WBS.

Network diagrams are awkward for managing budgets and personnel assignments. WBSes are awkward for scheduling. Thus, the use of both a WBS and a network to describe and control a project offers more powerful options.

If a task list or a WBS is done first, completing the network for a project is easy, because the tasks used to create the network have already been identified. Because tasks and milestones must be identified for a project in order to create a network, first create a WBS to identify the tasks in a project and then create the network diagram to show the sequence and relationships between tasks.

To review, a properly sequenced network diagram will:

➤ Show the sequence of tasks in completing a project.

➤ Identify milestones in the project that can be used for monitoring progress and accomplishments.

➤ Show the interrelationships of tasks in different parts of the WBS hierarchy.

➤ Establish a vehicle for scheduling tasks (covered in Chapters 12 and 13).

There are two central concepts that must be understood before a network diagram can be created for a project: the concept of precedence and the concept of concurrent (or parallel) tasks.

Precedence Relationships in a Project Network

Precedence defines task sequencing order and how tasks are related to one another in the plan. If one task must be completed before the next task can be started, the first one has precedence over the second. For example, in the newsletter project, the articles must first be written before they can be reviewed. In a network diagram, this precedence is illustrated by drawing one task after another. There are other precedences in the project as well. For example, the newsletter must be designed before it can be assembled and it must be assembled before can be printed.

Project Lingo
When one task must be completed before another task can be started, the first task is said to have *precedence* over the other.

Time Is Money
If a task does not have a clear precedent (that is, if it is unrelated to any tasks performed previously), it can stand alone with an arrow pointing to it from the Project Start box. Such tasks might have significant float (explained in Chapter 13) and provide you with additional scheduling flexibility.

Though some tasks must precede others, many tasks can be started in parallel with other tasks. This leads to the other important diagramming: the concept of simultaneous activities. Many project tasks can be worked on simultaneously as long as suitable resources are available. For example, it is possible to begin writing the newsletter articles before the format and masthead have been designed. However, both completing the articles and designing the format are precedent to assembling the newsletter. In a network diagram, it is possible to identify concurrent activities by drawing them parallel to each other in the same plane.

The concepts of precedence and simultaneous work are important because the relationships between tasks ultimately will establish the basis for scheduling a project, which you will learn about in Chapters 12 and 13. Adjusting the parallel activities and the precedences alters the time and resources required to complete a project. The goal in developing the network diagram is to identify activities that can occur in parallel and to specify the precedences that exist among the activities. This leads to the development of an optimum sequence of tasks for scheduling purposes.

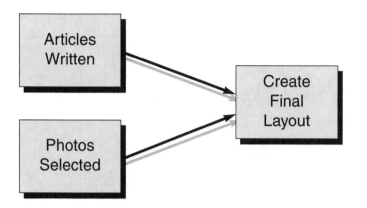

Two simultaneous tasks that are precedent to the same task.

How It Works: Symbols and Conventions

We have found that simple is better in most project management situations. Therefore, the networking diagramming techniques we recommend are simple ones. Still, in every networking method there are specific symbols used in the charts, which can seem complicated if you're new to the idea of a network diagram. But stay with us. The system we recommend is based on a simplification of a diagramming technique called *precedence diagramming*. If you work through the steps, you'll see it isn't as difficult as it looks at first glance. It's really just lots of lines and boxes—and most people learn how to draw those in kindergarten.

Boxes hold the description of each task. Lines connect the tasks to one another, as you can see in this diagram. The tasks are laid out horizontally from left to right to coincide with the time sequence in which the tasks will be completed. Groups of tasks that lead to specific deliverables are identified by boxes with rounded corners. These mark the milestones in the chart.

Network diagrams are really only a simple matter of linking tasks in boxes with lines. Just put the tasks in the right order and draw lines between them and you have a network diagram. Of course, where you put the boxes and how you draw the lines all mean something—so make sure you get it right, or you'll have the truck pouring concrete before the carpenters build the frame to hold it.

Diagramming the Relationships

So that everyone who uses network diagrams can figure out what's going on, there are a number of basic conventions (rules) in putting tasks down in a network diagram. Here are some of them:

➤ The defined sequences of tasks are represented by placing tasks in horizontal order from left to right in the network.

➤ Tasks that can happen at the same time are shown in columns. These are called "parallel tasks" because the work can happen in parallel with other work on different rows.

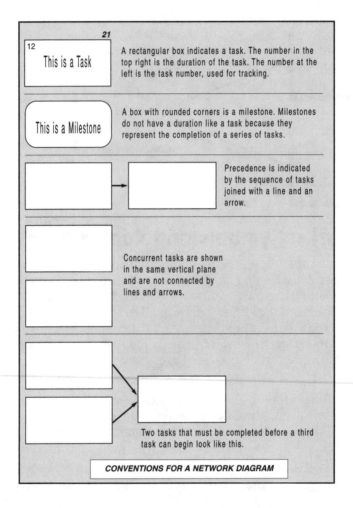

CONVENTIONS FOR A NETWORK DIAGRAM

➤ The precedences between tasks and milestones are shown by drawing lines from task to task, indicating that the task on the left must be completed before the task on the right can begin. The task that must be completed first is called the *precedent* task. The task that starts after the precedent task is called the *dependent* task. That's why the network diagram is said to reveal the dependencies among tasks. (Getting pretty technical? Don't worry. That's as hard as it gets.)

➤ Lines among tasks can cross the rows to show how tasks in the various sequences relate to each other.

There are other relationships among tasks that should be clearly explained in a network diagram. Here are some of them:

➤ One task may depend on the completion of multiple tasks or milestones. The precedences for all of these tasks must be shown by drawing lines from the precedent tasks to the dependent task.

➤ A task may start independently of some tasks but still be dependent on others. Lines are only drawn between tasks with dependency.

➤ A task without a precedent task or milestone can logically be started at any time after the initial "start project" task because it has no other dependent relationships. Put such a task in its own row.

If you look at the complete network diagram earlier in this chapter, you can see most of these conventions put into action. You'll also notice that it's pretty easy to figure out what's going on when you follow the rules.

Five Steps to Create a Network Diagram

By convention, most network diagrams start with a box labeled "Start Project" and end with a box labeled "Project Finished." All you have to do is fill in the tasks in between… But as you guessed, there's probably more to it than that. Actually there are five steps, explained in the next sections, that can be followed to produce a network diagram for any project. Before you start, however, get lots of scratch paper, sharp pencils, and a good eraser. These tools help as you try to figure out the sequences and relationships.

Don't expect to get things right the first time, either. Network diagramming takes practice. Even after you get it all put together, you should have some other folks from the project review your efforts. Now, with all that in mind, the following sections describe the steps to follow.

> **Words from the Wise**
>
> "Begin at the beginning," the King said, gravely, "and go until you come to the end; then stop."
>
> —Lewis Carroll, *Alice's Adventures in Wonderland* (1865)

Step 1: List the Tasks Using the Task List or the WBS

You have already learned how to create a task list and WBS (refer to Chapter 9). For a network diagram, each task should have a unique identifying number or other code. A network diagram will lay out the work units or individual task level in your WBS. Higher WBS levels will be identified as milestones (see step 3).

Step 2: Establish the Interrelationships Between the Tasks

To determine the sequences and precedences that need to be diagrammed for the tasks, ask the following questions about each task:

➤ What tasks must precede this task? That is, what other tasks must be completed before this one can be started?

➤ What tasks follow this task? Or, what tasks cannot be started until this task is complete?

➤ What tasks can take place concurrently with this one? Or, more simply, what tasks can be worked on at the same time this one is being completed?

The precedences and dependencies should be noted in a simple list. Some of the precedences won't become apparent until step 4, however, when you actually draw the tasks and link them together. If you don't identify all of the precedences now, it's fine. Just list them as you discover them to form a record. This list of task numbers and their precedences is especially useful if you use computerized project management programs.

Step 3: Identify the Milestones You Want to Specify

Milestones summarize a sequence of tasks or specify a key accomplishment during the project (refer to Chapter 9). Milestones are not tasks. Milestones do not take effort; they are just convenient markers for summarizing work that has been performed to that point on the network diagram. The top levels in the WBS are a good source of milestones for the project. Milestones also have defined precedences and sequences. You can draw a network of only milestones, or you can combine milestones with activities to display a complete project—or you can leave the milestones out of your project altogether (recommended only on small projects).

Here you see the network shown earlier for the sales office project laid out as a milestone network.

Milestone Network for San Francisco Sales Office Project

Step 4: Layout the Tasks and Milestones as a Network

Some experienced project managers start from the last task in the project and work backward when charting the project. Many people find it easier to identify preceding tasks than successive ones. However, there are many arguments for starting with the first task and working forward because this is how the work will actually be done. The outcome is the same—the approach used is a matter of preference.

Step 5: Review the Logic of the Network

The network review process is important because it is through adapting sequences and precedences that an optimum order of project tasks can be identified. To review the logic of the network, look at each task and each connection and ask yourself the following questions:

➤ Are the tasks properly sequenced?

➤ Are all the precedences identified?

➤ Are there some precedences that aren't really required? Or, are there tasks that can be completed concurrently (in parallel) that are incorrectly shown as sequences?

➤ Are all of the tasks really necessary?

➤ Does the completion of the tasks in the network represent the accomplishment of *everything* necessary to meet the project goals that have been specified?

Time Is Money

When establishing a network diagram using a computer, before using the software's demand for start, duration, and finish dates, take some time to roughly diagram the basic network on paper. This will help you understand the basic precedences and will assist you in building the chart correctly once you begin the computer entry procedure.

Along the Critical Path

To make tasks and sequences easier to find in your network, be sure to identify each task and milestone with unique numbers or other identification labels. In computerized project management programs, tasks are always numbered, as well as identified by task description. The same method of identification or numbering used in the WBS is usually appropriate; however, it is common in networks to skip numbers between tasks to allow flexibility in the network when requirements for new tasks or different ones may become apparent later in the project. For example, instead of numbering tasks as 1, 2, 3, and so on, it might be better to number tasks as 10, 20, 30, 40... Then, when you need to add new tasks between task 10 and 20, you can number them 10.1 and 10.2 without disturbing the logical numbering sequence of the original tasks. The numbering system should be flexible because projects almost always have changes that need to be represented in the network.

The sequences of tasks you put in your network are not absolute. Experienced project managers often revise and adjust the networks until they are optimized. People often find when they begin mapping precedences that tasks have been left out of the WBS. Add

High Water!
If a task defined in the WBS doesn't seem to fit in the network diagram, that usually means it's out of place. The task could be too small to include in the network diagram, or it could be too large and require further breakdown into more elemental tasks. If you change a task's status, make the change in your WBS so it and the network diagram match.

these new tasks, and make sure to note them in the appropriate place in the WBS. The network and the WBS should always match. In reverse, if you find that some tasks are redundant, remove them.

Be careful not to sequence tasks in an arbitrary order. Just because you've always done something a certain way does not mean it is the best way to do it. Try to look at the network from a new point of view; find better ways to get the work done. A network diagram provides a great opportunity to do this. Can the tasks be sequenced differently for better use of resources? Can some tasks be "split" into two or more tasks to make the organization of work more flexible? It is usually a good idea to have objective outsiders review the sequences, in addition to the project team, to avoid bias in the sequence of the work. Sometimes a person outside the politics of a project can identify a better way to complete the work.

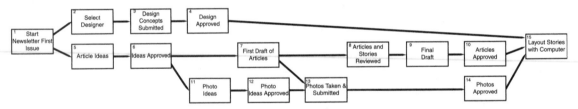

Even a relatively simple project to develop a newsletter has parallel tasks and dependencies that are best under-stood through the development of a network diagram.

Complex Time Relationships for Critical Projects

Most of you won't need to master this, but there are some advanced concepts in network and precedence diagramming that are important for some project managers to consider—especially in construction and engineering projects.

The optimum way to represent precedences in projects is not always a simple matter of completing one task and then starting another one. Your precedence diagrams also can specify complex timing relationships between tasks. By overlapping tasks in the diagram and using arrows to represent specific timing, relationships can be shown where tasks must be started at a certain point after another task is started. This is especially important in complex construction projects. For example, using precedence diagramming techniques, you can show complex task sequencing requirements, such as:

➤ A task that must not start before a specific task has been in progress for at least two days

➤ A task that must be completed at least five days before another can begin

➤ A task that must start three days after the first task but that must be finished at the same time as the first task

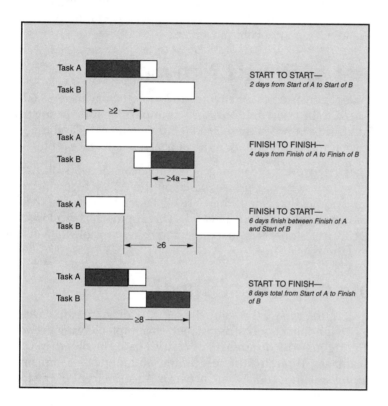

Complex precedence diagramming conventions for showing lead and lag times between tasks.

For most business projects it is not necessary to define these sorts of complex lead and lag times at the sub-task level. Simple precedence relationships are adequate for all but the most complex scientific and construction projects. However, they are mentioned here because the terms are often referred to in computerized project management systems or in other project management literature. You should know what the terms mean even if you don't use them. As a project manager, its a matter of pride (and being knowledgeable).

Project Lingo

Lag is the amount of time after one task is started or finished before the next task can be started or finished.

Lead is the amount of time that precedes the start of work on another task.

When Is Enough Enough?

Goals and constraints establish the scope for your project, which you learned about in Chapter 6. In creating a network, as in creating the WBS, the project goals and scope establish the level of detail for defining the work that must be completed. Even so, the question arises in developing every network as to how many tasks should be included. There are no hard and fast rules, but the experiences of early project management practitioners revealed that after a certain point the marginal return in control offered by more detail is far outweighed by the additional work required to develop and maintain the network. At some point in every plan, more detail becomes a negative rather than a positive attribute. The best advice is to use your judgement.

Slaying the Goliaths of Project Networks

Some giant networks for major construction or engineering projects may have 25,000 or more tasks that really do need to be tracked. It obviously is impossible for any one person to understand all the relationships between these 25,000 individual tasks—and the network diagram would take up an entire wall or more of a large conference room.

One way to make such a large network more manageable is to create network diagrams for each major sub-project or milestone of a project based on the WBS. These milestones can then be summarized in another diagram. If there are dependencies between the milestones, these can be noted in the milestone network. This approach also allows people responsible for specific milestones within a project to be responsible for a detailed network of his or her own sub-project.

When Is a Network a Waste of Time?

The more complex a project is, the greater the value the network diagram is in developing a schedule and a budget. Though there is a cost associated with implementing network management of a project using network diagrams, this cost is relatively low when compared to the potential advantages. Typically, the cost in time and money for implementing a network-based planning system is somewhere between .1 to 1 percent of the total project—the percentage gets smaller as the project becomes larger.

The value of using network diagrams is not universally accepted, however. Wags often argue that taking time to develop a network is a waste of time. And there has been some research that indicates that the use of PERT/CPM (see the following section) or other related methods has no significant effect on the technological performance or final deliverables of projects. In other words, projects that were managed without the use of network systems in these studies seem to get the same amount and quality of work done.

However, most studies indicate a significantly lower probability of cost and schedule overruns when network diagrams are used. In a business world concerned with profitability and performance, this seems like a pretty good reason to employ the network technique for organizing and scheduling work—because it reduces the risk of going over budget or running late.

Three Major Network Methods and Others You May Encounter

We've discussed the basic precedence diagram because we think this is the easiest, most effective networking diagram for most small to mid-sized projects—the projects most people manage in everyday business. But, even if it's just to impress your boss through using nifty acronyms, you should know that there are related systems of network diagramming and scheduling techniques used in industry today.

The two most common forms of networking systems are PERT, short for Performance Evaluation and Review Technique, and CPM, the acronym for Critical Path Method. The techniques are similar in principal to what you've already learned: the differences lie in how the projects display information and deal with scheduling uncertainties. And, given that these techniques were developed by engineers for engineering projects, there are a lot more symbols used to represent the relationships between tasks in a network.

Until PERT/CPM techniques were developed, Gantt charts or other bar charts were the best tools available to represent project sequences. Gantt charts show a graphic representation of work on a time scale. You will learn more about Gantt charts as a useful way to represent the overall project schedule in Chapter 12. Gantt charts are really just timelines that show tasks in parallel. They can't show the dependencies between tasks that are represented in networks.

THIS WAY

Along the Critical Path

One of the first pioneering efforts to show the interrelationships among tasks on a project was undertaken by the science management team of Morgan R. Walker and James E. Kelly in the mid-1950s at the E. I. Du Pont Company. Their joint efforts resulted in the Kelly-Walker network technique. However, in later publications of their work, they referred to the method as the Critical Path Method. Du Pont tested the CPM method in the construction of a major chemical plant and several maintenance projects that were completed by the middle of 1958. It is claimed that Du Pont credited over one million dollars in savings to this technique in the first year it was used.

During the same period of 1957-58, the management scientists of the Special Projects Office of the U.S. Navy, along with the firms of Lockheed and Booz, Allen, and Hamilton, developed a similar network system called PERT, which stands for Program Evaluation and Review Technique. The system was developed to help coordinate more than 3,000 people involved in the development of the Polaris missile. The use of PERT is credited with reducing the time required to complete the project by two years.

CPM is often cited as better for construction type projects. It is argued that PERT is more appropriate for research-oriented projects. The primary reason for this is because of the different approaches the two systems use for scheduling, not because of the networks, which are largely the same in terms of sequencing possibilities. In CPM, one time estimate is used for creating the schedule; PERT uses a more complex system based on three time estimates that are used to determine the most probable time for completion.

This more complex time-estimating approach is deemed by some as more appropriate for research projects with high degrees of uncertainty and risk. For most general business projects, these differences are not critical, and some people call all network systems by the name PERT/CPM because of their similarities.

Circles or Boxes? Who Cares?

Okay, this next part is for those who just want to know more about the PERT/CPM differences. It might get a bit technical—you can opt out now if you just want to get your project plan done. See you in the next chapter.

Still with us? Curious? Glutton for punishment. Well, in any case, here's the scoop on PERT and CPM.

Traditionally, PERT/CPM networks used circles and arrows to describe work in a project. The two systems use the same basic diagramming conventions you've learned about already as a way to link tasks, except that the arrows represent tasks (called "activities" in PERT/CPM) and the circles represent something similar to milestones (called "events" in PERT/CPM). These two concepts, activity and event, are central to the traditional PERT/CPM diagrams. An activity is a specific project task that requires resources and time to complete. An event is a specific end state for one or more activities that occurs at a specific point in time. An event occurs as a result of completing one or more activities.

AOA and AON

There are two methods of representing activities and events in PERT/CPM networks: activity on arc (AOA) (also called activity on arrow) and activity on node (AON). The use of method is largely a matter of preference. In AOA, the arrows are the activities and the circles (called "nodes" in PERT/CPM) are the events. In the AON method, the activities are the circles and the lines demonstrate the precedences between the activities. Some of the traditional ways of diagramming tasks in a PERT/CPM chart are shown in the diagram.

Simple precedence networks using boxes as shown here are really just another version of an AON PERT/CPM network. We think the boxes are a lot easier to use. (Bet you do too at this point.) We've found that most mid-sized business projects are easier to describe and understand using the boxes than by creating complex number, circle, and arc networks. In fact, most computerized project management programs now offer boxes to replace the circle/arc format.

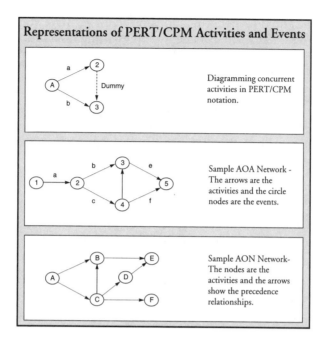

Representations of PERT/CPM Activities and Events

Diagramming concurrent activities in PERT/CPM notation.

Sample AOA Network - The arrows are the activities and the circle nodes are the events.

Sample AON Network- The nodes are the activities and the arrows show the precedence relationships.

We're glad you made it through all this, because it's important for an informed project manager like you to be familiar with some of the other diagramming options in project management. As you get more experience, you might want to experiment with these other diagramming techniques for your networks. (We also suggest you get a comprehensive book on PERT/CPM techniques before you do.)

Tried and True Networks

Over the years, and even with the advancements in computer software, some of the representational techniques in PERT/CPM and precedence diagramming have been improved or have been modified and expanded. Still, the simplicity of the original systems has withstood the tests of time and application, and no truly substantive changes have been made in the original methods.

Some computer systems for project management combine the advantages of the various network methodologies into programs that give project planners the option of representing projects at various levels of detail and complexity, using modified and/or expanded network representations. However, the true innovation of putting the tasks together in precedences and showing how all the tasks relate to one another through time is still the most important thing to know about creating a network diagram—even if you use a computer program.

As long as the logic and precedence relationships remain intact, it doesn't matter whether you use circle, boxes, or any other shape for representing tasks and milestones. The important thing is to understand how all the tasks in a project fit together—only then can you create a viable schedule.

In Chapters 12 and 13, you'll learn how to turn your network diagram into a schedule you can be proud (and confident) to present to management for approval. But before you get to scheduling, it's important to figure out exactly who and what you need to do all the work you've drawn on in the WBS and the network. That's what your going to learn in the next chapter.

The Least You Need to Know

➤ The network diagram is not always necessary on small projects, but it's a good tool on most projects to establish the order of steps and the relationships among the various tasks in a project.

➤ As a project manager, you predict the future. The tough part is making the future match your predictions! A network diagram can help.

➤ The task-in-box method is supported by most project management software and is relatively easy to use.

Chapter 11

Getting Who and What You Need: People, Supplies, and Other Stuff

In This Chapter

➤ Determining exactly who and what you need

➤ Getting bids from outside vendors and suppliers

➤ Choosing the best vendors and suppliers

➤ Checking price and availability

After the tasks have been defined and a basic network established, a complete list of resources required for your project can be developed. Why wait until you have the list of tasks? Because before listing the tasks, you might not have realized that you need an electron microscope and an electron microscope operator in order to clone sheep. But with all the tasks identified, you can choose exactly who and what you need to get all the work done on your project. Even the sheep.

This chapter explains how to scope out required skills, assess current resources, and develop a complete list of people and materials required to complete each task on your project. In addition, this chapter offers guidelines for filling the gap in people skills and material resources when adequate resources are not readily available.

You'll actually be doing most of your hiring and material selection after the plan is approved and you move to the project execution phase (that starts with Chapter 16), but you need to verify costs and resource availability *before* the plan can be put into effect.

After you determine all the resources you need and how to get them, you'll have to schedule all this stuff to be in the right place at the right time. That's what the network diagram described in Chapter 10 helped you do. It showed you how to assign dates to tasks so you get the resources you need at the time you need them. But, before you can do that, you need to know who and what needs to be scheduled.

From Core Team to Complete Team

Remember, at this point you are only *planning* the project staff and resources. You're probably already working with a subset of the project team, often called the *core project team*, which includes the managers, stakeholders, and key personnel. The core team is the group you identified to help initiate and plan the project. (Do you remember doing this in Chapter 8?) But all the resources for your project cannot be identified during the project initiation phase. You just don't have enough detail on the project to know who and what you need until you have listed the tasks.

Only now, when you have the tasks and the work breakdown structure (WBS), can you identify all the resources required to complete the project. The core project team may help you do this. However, it isn't until after the project plan is approved and the execution phase begins that you'll actually start working as a fully functioning project organization. (You'll learn how to organize the project people during the execution phase in Chapter 18.)

The Seven Resources You Need

As you proceed with figuring out who and what you need to complete the project, you'll have to consider the seven fundamental resources that are required to implement almost any project. These include:

➤ People

➤ Money

➤ Equipment

➤ Facilities

➤ Materials and supplies

➤ Information

➤ Technology

These are the seven things that you and the core project team need to identify for the entire project. And to figure out resources, there are two basic questions you and the core project team need to answer before a complete project plan can be approved:

➤ What people, materials, equipment, and other resources are needed to complete each task on the project? You answer this question by determining the needs for each task on the project network or WBS and developing a list of everything and everyone you need. (More about ways to do this throughout the book.)

➤ Who and what from the list are already available for the project? Remember, you already thought about the project team back in Chapter 8.

> **Words from the Wise**
>
> We live in a world of things, and our only connection with them is that we know how to manipulate or to consume them.
>
> —Erich Fromm, *The Sane Society*, 1955

Three More Things to Consider

After you (and the core team) answer the questions in the previous section, you still need to know three things before you can complete your plan for project resources. Those are:

➤ *The cost estimates for each resource,* including the overhead assigned to your project for that resource during the course of the project, if applicable. For people, this could be their hourly rate. For outside resources, it's a good idea to get bids and estimates for services, supplies, and equipment in advance of approving the plan. (You'll learn more about this later in the chapter.)

➤ *The availability of each resource.* For people, this means knowing their work availability, holiday schedules, and commitments to other projects. For other resources, this means verifying the general availability of the supplies or equipment during the timeframe of your project.

➤ *The estimated quality and output of people and equipment resources.* This is important because it allows you to make trade-off analysis among similar resources. If time is most important, choose the fastest resource. But if a slower resource really saves money in the long run, and if you have the time to spare in the project, then a slower but cheaper resource might be a better selection. If you don't make these estimates in advance, you won't be able to put the best budget and schedule together for your project.

These estimates and availabilities will allow you to put together an optimum schedule and budget. Without them, you'll just be guessing, which is not a good idea when you're trying to plan the cost of a project.

People First, Please

Always start with the people on a project before you move to other resources. Even in a small or routine project, choosing the right people to successfully complete the work can be difficult, risky, and potentially time-consuming. Still, without people, the project will never happen—regardless of the cost and availability of equipment and supplies. Thus, it's important to seriously consider the needs of personnel, even on the smallest project. People are, after all, the common denominator in making projects successful.

Three Questions to Ask About the People You Need

In any project, there are three major questions that must be answered regarding the people used to complete the work on a project:

➤ What skills are required to complete the tasks on the project?

➤ Where will the people come from to complete the tasks?

➤ How should the people working on the project be organized?

The first two questions are the most important at this stage because the answers affect the number and cost of people required for the project. The organization of the project (covered in Chapter 18) comes later; however, some general thinking about the organization is necessary, because the organization of the project can impact the need for supervisory personnel and other support people. It's a good idea to have some general organizational strategies while you're planning for resource requirements.

Matching Skills to Tasks on the WBS

The questions about people skills can be answered with confidence using a structured approach that starts with the project's WBS or network. For each task in the project, answer questions similar to the following:

➤ Is there a specific technical skill or combination of skills required to complete this task?

➤ How much experience should the person or people have to complete this task?

➤ Does a person need to have specific experience doing this task or can general experience be applied? If so, what general experience is required?

➤ In addition to technical skills, are there any specific interpersonal skills required to complete this task effectively, such as good written or verbal communication skills, diplomacy or negotiating skills, or management ability?

➤ How many of these skilled people will be needed for each task and how would they be organized by job title and job function?

Worksheet for Determining Skills Required for Project Tasks

Project: Newsletter   Date: Jan 7

Completed By: Joe

TASK	SKILLS REQUIRED	POSSIBILITIES
1. Assemble story ideas	Knowledge of customer issues Knowledge of new sales	Members of technical support and sales development staff - ask Ingrid and Roger
2. Meeting to approve story ideas	Good judgement Understanding of the project goals	Department managers
3. First draft of stories	Writing skills Word processing Good interpersonal skills with staff	Staff writer - perhaps Gail or Julie Members of support or sales staff - perhaps John or Sarah Freelance writer Advertising agency
4. Stories reviewed.	See Task 2.	Same as Task 2.
5. Final draft of stories.	Same as Task 3.	Same as Task 3.
6. Final draft approved.	Same as Task 2.	Same as Task 2 and Project Manager
7. Layout stories and illustrations on the computer.	Desktop publishing skills. Illustration skills. Design background. Familiarity with corporate communication guidelines.	Staff designer - perhaps Steve or Gail Freelance designer Advertising agency

You can use a worksheet like this to list the people and other resources required to complete each task in your project.

List the skills and experience next to each WBS level or use a worksheet like the example shown for the newsletter project. After this is done, identify where the people will come from. (You learned about many of the sources for obtaining people in Chapter 8.) The source of the people will affect their cost and availability—maybe even the quality of the output; these are all things that will affect the schedule and budget you have yet to create.

Words from the Wise

For art and science cannot exist but in minutely organized particulars.

—William Blake, *Jerusalem*, 1818–20

Wow! This whole thing is sure interrelated. That's why you need to put your thinking cap on while you're planning. The better you understand your choices, the better chance you'll have at making good ones.

A Skills Inventory Can Help

Before you decide whether to use existing staff, hire new people, or use outside vendors in your project, you should develop a skills inventory of people in your own organization as suggested in Chapter 8. Such an inventory in a large organization often is maintained by the personnel or human resources department, although this normally lists only the technological skill levels and formal educational background of people in the company.

Managerial and communications skills are not available in most company skills inventories, and would be suspect even if they were. Skills in communication and management should be assessed after you have experience working with a person, or through talking to people who have such experience.

Time Is Money

A database program on a personal computer can be used to maintain the skills inventory for your project. The skills can be assigned codes for easy sorting. Some of the more sophisticated project management programs allow you to include skills inventories as part of the project data. The programs even offer suggestions for staffing each task on the project.

Developing a skills inventory can be an informal process or part of a formal personnel review system. The end result of completing a skills inventory will be a listing of the technological, management, administrative, and human skills for each staff member in your organization. If you have a complete, up-to-date skills inventory, you can easily match the skills required on your project to the people who have those skills.

A skills inventory is something that must be kept up-to-date to be useful. It is also something that can be used for many projects, so developing a regular procedure for keeping it up-to-date is worth the effort. Skills inventories also can help you identify people for your project whom you might overlook if you rely on memory or intuition to establish your project team. A simple form can be used to create a skills inventory and cost analysis of people available for your project. We provided an example in Chapter 8.

Call on Your Contacts and Supplier Networks, Too

If you will be working on many projects, build and maintain a network of contacts and suppliers as well as an inventory of your own organization's skills. If you will be producing different kinds of printed projects, for example, interview a variety of printing companies in your area and become familiar with their pricing structures and quality of work. If you will be hiring a large number of temporary manufacturing services, keep a list of temporary agencies who supply these types of services.

You can develop your own skills inventories and ratings for these contacts and vendors, just as you would describe your own internal staff. Then, when a project comes up, you are ready with a list of people and vendors who can fill your project's needs. This extra time up front on your first project may pay off in later projects.

A Lifesaver After the Project Starts

Skills inventories and contact lists are useful after the project starts as well. What happens if a key staff member assigned to your project quits or gets sick? Pull out your skills inventory to identify potential replacements. If you don't have a network and skills inventory ready, you will waste valuable time trying to find someone who can take over for the lost resource, and the project may suffer delays or other problems as a result.

The Best of the Best: Making Your Selections

After you have considered your options and the talent available to you, create a list of possible people and vendors for each task on your list. This list should include the alternatives available. In large, complex projects, the alternatives should be ranked in priority order, and the strengths and weakness of each choice should be well understood. A worksheet like the one shown previously can be useful in identifying people and their strengths and weaknesses for a project team. (Don't publish this list!)

If you depend on your skills inventories, you will discover that there are almost no perfect matches of people and project requirements on your list. Because no one can perfectly fit your needs, the selection process usually involves trade-offs. For planning purposes, identify people with the closest match of required skills and ask yourself if the skills deficiencies are workable. Can you use two people who complement each other's skills on the project? Can you make up for the lack of skills in other ways? The more critical the tasks, the more important the match of skill requirements to people becomes.

Sometimes You Have to Compromise

Obviously you want the best people possible for your project; but even after making compromises and trade-offs, it is not always appropriate to use your first choice person for every task, especially if another person's skills are adequate.

For example, there might be two designers who could be hired to create a newsletter. The first designer is truly exceptional in creativity and works fast. The downside: this person is also very expensive. Another designer has adequate creative skills and is much less expensive.

Because your newsletter project requires a relatively straightforward design, the use of the first person would not be a good choice, because the project budget would be exceeded. Thus, the most technically qualified person in this case is not a good choice because of the budget constraints on the project. Every choice involves risks and trade-offs.

Time Is Money
Keep in mind that as you develop the rest of the plan, your resource choices will affect the quality, the schedule, and the budget for your project. If you aren't able to get the resources you planned to use, you'll have to adapt the objectives, schedule, or budget accordingly. It's a good idea to verify the availability of as many resources as possible before the project plan is approved.

107

Why is this so complex? Because people are involved; things are almost never easy when people are involved, and never totally predictable. You'll have to make choices based on your own interpretation of the most important needs and your best guess of what you expect to happen with these people. It's the best you can do. With experience, you'll get closer to getting the right people for your jobs (but you'll still get surprises on occasion—that's why things never get boring in project management).

Planning for Outside Vendors and Suppliers

During the planning phase (where you are now), you need to determine the list of probable vendors for your project and get estimates of cost and availability. Before you talk to vendors, you need to be crystal clear about the tasks and work you want them to produce. It's usually after the plan is approved that you'll make your final vendor selections based on these estimates.

You want to know that the estimates are good ones—and that the eventual commitments will be met. You should follow these guidelines for getting the best estimates for your project:

➤ Whenever possible, get written estimates from suppliers with whom you have extensive and positive experience.

➤ Save money by renting equipment required for the short term, be it a massive backhoe or a miniature electron microscope. But don't forget to get estimates for the rentals for your plan.

➤ Make all providers (people, materials, and equipment suppliers) bid competitively.

➤ Consider out-of-town suppliers. What sells for $12,500 in Manhattan may go for $3,000 in Phoenix. (Be sure to take shipping and interstate tax requirements into account!)

Talking Turkey

Time Is Money
Many organizations have an approved vendor list. These are companies that your people frequently buy from, work with, or hire regularly. Look outside the list for a better deal if this won't cause political ripples.

Now you can get to the bottom line of working with outside suppliers. No estimate is set in stone unless you're working with a government provider or looking at a seller's market. (If you need 500 carpenters who are already busy rebuilding frame homes after a natural disaster, you'll have little negotiating power over the price of building your new corporate headquarters. Timing can be everything in a bidding situation.)

Negotiation is a fine art. There are many good books on the topic. Read a few. For a complete and free education, spend time at a flea market and watch as expert negotiators go up against the most set-in-concrete pricing scheme and drive the prices down. Or better, watch your organization's best salespeople at work. They wouldn't make those big salaries if they didn't know how to negotiate.

Snakes and Consultants

You may have to get estimates for service providers or consultants for your project because you don't have all the people you need within your own company. Choosing the consultants and service providers for a project can be a tough call. Experts, consultants, and even temporary labor hide behind a salesperson's persona.

Good consultants are masters at selling themselves, otherwise they would be out of business. Remember, just because someone proclaims himself an expert doesn't necessarily mean he has a track record to back up the claim. Make sure the vendors you choose have been around the block a couple of times.

Even hiring low level labor must be handled carefully. The temporary agency's polished salesperson may overwhelm you with smooth promises and glossy brochures, but eventually you'll just need grizzly old ditch diggers to dig those ditches. Remember, the gloss and polish you paid extra for probably won't make any difference if you just need good ditch diggers.

Because talk really *is* cheap, you must be careful of whomever you hire. Unfortunately, you won't really know what you have in hand until they perform—or fail to perform. Check the references and get performance guarantees in the contract before you sign on the dotted line.

> **Project Lingo**
> Here's the old joke about consultants (more true than it should be): a *consultant* is an unemployed person who has a watch and a briefcase.

> **High Water!**
> You've probably seen that old film footage of the Tacoma Narrows Bridge in Washington state. It started swaying in the wind on completion day and quickly crashed to the river below. Someone learned an expensive lesson in checking out vendors before counting on their performance. Don't wait for your own disaster to make the same discovery.

Choosing the Outside Sources and Suppliers

You need good estimates for your plans and good working relationships with your vendors to get these estimates. Work with suppliers, study the goods or services they sell, and check up on their reputations. Never let a powerfully persuasive salesperson push you into a commitment before the plan is approved. It may be harder to resist than you think when a honey-voiced merchant visits and applies rose-colored glasses to the top of your nose.

Time Is Money

Equipment suppliers would rather be paid at least some money for what they already have standing around than to have the stuff collect dust in wait of a well-heeled customer. Ask for a discount and expect to get it unless you're renting surfboards for a company party in July at Malibu.

If you follow these simple steps, you'll get more accurate estimates from suppliers of all sorts of goods and services:

1. Get written estimates on your service, supply, material, and equipment needs. On large projects you may want to put together a formal RFP (request for proposal) to attract the maximum number of potential suppliers. Advertise the RFP, if that's what it takes to get good estimates and quality vendors. Offer detailed specifications of your project and its needs by return mail or fax. Vendors will assume bidding is competitive, although the words "Competitive Bid" stamped (in heavy red ink, of course) on the RFP will help get the point across.

2. Fully explain, demonstrate, and document your requirements for equipment, materials, and supplies for the estimate or in the RFP. Be as precise as the following sample bid request for copy paper: "Bid required for bright white copy paper suitable for laser printing, 20 pound bond $8^1/2$" by 11", quantity 100,000 sheets packaged in 500 sheet reams, 10 to a box. Recycled paper consisting of at least 40 percent recycled paper is preferred. Please indicate the percentage of recycled paper used in your paper. Enclose a sample, please."

3. Include delivery mandates in the description of your needs. (Ordinary but unavailable materials have sunk more than one project.) These specifications indicate when the goods must be delivered and to where or the contract is void. If they turn out to be a no-show, you're still in trouble project-wise, but at least you won't owe a bill for a shipment that arrives three weeks too late. (You won't be able to specify dates, however, until you complete the schedule in Chapters 12 and 13.)

4. Make sure the vendors know that acceptance clauses will be inserted in the final order for goods. This means that goods that don't meet specified standards will be returned and replaced at no cost to you. Also, make sure the vendor will be responsible for picking up the shipping tab for return freight if materials or supplies are inappropriate or substandard on delivery.

5. If getting estimates from consultants or other service providers, ask for a formal proposal for their services. When hiring a packaging expert, for example, you might ask competing designers to create rough illustrations of how they would package your project.

6. When hiring consultants or service providers, ask also for a description of their current workload. Many will boast about current projects without realizing that what you're looking for is a person with the time to take on your tasks. Although it's true that the busiest may be the best, when it comes to managing a project, you

need adequate share-of-mind for your work and committed schedules from the vendors. Thus, a vendor who is a close second in quality but who has fewer commitments may be a better choice.

7. Check references, compare estimates, and use the estimate from the most likely choice of vendors for the rest of your planning purposes.

The Ghost in the Machine

Sometimes you won't be given the opportunity to get estimates or order resources without going through the purchasing department. This can be a relief—it takes the work out of your hands. But the purchasing department is the bane of projects (and project managers) more often than not.

If you're lucky, you'll find a professionally run organization with experienced purchasing agents who take the time to understand your needs and handle your bid requests with aplomb. But, be aware that you may be faced with the uphill task of (literally) fighting with your organization's purchasing personnel to place an order.

The only way to know what you'll be up against during a project is to test the waters. Begin by ordering something simple, such as a desk for a team member. The resulting cooperation of the purchasing department—or lack thereof—will let you know if you need to add tasks to your project that read: "Work with purchasing to explain need, secure bid, and gain approvals to order desks."

Sadly, in our 25 years of experience with purchasing departments, many are run by bureaucrats who slow the estimating-buying cycle to a crawl as six signatures of approval are required to order a new light bulb for an overhead projector. Too many purchasing departments work with favored vendors who make the purchasing process easy for the purchasing department but costly for your project. The department may choose vendors based on who buys them the best lunch in town rather than price, timely delivery, and a workable approach to handling problems. Remember, it's not *their* project they're purchasing for—it's *yours*.

> **Time Is Money**
> "Money talks" is one of life's truisms. (We'll skip the second part—you already know the sentiment.) You'll find that it's especially true when you control a project budget of which outside providers want a share. Avoid taking money, gifts, or vacations of any kind on a vendor's tab. This keeps the bids on the level and the lawyers out of your life.

The best way to solve problems with a recalcitrant purchasing organization is to learn their procedures, follow their processes, and make friends in the department. If the department causes more problems than it solves, try to work around it when you can and learn to work within the process when you must. The test of the project manager's mettle will be to make it all work, easy and hard.

Use a worksheet like this one to define precisely what materials and supplies you want. Be specific.

Equipment and Supplies Worksheet

Task Numbers [   ]   Date Prepared: [   ]

Completed By [   ]

Required	Responsible Person or Vendor	How Much Is Needed?	When Is it Needed?	Check If Available
MATERIALS:				☐ ☐ ☐ ☐ ☐ ☐
EQUIPMENT:				☐ ☐ ☐ ☐ ☐
SUPPLIES:				☐ ☐ ☐ ☐ ☐
SPECIAL SERVICES:				☐ ☐ ☐
OTHER:				☐ ☐ ☐ ☐ ☐

Don't Skimp on the Team's Needs

Your project demands the best equipment you can afford. Before you rent those bargain 386 desktop computers for $9.95 each per week, consider your hard working (and well-chosen) project team. With inferior equipment, less work will get done, and the staff might become alienated because they assume no one cares about their productivity. Is this saving money? We don't think so.

Give your people the right tools for the job. Provide them with modern equipment, a comfortable and safe place to work, and quality supplies as necessary. For special needs, ask project participants what they need, and do your best to furnish that high-powered workstation or linear accelerator, if necessary. Obviously, people might ask for more than they really need, so give the choices some thought. Still, giving people the right tools is essential to completing a project on time and within budget. You need to sort out wants from requirements, and then make sure your project gets all of the latter.

From the Plan to the Stuff

For planning purposes, getting the bids for supplies, materials, and equipment may be enough to establish a budget and schedule for your project. After the plan is approved and you have the go ahead to proceed with the project, however, you'll have to choose the specific vendors you want to use on the project. At that point, you'll need to check references (if you haven't already), compare bids, and verify delivery dates, and then choose the best vendor (probably in conjunction with the core project team). Then, by all means, get an attorney or the corporate legal counsel to draft the actual work agreements with any suppliers or outsider vendors, and require vendor signatures on the agreements *before* work commences or money is exchanged.

For now, with the resources completely documented, you're ready to draft a schedule and budget for your project. The saga of the plan continues...

Time Is Money
Never let contractual paperwork wear you down to the point where you acquiesce to an inequitable deal. Just because you're tired of the salesperson's heavy hype or you're simply tired of looking, don't give in. Keep looking for a vendor with realistic prices—or call in another negotiator from your company to help turn the deal into something workable.

Words from the Wise
Give us the tools, and we will finish the job.
—Sir Winston Churchill, radio broadcast, 1941

The Least You Need to Know

➤ After you have all the tasks for a project identified, you should identify the specific resource requirements for each task, including people skills, material requirements, information needs, and other resources.

➤ Before you get your project plan approved, make sure you've verified the cost estimates and availability for all the resources for your project. Otherwise you can't put together a reasonable schedule or budget.

➤ You can guess what people can do for your project, but you'll never be sure until you work with them.

➤ Getting accurate estimates from suppliers of people, materials, and equipment requires a clear description of your needs and careful review of the vendors' capabilities.

➤ You should always check out vendors before you sign a contract.

➤ *All* fees are negotiable.

Chapter 12

Project Start to Finish—Establishing the Time to Get Things Done

In This Chapter

➤ The importance of accurate scheduling

➤ Building estimates from experience

➤ Four ways to correctly estimate tasks

➤ Schedule inflation and how to avoid it

➤ The confidence factor in scheduling

Time is of the essence. When it comes to managing a project, everyone wants results ASAP. Tomorrow at the latest! Next week? Impossible! But if you put together the wrong schedule, that's what your project is going to be. Impossible.

Scheduling is often the most difficult and most risky aspect of project planning. All too often, you are rushed through the process, forced to use guesstimate numbers, pie-in-the-sky expectations, and then render a solid schedule that you will not only be expected to keep, but also will be held accountable for on your next performance review.

As you would assume from reading earlier chapters in this book, the schedule is intertwined with the task list, the network diagram, and eventually the budget. Change one and you invariably influence the others. We have separated the schedule and the budget in the next few chapters—but in reality, you should work on both at the same time. The schedule and budget work together to float a project or sink it.

The Schedule or the Budget: Which Is First?

Some naive project managers are inclined to start with the budget first, but we don't recommend it. Because time is money, the schedule will affect the final budget in many ways. That's why we talk about scheduling first. The best project managers establish the schedule before finalizing the budget, even if everyone thinks they're nuts. It's best to try to determine how much time is *really* required to complete a project before you let your (lack of) money get in the way of your thinking.

The experienced project manager, hair graying, can look at a task, understand what's required, and provide a reasonably realistic guess of the time requirement as if pulling the number from the air. You will get to that point someday, with the help of this book, and with a few projects under your belt. But until you get that experience, you can establish a reasonable schedule using this and the subsequent chapter's advice as a procedural guide. Maybe more importantly, in the following pages, you also will learn how to deal with external pressures (such as bosses and customers) that demand unrealistic dates. And no matter what your manager says, you can't build Rome in a day.

Building a schedule also verifies the project's viability. If, when assembling the schedule, time is not on your side, you may need to work out an extension with management or an increase in resources. Working on the schedule might also reveal missing tasks. Remember: it's all interrelated, so expect to adjust the network, task list, and budget as you adapt the schedule.

The Schedule Synchronizes the Project

Accurate, realistic, and workable scheduling is what makes a project tick. The schedule shows who is doing what, and when they are supposed to be doing it. Scheduling involves converting the well-organized and sequenced tasks in your work breakdown structure (WBS) and network diagram—and the list of resources and vendors you developed in Chapter 11—into an achievable timetable with start dates, finish dates, and assigned responsibilities for each task.

The steps in creating a schedule are carried out sequentially and include:

1. *Establish the scheduling assumptions.*
2. *Estimate the task effort and duration* (the time to complete each task on the network diagram) based on the resources you have at hand or can afford. Here you need to estimate the duration of a task over a number of days.

    Sometimes duration and effort are the same. If it takes eight hours of effort for a secretary to stuff envelopes over one day, then the effort is one work day and the duration of the task is one work day. Sometimes duration and effort are very different. It may take only four hours of meeting time to get the building inspector's approval of a building's wiring, but these meetings happen over a period of two weeks. Thus, the effort for getting the wiring approved is four hours, but the duration of the task is two weeks.

It is important to know both the effort and the duration required to complete a task in order to create both an accurate schedule and a detailed budget for a project.

Duration stands out in project management terms because the accumulated duration of tasks along the critical path in the project plan directly affects all the subsequent tasks in the project. (You'll learn about the critical path in Chapter 13.) For now, just know that you need to estimate both the effort and the duration (time span) of each task in you network diagram or work breakdown structure (WBS).

3. *Determine calendar dates for each task and create a master schedule.* For a complex project network, you also will need to determine the critical path and float for each task on the project (you'll learn how to do this in Chapter 13).

4. *Adjust the network dependencies and individual resource assignments as necessary to optimize the schedule.*

5. *Chart the final schedule.*

Project Lingo
Duration is simply the time it takes to complete a task. In a schedule, the duration is an estimate; when the project is done, the duration is the time it actually took to get things done.

Estimating Time: Your Best Guess at Effort and Duration

Of all the steps in scheduling, estimating the task durations is the most important. Unfortunately, estimating the duration of tasks is like trying to predict the future. You can only guess—but there are better ways to guess than others. Estimating the duration of tasks is the most important aspect of the project scheduling process. Without accurate task duration estimates, the entire plan and project might crumble around you.

When estimating duration for tasks, there are five options you can use to make the estimates (guesses) as good as possible. These include:

➤ Ask the people who will actually do the work.

➤ Get an objective expert's opinion (for example, from someone who isn't working on the project).

➤ Find a similar task in a completed project plan to see how long it took to get done.

➤ If you have time and the task lends itself to this type of verification, perform a test session of the task to see how long it really takes using your resources.

➤ Make your best educated guess. This is the last resort when you're under pressure, so make sure the guess is more educated than it is arbitrary. To do this, try the preceding options instead.

Who You Gonna Call?

To get reliable estimates on the duration of tasks and effort required, you will likely need to ask other people about the time it will take them to get things done (unless you're completing the entire project on your own, of course). The following sections describe some of the people you can ask to help determine the task duration and effort estimates for your schedule.

Representative Team Members for Each Part of the Project

Seek out the most experienced team members who will be completing work on your project. Have them estimate the task durations in their areas of expertise; then, adjust the estimates based on your own experience. Remember, some team members will pad their estimates a little or a lot, and some will be over confident about their abilities to accomplish miracles. You must adjust the duration in the final plan to account for these idiosyncrasies if you want to come up with the optimum schedule.

It's often useful to sit down with all the team members to estimate task durations. Even if nothing useful (to you) comes of the sessions, they serve to build camaraderie and give you a better understanding of the project from the team member's point of view. It's also an excellent technique for assembling a rough-cut schedule in a hurry.

Outside Vendors and Service Agencies

You must get estimates directly from any outside service providers and consultants who will work on your project. Never estimate their time for them. You can negotiate their estimates, but if you tell a vendor without their input, you'll never get the schedule you demand. You should politely demand a written estimate that fixes the cost and commits to a schedule (unless the project runs off the rails or changes in nature, of course). Shop price! Shop time! (You read about this timely topic in Chapter 11.)

Experienced Managers or Experts

Those in your organization who have handled similar projects can provide excellent advice and study cost estimates for problems. They also might be able to provide exact estimates if a project they worked on has elements common to yours. Or, they may be much more experienced project managers and willing to help. If no such experts exist within your company, you could get advice from a consultant or colleague in another company who can help verify your duration estimates.

Management and Other Project Stakeholders

If you want your managers and stakeholders to buy into your schedule, you need to give them an opportunity to help plan the schedule (or at last review it before you submit the project plan for approval). By bringing stakeholders into the process, they'll see that you will efficiently use your time and wisely spend their money. Their involvement will assist you in getting the final plan approved because they'll already have a grasp on the realities of the schedule.

Weighing the Risk

After getting information on task durations from various sources, you'll need to use your judgment to determine the duration you'll actually assign to the schedule. Each of these durations will have a risk associated with it. It's often useful, then, to come up with a best-case schedule and a worst-case schedule based on these risks.

Best Case and Worst Case—Compromising Between the Two

In estimating every task, assume that the actual time required will fall somewhere between that of flawless execution and that of major disaster. The best approach is to establish a compromise between the two. Some project management methodologies, such as PERT (refer to Chapter 11) provide the mechanics for estimating all three. These include:

➤ The optimistic estimate: everything goes like clockwork and without problems.

➤ The realistic estimate: a few problems crop up and subsequent delays compromise the optimistic estimate.

➤ The pessimistic estimate: allowances are made for many elements to go wrong, substantially delaying or jeopardizing the task. Note: the pessimistic estimate assumes that the project is going ahead. A complete disaster could still occur that would sink the project's timetable and budget.

Ultimately these three estimates will be used in combination with each other to come up with a "most likely" schedule based on your confidence in the estimates.

The Confidence Factor

Just how reliable are your estimates? You might be comfortable with the timetable for delivery of a photocopier and other office equipment to a new company headquarters, but be unsure how long it will take to complete the electrical wiring for the building. You're even more uncertain about the task to design a new logo, which takes lots of creativity and political approvals.

For every task duration on your list, you'll have varying degrees of confidence. The tasks with the highest degree of confidence are usually those you've performed previously or that you'll do yourself. Those you have no direct experience with represent tasks you aren't sure of. A task with complete confidence might rate at 99 percent. (Remember, no estimate can be perfect in scheduling; there is always the risk of the unknown, unexpected event.)

The degree of confidence is also influenced by the complexity (or simplicity) of the task, and how much the task is dependent on the completion of preceding (possibly complex) tasks.

High Water!
Don't pad the schedule just to cover your uncertainties. Too much padding is as bad as agreeing to complete the impossible in no time at all. A little padding (called contingency planning) is standard practice in all project plans—because no one can foresee the future. But padding adds expense and time to your project.

Remember that if you do the estimates alone, your team members may not buy into them. You could create and sell a schedule to management that team members cannot support (or deliver). Make sure team members are involved in task estimating.

An "iffy" task that has risk associated with it may have a confidence rating of 10 percent or less. Use your confidence in tasks to determine the best/worst case scheduling scenarios described in the previous section.

If many of the estimates have low confidence associated with them, move your schedule dates toward the worst case scenario. If most of the estimates are high confidence, a schedule closer to the best case estimate is the best choice. Further, the more complex (and interdependent) the tasks, the more you might want to learn towards a worst-case scenario.

If you do add a little protection to your schedule for risky tasks, never make your padded time estimates too obvious. ("Trip to grocery store for product rollout party supplies: seven days.") This tactic won't win you any popularity contests with management. Such obvious protection schemes will have management sniffing through the entire project for inflationary tactics at all levels, including the budget. Ultimately, you'll lose not only credibility, but the real resources and time you need to get things done.

If your schedule starts looking like it will take too long to get things done, try adding more people or resources to the plan; however, this impacts the budget and some tasks could suffer from the too-many-cooks-in-the-kitchen syndrome. More people doesn't always mean you'll get things done faster. More people always has unforeseen costs in management time and coordination, so make sure that adding people is really a good solution to adjusting the schedule.

Details, Details...

After estimating the task durations and taking judgment on the estimates, you must decide on the level of detail you want to put in the schedule. Usually, the scheduling level should relate to the levels in your WBS or network diagram. For example, you can probably schedule a small project down to the day or even the hour on first go around, but you won't be able to schedule a megaproject any finer than by the month or week.

For planning purposes the schedule may be produced in weeks or months or maybe even years for a megaproject. As work on the project proceeds, you can schedule the work at finer levels. Obviously, scheduling a megaproject to the hour from the beginning of the project would produce silly schedules and mounds of useless paper. Alternately, inadequate schedule detail at the beginning of a small project might leave team members thinking they have more time to get things done than they really have. It takes practice—you'll get the hang of it.

Putting It Down on Paper

Once the assumptions for the schedule (that is, the number of people and the task sequences) and the durations are nailed down, you can begin assembling a reasonable schedule. For a simple project with few dependencies, you can simply list durations on the project task list. For more complex projects, use the WBS and the network diagram to schedule your project.

Scheduling with a network diagram is conceptually simple. Just estimate the length of time each task will require for completion (this is called *estimating task duration*). Then, you simply add all the durations of all the tasks on the project to get the total time required to complete the project. Just lay the days out on a calendar and, voila!, you have a schedule. To show you how it's done, we've provided the following example of a network diagram and task list with durations.

Project Lingo
Project duration is the time, usually in days, that it takes to complete the entire project, from starting the first task to finishing the last one.

Of course, nothing is ever as simple as it sounds. You need to take into account work days, holidays, vacations, parallel tasks, and other special circumstances. That's why scheduling a large project is easier with a software program designed for the job. (Read Chapter 28 for more information about project management computer programs.)

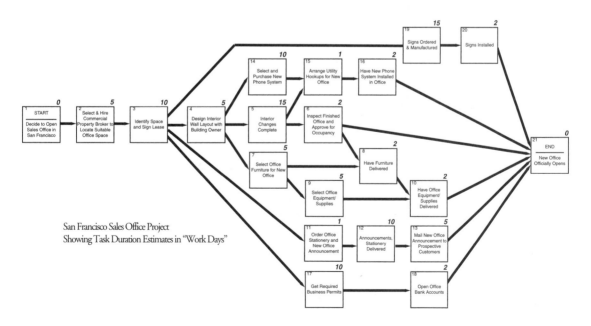

San Francisco Sales Office Project
Showing Task Duration Estimates in "Work Days"

This is an example of a task list and a net-work diagram with the durations added. On a simple project, that's about all there is to creating a schedule. A complex project is too much for mere mortals—using a computer program is a good idea.

121

Schedule Charting Pros and Cons

There are several schedule-charting formats you should be aware of. The trick is choosing the format that best suits your project. Here are some of your options for displaying the schedule:

➤ *Listings*. Schedules that follow the formats in the sample forms are useful for most projects and are necessary for keeping track of progress as the project proceeds. For manageability and control, break these schedule listings into sub-projects if the project is extremely large, and combine them with a milestone schedule.

➤ *Calendar charts*. Annotated calendars can be extremely useful for keeping track of schedules for many small projects. Multiple projects or different team member tasks can be entered in various colors on the calendar. Calendars are a good communication tool when displayed in a central location where many team members can see the dates. Large display calendars with re-usable, washable surfaces are available in many business supply stores for this purpose.

➤ *Gantt charts*. Gantt charts are best used as a visual overview of project timelines; however, they don't show task relationships and should not substitute for a network diagram or master schedule listing. Gantt charts can be very useful in initial schedule planning, for simple projects, or for individual timelines on a complex project involving many people. These charts also are good for comparing project progress to the original schedule.

➤ *Milestone schedules*. In Chapter 11, you learned that milestones can be assigned to summarize major paths on a network. Milestones also can be used to chart an overall project schedule. A milestone schedule doesn't have enough information for managing a project, but it can be useful for communicating an overall schedule on a large project to upper management or other people who need an overview of the project without task details.

In complex projects, most project managers use more than one schedule format because it allows them to view the project in different ways, depending on the focus of the analysis that is required. Gantt charts are good for an overview, the calendar schedule is useful for the details, and individual schedules are needed for unambiguous communication to team members about their respective responsibilities.

Even on small projects you might want to use two or more charting options to represent a project. This can help you view the schedule from different perspectives and help communicate the schedule to people with different ways of looking at things.

More on Gantt Charts

Gantt charts—sometimes referred to as *project timelines*—are the most commonly used scheduling charts in business because they're easy to produce and easy to understand.

Gantt charts ordinarily have a list of dates at the top and a list of tasks down the left side. A line on the Gantt chart shows the date where each task begins and ends on the chart based on its precedence and duration. The level of scheduling detail you display in your Gantt charts will be determined by the time periods you use on the top: daily, weekly, hourly, monthly, or whatever is appropriate for your project. If a project takes a year or more to complete, you may want to use a monthly or weekly Gantt chart. If your project takes 30 days or less, a daily Gantt chart will provide more useful information. Gantt charts are most effective if you can present the whole chart on one document, such as a 8"×10" or 11"×17" paper.

Be aware that Gantt charts don't show the interrelationships among tasks. You need a network diagram for that. Also, a Gantt chart alone may not provide enough detail to communicate schedules to individual team members in a complex project. The following Gantt chart shows general float time among tasks, but not the precedences.

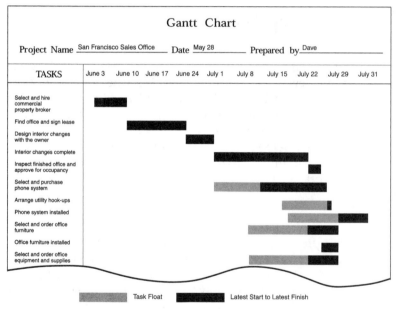

Gantt charts are useful for envisioning the entire project through time.

A Detailed Gantt Chart Showing the Schedule for the San Francisco Office Project

Scheduling on the Network Diagram

In addition to creating a Gantt chart, some people like to annotate the schedule dates directly on the network diagram. Although this is a good reference tool for reviewing the entire project, it is awkward to use as a working schedule when assigning responsibilities to individual team members. Therefore, you also should use a schedule listing in addition to the network diagram to display and communicate the schedule details.

Of course, many variations of schedule formats can be used to accommodate individual preferences. It is important that the key information, including task descriptions, start dates, expected finish dates, and assigned people, be easy to read and interpret. As project manager, you need to be able to create a personal timetable for each individual on the project team. Each individual who will be working on the project also needs to be able to relate his or her personal timetable to the master schedule.

Revisions and the Schedule

Assume that your schedule (and every other aspect of your plan) will require several revisions. As feedback arrives from both team members and outside resources, you might redraft the task estimates and dates several times until you come up with a workable, approvable timeline (schedule) for the project.

High Water!
If you must share your preliminary drafts of the plan with management, stamp "DRAFT" or "INCOMPLETE" in bright red letters on each page. That way, you won't be held to the shifting sands of an unfinished plan by senior managers who assume an early version of the project plan is final.

Learning Takes Time

Even in the most routine jobs, some time is required for learning the procedures in the new company and adapting to the new work environment. This is true of some consultants as well, who must become familiar with your company's way of doing business before they can get down to work. When you schedule a project, allow for these various training and development requirements. You might even want to identify training activities as specific tasks in your WBS or network.

The Heat Is On

Instead of caving in to unrealistic pressure, you need to be comfortable with estimating the time each task will require. Unfortunately, no one will make it easy for you. Team members may pull a date or time block (hours required) out of a hat at the same time senior management wants the work completed the day before yesterday. Every project is a rush. With that in mind, how do you, as project manager, avoid succumbing to unrealistic expectations and unrealistic goals? Assuming that those commissioning the project are semi-rational human beings, your best tool is the schedule. Actually it's all a game. Management will constantly challenge costs, time, and resources. You must make them believe—through a well-documented schedule and plan—that your estimates are realistic and not unduly padded.

Team Member Estimate Errors

Chances are that you're counting on team members to provide the best and most accurate scheduling estimates possible. But, rather than carefully thinking through the process they are responsible for, some of the team might simply choose a number and feed that into your plan. If it's unrealistic, you're stuck with it.

Avoid this problem by presenting copies of the scheduling worksheet found in this chapter. Team members will have to turn their brains on to complete it. Even a cursory review of the worksheet will point out those who haven't done their homework. Send them back for another pass before adopting their time and date estimates. And make sure they consider elapsed time. For example, if their task is to evaluate a new software package, they need to build in time to order it, install it, test it, and go through some conversations with support staff. What looks like four days of effort (32 hours) could result in a duration of 12 days when all the "dead" time between activities is accounted for.

Dictate Doesn't Mean Doable

Sometime you'll be asked (actually told) to shorten the schedule—even though you know it's impossible to get the work done any faster. Before you cave into dictate, sit down with everyone pressuring you and go over the schedule day by day if necessary. Be friendly and cooperative and explain each task and the assumptions about your time allotments represented in the schedule. Bring in expert project managers or technical team members to explain the more opaque tasks.

Your goal for this process is to communicate why the project requires a certain amount of time. In a truly impossible situation, you might need someone senior to you to go to bat when others attempt to force an unworkable adjustment to the plan on your shoulders.

The Just-In-Time Strategy for Scheduling Resources

The just-in-time strategy for getting materials and supplies is credited to the Japanese, but the technique is now common practice worldwide. Just-in-time delivery depends on accurate scheduling and project coordination. With an accurate schedule in place, you can order just what you need and get it delivered exactly when you need it. That means that supplies, equipment, and even people arrive only when the project is ready for them.

By having goods delivered (or people hired) exactly when they're needed, you save money for storage, reduce up-front costs for ordering materials, and are assured that you don't have extra stuff on hand that has cost you extra money.

The key to making this approach work is, you guessed it, communication. Having a contract with suppliers that lets you adjust dates is the essence of just-in-time delivery. That way, you don't have to warehouse 1,000,000,000 chicken feathers when the tacky straw hats you planned to adorn don't arrive from the supplier. You need to make just-in-time delivery a mandatory contract clause: no delivery until a written request is made and guaranteed delivery within a set number of days or hours when you do put the order in.

The window for just-in-time delivery must be agreed upon in advance—or the whole schedule falls apart. A temp agency hiring 20 people for your project will want enough time to hire the needed people, but notify them if the project goes late. The maker of

6,000 bicycle seats won't want to wait three extra months because the frames come in late from France. They'll want them out of the way and expect payment as well. You, as project manager, must ensure that people and supplies arrive appropriately according to the original or revised schedule.

The Least You Need to Know

➤ Scheduling involves estimating the task durations for the project and plotting the dates on a calendar, accounting for holidays, special events, and unknown circumstances.

➤ No schedule is ever perfect, but the goal is to make the best estimate possible. You do this by using your own judgment and the experience of others to help you make your estimates.

➤ The project's schedule in part determines the budget. Thus, you must work cyclically on the schedule and the budget until you get them right.

➤ The detail in your schedule should reflect the size of the project.

➤ The Gantt chart is an excellent tool for studying overall schedules, but it doesn't show the interdependencies among tasks that are shown on the network diagram. Thus, using both in a project plan is a good idea.

➤ Time estimates should be based on best case/worst case scenarios. Your degree of confidence in the accuracy of these estimates should dictate the ultimate schedule, which should be a compromise somewhere between the two extremes.

➤ Just-in-time logistics can save you money without extra charges for early delivery or storage fees.

STEP 1

Chapter 13

The Steps to the Critical Path

> **In This Chapter**
>
> ➤ Understanding the critical path
>
> ➤ All about float and slack in a project
>
> ➤ Important adjustments necessary in complex project schedules
>
> ➤ Ways to adapt a project to meet a forced schedule

In Chapter 12, you learned the good news: scheduling is a simple matter of estimating durations for tasks and then plotting the dates on the calendar. Now the bad news: even using computer-based project management software, scheduling a complex project is well, complex. Because an accurate schedule is essential to managing projects of all sizes, the process is not one in which you should attempt to cut corners. You need to consider some of the complexities of scheduling before you finalize your project plan. That's what this chapter is all about—the complexities of project scheduling.

For complex projects, computers have a significant advantage over manual scheduling. Yes, you learn how to calculate the critical path and float in a complex project schedule in this chapter, but you should get a computer program to help on projects of more than 10 or 15 tasks (see Chapter 28). Then you can easily change and revise the schedule as you work through the issues and changes in a project.

The Scheduling Process Step by Step

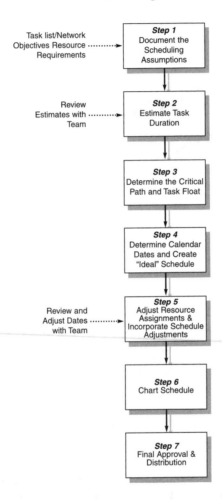

Task list/Network
Objectives Resource ·········▸
Requirements

Step 1
Document the
Scheduling
Assumptions

Review
Estimates with ·········▸
Team

Step 2
Estimate Task
Duration

Step 3
Determine the Critical
Path and Task Float

Step 4
Determine Calendar
Dates and Create
"Ideal" Schedule

Review and
Adjust Dates ·········▸
with Team

Step 5
Adjust Resource
Assignments &
Incorporate Schedule
Adjustments

Step 6
Chart Schedule

Step 7
Final Approval &
Distribution

Words from the Wise

Nothing is so difficult but that it may be found out by seeking.

There is nothing so easy but that it becomes difficult when you do it reluctantly.

—Terence, *The Lady of Andros*

The Scheduling Assumptions for Your Project

From earlier chapters, you already know how to clarify goals and objectives before the project plan reaches its final stages. For the same reasons, it's important to specify scheduling assumptions before the schedule is completed. Answering the following questions should help in this process. We've included a simple worksheet that will assist you in determining the assumptions germane to your project.

➤ Are there a fixed number of resources to be used on the project, or can you add them to meet the schedule priorities?

➤ Is there an absolute date by which the project must be completed or become worthless? (For example, designing a new tradeshow booth for the big July show: If the booth is a no-show, then the time and money used to design and build it as well as the cost of the tradeshow floor space gets flushed down the toilet.)

➤ Can the completion date be negotiated based on a realistic schedule of when all the deliverables (goals) can be met?

➤ Will people work standard workdays or will overtime be allowed and/or expected? Watch for holidays or expect to pay extra for resources working on Christmas Day!

➤ Are all resources currently trained and available, or will your project require hiring additional people and acquiring new equipment? If training or hiring is required, it should be scheduled.

> **Words from the Wise**
>
> The best laid schemes o' mice an' men Gang aft a-gley. An' lea'e us nought but grief an' pain For promised joy.
>
> —Robert Burns, "To a Mouse" (1785)

Scheduling Assumptions Worksheet

Project Name San Francisco Office Project   Date May 22

1. Are all the resources currently available for this project?
   If no, list the resources required that are not available:
   People Leasing Agent Needs to Be Found   ☐ YES
   Equipment _____   ☒ NO

2. Is there a due date when the project absolutely must be complete?   ☐ YES
   If yes, enter date: _____   ☒ NO
   Reason: _____

3. Will overtime be allowed?   ☐ YES
   If yes, how much? _____   ☒ NO

4. Are there any holidays or other breaks during this project?   ☒ YES
   If yes, list dates: July 4   ☐ NO

5. Have additional resources and people been approved for this project?   ☒ YES
                                                ☐ NO

6. Have the work schedules and availabilities of all resources been documented?   ☒ YES
                                                ☐ NO

Notes: Follow the Phildelphia Office Plan as Reference

Use this worksheet to help detail the assumptions about the schedule for your project.

Some examples of assumptions are: A network expert from the organization will be available from August through October; new milling machinery will be operational as planned by January 25th; there will be no major changes in procedures for tracking inventory within the next six months. Assumptions protect the project from being severely impacted by planned change in other parts of the organization that the project manager is not aware of. Worst case, they reveal these, so you can build them into your plan.

Large projects require that you document your assumptions in writing. That way, you are less likely to forget something. You can make your own worksheet with a word processor if you need a lot more room. Simple projects don't always require documentation of the assumptions, but you should have a verbal agreement among your team and outside resources on them. Need to rent a specialized piece of expensive equipment? Your assumptions should ensure availability within the time window you specify. Some equipment requires an experienced operator and the vendor providing the equipment might insist on you using and compensating their operator or technician.

Time Is Money

When scheduling a project, you must allow for those times of the year when work slows due to vacations and holidays. In the U.S. and Canada, work barely crawls in late summer as people vacation and during the holiday season, Thanksgiving, and December 15 to about January 3. Other holidays may briefly slow progress as well. Major religious holidays might have to be accounted for in your plans.

If additional resources are required, you must budget for them and get budget approval from senior management. Increasing headcount is always a tough assignment, unless the team members are hired as temporary employees or through a temp agency.

If you are managing a project for a large organization, chances are the personnel department will help you with the hiring paperwork. Specific forms must be completed by you and approved by any number of management levels. You also need to make sure that the hiring tasks are part of the network and the schedule.

Estimating the Time to Complete Tasks Based on Available Resources

After the assumptions are understood and agreed to, you can proceed in assembling the actual schedule. Start by estimating the length of time each task will require for completion. Remember, you need to estimate both labor hours (for budgeting purposes) and the total duration of the task in days or partial days. You learned about estimating task and effort durations in Chapter 12.

It is the duration (number of days) of the tasks that, when added together, establish the time required to complete the project. Enter each task duration into the scheduling worksheet included later in the chapter.

To complete the estimating process, it's necessary to work with the network diagram and task list developed for the project. You will need to revise your plan when you choose to combine two tasks into one or split one into two or more. You also might think of tasks that were forgotten earlier in the planning stage. Should you modify the plan, include your changes in all associated documents, such as the work breakdown structure (WBS).

How to Determine the Critical Path on Any Project

When you have determined task durations and are confident in your estimates, it's time to assemble a schedule using real dates. But, on a large/complex project, one more step remains in the way to assembling a working schedule. On projects with multiple parallel tasks and subprojects, a critical path must be determined to identify the time required to complete the project. (Most small projects with few tasks can skip this step.)

> **Time Is Money**
> Each version of your schedule should be time and date stamped, either by the computer or by hand. That way you won't mix up an old version with a new one.

Critical Path and Critical Tasks

The critical path is a sequence of tasks that forms the longest duration of the project. If a task is delayed on the critical path, then the project is delayed. For example, when opening the new sales office, the interior build-out can't begin until you've negotiated and signed the lease.

Tasks not lying on the critical path are more flexible. You can install the telephones any time from the completion of the build-out to the office's first day in operation. That's assuming you have enough time to accommodate the install between build-out completion and an opening day party for customers.

Adding together the duration of tasks on the critical path determine the total time the project will take. Because each task on the critical path must follow its predecessor in order, any task that is late on the critical path will cause the project to be late—and all tasks following a late task on the critical path will be late. Yes, the delay will hold up the entire project. That's why the critical path is, well, *critical*.

> **Project Lingo**
> The difference between the time available for a task and the time required to complete it is called *float*. Float is also known as *slack* or *slack time*. Latest finish – earliest start – duration = total float. If the total float for a task equals zero, then that task is on the critical path. The amount of float is the amount of flexibility for starting a task.

Float

Tasks not on the critical path also must be completed. You can't build a house and ask someone to move in before the water and sewer are connected, but such tasks can occur later in the project's timeframe without substantially delaying those downstream. This gives them a flexible start and finish date, which in project management lingo is called *float*.

Establishing the Critical Path

The critical path is easy to determine in a project that has been documented with a good network diagram. Simply add each parallel path's tasks together and the path requiring the most time to complete is the critical path. In the example shown for building a sales office, the longest path requires 41 days. That makes it the critical path. Critical tasks—those on this path—not completed on time will delay the project, unless you can make up the time further down the critical path or an on-the-path task finishes ahead of schedule.

Critical Path: Myth or Reality?

The concept behind critical path is simple: if you delay a task on the critical path, the project is delayed. This seems to make perfect sense to most people new to project management. The path on the project has to go from beginning to end.

High Water!
When its tasks go late, the critical path becomes the roadblock to project completion. That's why you should put extra effort into estimating these tasks. If you lack confidence in the task schedule or resource availability, delay the project until everything fits in place. If the project is already underway, put your best people on the tasks and focus your energies on catching up.

Unfortunately, as in all things involving people and plans, there are complexities. First, some tasks on the critical path may be less important than others. Some of the tasks may be there for mathematical reasons (which you'll learn about in a bit), not managerial priorities. For this reason, many managers also create a "Managerial Task List" which is a list of the most important tasks on the project. This managerial task list, along with the mathematical list of critical tasks, can be used to focus attention on the important work of the project.

And always remember that regardless of the mathematics of it—or the managerial importance—when you change task dependencies, duration estimates, and other network details, you need to reevaluate the critical path and reassess the schedule. There's no way around it. You can't change the sequences without impacting the schedule.

Use the Critical Path Worksheet to Calculate Path and Float

If you're new to project management, the calculation of the critical path initially sounds complicated. But it's really simple, assuming you've done your homework by correctly listing, estimating duration, and assigning precedence to each task. If you're using a computer-based program, it will probably identify the critical path automatically. Otherwise, the steps are as follows:

1. *List the tasks and estimated task durations on the worksheet.*
2. *Calculate the earliest starting number for each task.* The earliest start is the number of duration days at the point where all precedent activities before it in the path have been satisfied. The first task begins on *day zero*—a D-day of sorts for the start of any project. Assume that each subsequent task begins after the finish of the preceding activity. It works like this:

Earliest start = least number of days from the beginning of a project before it can begin.

In the example, the earliest start for the task "Install entry system" becomes 0 + 5 + 10 + 5 = 20, because 20 is the total of all durations that immediately precede the beginning of that task on the network diagram.

Critical Path Worksheet

Project Name Philadelphia Sales Office Project   **Date** January 25

Task	Duration	Earliest Start	Earliest Finish	Latest Start	Latest Finish	Total Float
Select and hire commercial property broker	5	0	5	0	5	0
Find office and sign lease	10	5	15	5	5	0
Design interior changes with the owner	5	15	20	15	20	0
Interior changes complete	15	20	35	20	35	0
Inspect finished office and approve for occupancy	2	35	37	35	37	0
Select and purchase phone system	10	20	30	28	38	8
Arrange utility hook-ups	1	30	31	38	39	8
Phone system installed	2	31	33	39	41	8
Select and order office furniture	5	20	25	29	34	9
Office furniture installed	2	37	39	37	39	0
Select and order office equipment and supplies	5	25	30	34	39	9
Office equipment delivered and set-up	2	39	41	39	41	0
Order and manufacture signs for new office	15	15	30	24	39	9
Signs installed	2	30	32	39	41	9
Order stationery and announcements	1	15	16	25	26	10
Stationery and announcements delivered	10	16	26	26	36	10
Announcements mailed	5	26	31	36	41	10
Get business permits	10	15	25	29	39	14
Open bank accounts	2	25	27	39	41	14

ALL TASKS WITH ZERO FLOAT ARE ON THE CRITICAL PATH

Use this worksheet to calculate the critical path and float for the tasks on your project. If you have more tasks than will fit on a page, look into getting a computer program (see Chapter 27).

133

3. *Calculate the earliest finish number for each task.* To do this, add the task duration (as a number of days) to the earliest start number.

   Earliest finish = earliest start number + task duration number.

   The earliest number to start "Install passcard entry system" is calculated as 20 + 10 = 30. Thus this task can't be done before day 30 in the project.

4. *Calculate the latest finish number for each task.* The latest finish is the last day a task can be performed without changing the end date of the project. The latest finish is calculated by first noting the largest number in the earliest finish column. This number is the total number of days in the project. Assign this number to the last task in the project and subtract the duration from the number of duration days in the path. To calculate latest finish, you work backward from the last day of the project—it's like calculating the earliest start from day zero, but in reverse. So, the latest finish for the "Install passcard entry system" task becomes, 41 – 2 – 1 = 38 because these are the total number of the durations between the task subtracted from the number of the last day in the project.

5. *Calculate the latest start number for each task.* The latest start is the last day in a project a task can begin and still be completed without affecting the end date of the project. In other words, if a task hasn't begun by this date, the project will be late. Determining the latest start date is simply a matter of making the following calculation:

   Latest finish – duration = latest start number.

   For the "Install passcard entry system" task, this becomes 38 – 10 = 28. Thus, if this task begins after workday 28 in the project, the project will be late if all the other task durations are correct.

6. *Determine the total float for each task.* Total float is determined by the following calculation:

   Total float = latest finish – earliest start – duration

   The tasks with zero float are on the critical path. Check this with the network diagram illustrating the critical path shown earlier. Tasks with float have some flexibility. In the "Install passcard entry system" task, the total float calculation is 38 – 20 – 10 = 8. Thus, there are eight days of scheduling flexibility associated with this task.

Even if you do use a computer to help you with your network diagrams and critical path calculations, it's important that you master the basic scheduling principles presented here. If you don't understand the basic principles of float, start dates, finish dates, and critical path, you won't understand how the computer derives the schedules it produces. And if you don't understand these concepts, you won't be able to appropriately modify the schedules to suit your project's priorities.

Calculate the Dates on the Calendar

With the tasks, durations, and start and finish calculations complete, it's time to assemble the actual schedule with dates on a calendar. Use the form included and make copies to accommodate all of your project's tasks.

The starting date of the project is determined by you, management, and your team. Using a calendar with room for notes, number each day in sequence. Those you don't plan to work, such as weekends and holidays, shouldn't be numbered. Remember too that tasks on the critical path should have the same earliest start date and latest start date, as well as the same earliest finish date and latest finish date.

Once all the dates are entered on the schedule worksheet, you will have assembled the *ideal schedule*. The ideal schedule is just that: it's the best-case schedule if all resources are available and ready when planned.

Ideal Schedule Worksheet

Project Name   Philadelphia Sales Office Project

Scheduled Start   June 3   **Calculated Finish**   July 31

Task	Responsible People	Duration	Earliest Start	Earliest Finish	Latest Start	Latest Finish
Select and hire commercial property broker	John, Dave	5	June 3	June 10	June 3	June 10
Find office and sign lease	Agent, Dave	10	June 10	June 24	June 10	June 24
Design interior changes with the owner	John, Dave, Agent	5	June 24	July 1	June 24	July 1
Interior changes complete	Owner	15	July 1	July 23	July 1	July 23
Inspect finished office and approve for occupancy	John, Dave	2	July 23	July 25	July 23	July 25
Select and purchase phone system	John	10	July 1	July 16	July 12	July 26
Arrange utility hook-ups	Jennifer	1	July 16	July 17	July 26	July 27
Phone system installed	Phone Co.	2	July 17	July 19	July 29	July 31
Select and order office furniture	Jennifer	5	July 1	July 9	July 15	July 22
Office furniture installed	Jennifer	2	July 25	July 29	July 25	July 29
Select and order office equipment and supplies	Jennifer	5	July 9	July 16	July 22	July 29
Office equipment delivered and set-up	Jennifer	2	July 29	July 32	July 29	July 31
Order and manufacture signs for new office	Dave	15	June 24	July 16	July 8	July 29
Signs installed	Dave	2	July 16	July 18	July 29	July 31
Order stationery and announcements	Jennifer	1	June 24	June 25	July 9	July 10
Stationery and announcements delivered	Jennifer, Printer	10	June 25	July 10	July 10	July 24
Announcements mailed	Jennifer	5	July 10	July 17	July 24	July 31
Get business permits	John, Jennifer	10	June 24	July 9	July 29	July 31
Open bank accounts	John	2	July 9	July 11	July 29	July 31

Use this worksheet to help you schedule your projects.

Normalizing the Schedule

You must review the schedule to determine whether the resources you assigned are actually available within each task's schedule window. After individual assignments are finalized and reviewed by the team, the schedule must be adjusted to accommodate any other necessary changes. It needs review and approval by senior management, as well, as part of the project plan.

When you use the critical path in a project, the tasks that are not on the path (called *non-critical*) can be scheduled in a number of ways to accommodate various needs of the organization. Three strategies are:

➤ Schedule all non-critical tasks at the earliest date possible. This offers a way of freeing up resources earlier for other projects or the later critical tasks.

➤ Schedule all non-critical tasks as late as possible. This shows how much work can be delayed without causing the critical tasks (and thus the project schedule) to slip.

➤ Schedule a subset of non-critical tasks, and as milestones are met, complete the rest of the schedule. This gives the manager scheduling flexibility and a way to assign resources to critical activities without causing political problems.

When assigning resources, the rules are simple:

➤ Make sure you know the specific availability of all resources (as much as is humanly possible).

➤ Assign the best suited, available people to each task.

➤ Use resources efficiently to ensure the smallest gaps in working schedules.

➤ Redo the schedule over and over until you get it balanced. (Get help in terms of experts or computer programs if it takes more than three tries.)

Time Is Money

If one unique resource commands the premier place in the project, you must wrap your schedule around its availability. For example, you can find plenty of typists and you can rent a crane from another company, but locating a qualified bio-mechanical engineer or getting time on a linear accelerator may limit your scheduling options.

Loading Up and Leveling Out

Many ideal schedules forget to deal with conflicting availability among resources, potential overuse of key resources, and the needs of other projects and priorities. For example, the ideal employee to supervise the alarm installation and testing may be unavailable the week you need her due to mandatory booth duty at a trade show in another city. If the task can't be rescheduled until her return, you'll have to choose someone else.

After working on your schedule, you will likely find that some team members have too much work—more than they can accomplish in a work week. Others may not have enough. The amount of work each team member or other resource is assigned is called resource loading. As you would expect, it's easy to overwhelm important resources with an impossible workload while under-loading others.

To compensate for overloaded workers, scheduled work is redistributed from resources with too much responsibility to those not fully booked. This is called *resource leveling*. As you level resources, skills and availability must be considered. If Shendyl, your computer network expert, has an unreasonable 164 hours of work scheduled per week, you can't redistribute the extra workload among three or four other team members who lack experience with computer networks. Instead, you need to acquire additional, experienced resources or adjust the schedule and ultimately the budget to accommodate the necessary changes.

Options for Adjusting the Schedule

Your options for reworking an impossible schedule with excessive resource loading include the following:

➤ Change the scope (size) of the project or add resources, keeping in mind that more people and materials will impact the budget.

➤ Give a task more time or spilt it in two, modifying resource utilization to make the process work.

➤ Move a task to a time when more resources are free. This will mean calculating the entire schedule again to make sure the moved task doesn't impact the critical path.

➤ Get more time in which to complete the project, and change the schedule and budget accordingly.

Project Lingo
The time individual resources (people, vendors, and so on) have committed to a project is called *resource loading*. A team member or other resource who has a large block of time committed to the project can't work on other projects. If the load exceeds their work week, you'll have to pay overtime or add resources.

Project Lingo
Resource leveling is the process of shifting the use of resources to even out the workload of team members and equipment. If Joe is required to work 86 hours a week on the project, you'll need to find other resources that can take on part of Joe's workload. Be aware, however, that resource leveling will likely cause changes in the network diagram, budget, or timing of a project.

Adjusting a Schedule to Meet a Forced Deadline

Many projects have a forced or dictated deadline. A customer may need a project completed by a specific date or an event must take place on the day it's scheduled or the effort will be a useless write-off. In the office project, a pre-announced opening party for customers won't be much fun if crews are still cutting and installing dusty drywall.

Such a project should commence as early as is possible in case unforeseen delays slow completion. If your careful scheduling shows that a project due date is impossible, you have three alternatives:

➤ Reduce the scope of the project.

➤ Add additional resources.

➤ Work out some way to extend the completion date (not always possible).

Chart the Final Schedule and See If It Works

When the final schedule is in place and approved (along with the rest of the project plan), it should be distributed to all team members and posted in a common area so team members can measure progress. This helps you maintain a healthy competitive attitude as the various team members rush to meet or exceed their schedule delivery dates. At that point, you cease to be a project planner and take on your role as project manager. Of course, you still need a budget before you have an approved plan. With the schedule in hand, the budget should be no problem. Read on. It's time to play with the money. It's not just politicians who love to do that. We will discuss how to use the schedule for tracking in Chapter 21.

The Least You Need to Know

➤ Understanding the concept of critical path is important in keeping a project schedule on track.

➤ When assembling a project, you must document your assumptions. Can you assume that Grand Central Station will be deserted at noon for your restoration and painting project?

➤ Holidays slow projects because team members' minds may be on family matters rather than work.

➤ Tasks on the critical path must start and finish exactly as scheduled to meet the project's finish date.

➤ For non-critical tasks, there's float—the extra time between the earliest date a task must start and the latest date it is possible to start the task and still meet the rest of the project schedule.

➤ Larger project schedules require not only the determination of the critical path but also resource leveling—moving resources around so no one is over- or under-booked with work.

➤ Resources, including supplies and equipment, must be considered and listed in the schedule with an eye on delivery dates and availability.

Budgeting Options for Your Projects

Time is money. Money talks. "Just give me money, that's what I want." As the Monty Python crew reminds us in *The Money Song*, "It's money, money, money, makes the world go round!" And, money *is* vital to every project. Much in the way water sustains life, money sustains projects. If funding dries up, so does the project.

Having a robust budget allows you to fix almost anything that goes wrong! Managing a project with a staff as intelligent as a bunch of Elmer Fudd clones? Has a key engineer run off to join a bizarre religious cult? Did aliens hijack the project's expensive equipment and take it back to the planet Surf? All of these scenarios can be remedied with the mythical unlimited budget or an unfavorable buyout of Fort Knox, Inc.

But, in the real world, most projects run on a tight budget. Funding is often inadequate for reasons we'll discuss in this and later chapters. Managers want blood from turnips. Things go wrong. Project delays waste budget dollars that you can't afford to lose. Inflation takes its toll as the project takes longer than planned. Every minute a project is delayed because of a sick participant, equipment failure, or a blizzard cooling delivery of vital project components, money is wasted. Project budgets have something in common with storing radioactive elements—they lose strength over time, even when not in use.

The Four Horsemen of the Project Apocalypse

Budgeting is one of the toughest aspects of planning (and later directing) a project. A multitude of largely uncontrollable factors (acts of God, shifts in an organization's priorities, and so on) inevitably make the process even more awkward than it already is. Your career might ride on the successful translation of x-dollars/resources into completion of project y. Success in part is measured by not having to return to the well for additional dollars, piasters, pesos, or extra dinero in any form. Budget pressure comes at you from four directions (sometimes all at once):

Project Lingo
Vendors low on cash or looking to soak you on future jobs might bid at a loss to blow away the competition and get the work. This is called *buying the job.*

➤ **Problem 1** Your Vendor's estimates are all over the spectrum. Do you have three quotes from expensive services but they're 50 percent apart? Are you getting a bargain or is the vendor taking the job at a loss to build cash flow (called *buying the job*) in hopes of repeat business charged at higher prices. You'll need to figure out why the bids differ. Are the assumptions different? Quality? Materials?

➤ **Problem 2** The occasional alligator among senior management will attempt to compress costs. He will do his damnedest to badger down your carefully calculated budget figure. Even if you know that the decreased budget is wholly inadequate, it's politically difficult to stand up to the big cheese. A misinformed senior manager might take the attitude of, "I'm going to cut this budget in half!"

Such an attitude may bring short-term glory to that senior manager, but it courts long-term disaster. It may be especially problematic if you are dealing with a senior manager who sees himself retiring (in glory, complete with golden handshake and stock options) before your long-term project is completed and the folly of his ways has been revealed.

➤ **Problem 3** Suppliers, consultants, even department heads lending you people will demand as much money as they can get. Negotiation is the key to keeping these people's hopes on the earthly plane. Remember that for all but the most esoteric services, someone else can be found to do it cheaper. Remind your would-be prima donna of this vital underpinning concept of capitalism. Try, "That's more than I can afford to spend. I guess I'll have to look around for someone else who is less expensive." That should do it if anything does!

➤ **Problem 4** The Twilight Zone—have you forgotten something? What key tasks have been left out of the project plan? This is common to every project, but a really expensive task can eat the budget of other project tasks. (If you see Rod Serling lurking in the shadows nearby, carefully review your task list!)

➤ **Problem 5** Not enough time to do it right. When the project manager has to turn out a budget quickly, that he or she does not calculate or estimate in a sufficient level of detail to permit correct tracking later.

All in all, budgets are affected by pressures from outside, within, and above projects. As project manager, you need to resist pressures that will negatively affect you plans.

THIS WAY

Along the Critical Path

These project caveats might seem difficult to deal with. What further complicates project budgeting is that problems might rear their ugly heads simultaneously. For example, Chansen's, a now defunct department store in Wyoming, simultaneously ran into three of the four horsemen. During a major remodeling to update an aging store, the budget first was set adrift, then ran aground. Here's what happened:

➤ Management squeezed too much money from the project budget. Demanding a complete remodel, funds were squeezed from a realistic project budget to make the firm's stockholders happier with the store's profitability (Problem 2).

➤ The architect refused to deliver the final plans until she received a substantially larger fee. Already unhappy with the number of changes she was forced to make gratis, she took a negative attitude. So, holding the blueprints hostage, she demanded more money for her labors (Problem 3).

➤ The store's escalators were not inspected previous to budgeting and later found in need of an expensive overhaul. No permit would be forthcoming from the city until they were repaired and brought up to modern code (Problem 4).

About this time, a desperate project manager was last seen thumbing a ride to points south. Can you blame him?

Developing Budgeting Skills

Like Charlie Brown's first attempt, your first kite probably ended tangled in a tree. But then, after a few kite-eating trees, you got better at launching and flying your creations (assuming you avoided the high voltage wires).

The experienced project manager can look over a project—one that's not too complex—and after spending a few minutes with a calculator, pencil, and paper, prepare an estimate that's amazingly snap on the money. As a newcomer, you might have to learn through bear-pit training. When you're in the bear pit, you either learn to train bears or you don't.

How do you establish a budget? It's initially easy. You follow the yellow brick road, or as in *All the President's Men,* "follow the money!" Instead of hassling the wicked witch of the west or Charles Colsen, you acquire the requisite estimates and then, fingers crossed, look at the project's totals. This is done task by task, step by step. Doing the budget for a small project, such as establishing an internal copy center, might take an afternoon. For large projects, a team might take months to bring expenses into line and to remember forgotten tasks.

The project budget should help the project manager control the project; however, it's common for the project manager to find the budget controlling him. A realistic budget is central to keeping control of the project. It's okay to have one that's a little too conservative, but like an alchemist, you can't turn lead into gold.

Building a Budget

The budgeting process can be intimidating to project managers. How much will it *really* cost? What if the price of widgets doubles on the Chicago Exchange? How can I control an important staff member who demands a salary increase? What if I make a mistake? (If you see someone at the office with the shakes, it's probably because he or she has either recently given up coffee or is assembling a project budget for the first time.)

The process of building a budget should be an orderly one; otherwise, it's impossible. You must carefully understand the components of each task and then cost out each one. Yes, you might make an error, underestimate (or overestimate), or blow it completely, but all you can do is try, using your best estimating capabilities. Even so, business conditions might change, the project might get bumped into a new direction, or a task might fail. So, what you are making in your astute budgeting is a set of assumptions that might change. Rub a lucky rabbit's foot while remembering the following:

➤ *Costs are tied to project goals.* Is your company's plan to build the cheapest notebook computer possible, even risking a 25 percent out-of-the-box failure rate? Or are they planning on a top-of-the-line model offering every feature and built to take a five-story drop without so much as dinging the case? Obviously, one is going to cost more to build than the other, and you must account for that in the budget. (Refer to Chapter 6 for more information on setting project goals.)

➤ *Costs are tied to time frames and schedules, and doing things faster usually costs more money.* Need a swanky $48,000 tradeshow booth for that important show next week? It can be done, but if you're using an outside booth builder, you'll have to come up with 200 percent rush charges to motivate them. (*Rush charges* are substantial extra costs tacked on when people have to sacrifice their nights and weekends because of your bad planning.) Substantial rush charges make a sizable dent in your project budget.

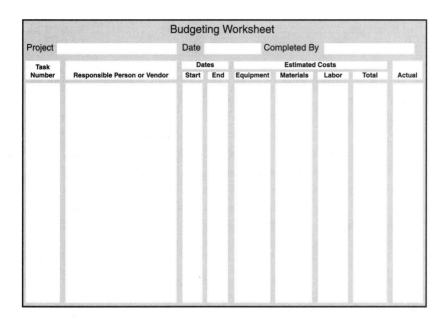

Budgeting Worksheet									
Project			Date		Completed By				
Task Number	Responsible Person or Vendor	Dates		Estimated Costs					Actual
		Start	End	Equipment	Materials	Labor	Total		

This worksheet can help you determine the costs associated with your project.

➤ *Costs require expert input.* With specific tasks at the ready, query the people who will be doing the work about their charges for time and materials (refer to Chapter 11). It's important that each contributor understands exactly what you are looking for. For example, if you run a winery, your 1,000-pound order of cork for the latest vintage might turn into two 500-pound pigs because the rep heard *pork*. That's why written information, sketches, and models from the rep, showing his interpretation of your requirements, are vital to ensuring that what you ordered is what's delivered. This is called the *answer back* process.

Project Lingo
Rush charges are applied by outside vendors when you rush them. A task that normally takes a film lab 24 hours will as much as quadruple the original charge if you must have your job done in two hours. So, a $150 charge could become a whopping $600. Imagine the rush charges on a $48,000 tradeshow booth like the one mentioned earlier!

You also will need budget input from the following:

➤ *Staff.* You need firm estimates for the time required for task completion as well as *all* supplies and equipment. These estimates must be specific. Do not assume, for example, that five company Macintosh workstations will be idle and available March 4 to 24. They might not be, and you'll have to pay a fortune to rent them.

➤ *Outside service vendors.* You must have hard numbers from outside service providers and consultants. Demand (politely, of course) a written estimate that fixes the cost, unless the project runs off the rails or changes nature. The latter might force the consultant to redo his work, and he should be compensated for it. As mentioned in Chapter 11, always shop price!

➤ *Other managers or experts.* Those in your organization who have handled projects can provide excellent advice and study cost estimates for problems. They also might be able to provide exact estimates if a project they worked on has elements common to yours. Or, they might be much more experienced project managers and willing to help out.

➤ *Your managers or owners.* Although sometimes unhappy about a project's bottom line, they might be able to provide advice from their own years managing projects. Plus, by bringing them in early, they'll see that you're carefully covering your bases and spending their money in an equitable manner. That observation will assist you in getting the final budget approved, because management already will have a strong grasp on the realities of the project and its budget requirements—not to mention faith in you and your abilities.

Project Lingo
If a process is highly technical, large, or complex in scale, ask for an *answer back*. In an answer back, the vendor takes your specs and builds a simple model that allows your experts to ensure that a clear understanding exists and no significant parts or systems were neglected.

Expert project managers estimate budgets accurately not because they have years of experience, but because they look at the budget and final costs of similar tasks on related projects. You can do it, too. If you furnished an elementary school last year and have a similar one to equip this year, base at least part of your estimate—accounting for inflation—on last year's costs.

➤ *Suppliers/service providers.* You must have supplies and equipment commensurate with your project's requirements. Shop price, but be careful about taking the least expensive option if quality is an issue. Building a neighborhood police station as a charity project? Supplier A might provide clean two-by-fours for the same price as supplier B's knotty, warped and generally misshapen lumber. Ask for samples.

➤ *Purchasing department staff.* Purchasing may or may not save you money. Purchasing is a department that might help you in your quest for success or stand in your way at every turn. Use them if they've proved helpful in a timely manner in the past. Avoid or work around them if they are difficult to deal with. You might need an order from senior management to avoid working with them. This tactic is a slap in the face to the purchasing people. Don't expect to win any popularity contests with them next time you order a box of number two pencils.

➤ *Experts.* Completely lost? Request (probably expensive) budget for someone with a special skill-set to assist you through a sticky project. Hire experts after carefully explaining their duties and setting a firm budget for their time. The best and least expensive experts are often those retired from a field after a lifetime of experience. You also can hire an expert project manager—not to take the reins, but to review results and proffer advice.

➤ *Standard pricing guides.* Many government regulated organizations and some private companies offer standard pricing in printed guide format. Need to know how much Federal Express charges to move an elephant from Zoo A to Zoo B? Just look it up in their free user guide (assuming you have the current guide!).

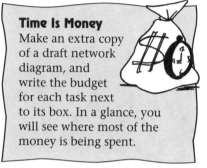

Time Is Money
The conceptual budget process: People + Resources + Time = Budget.

Time Is Money
Make an extra copy of a draft network diagram, and write the budget for each task next to its box. In a glance, you will see where most of the money is being spent.

Once these cost estimates have been gleaned and carefully listed along with the names of the contributors, it's time to do a task budget round-up. In this process, you take all of the estimates for Task A and combine them. (Use the worksheet included in this chapter.) Nancy in marketing might have provided one, Sid in engineering another, and Jerry in manufacturing a third. After you wrap up costs for all of the tasks separately, you can add the total of the entire plan to ascertain the project's total cost. Costs that are not available because Joanna in research is out of town must be guesstimated with a large highlighter used to indicate that the total is possibly fictitious. With a computer, most unknown/unverified estimates can be indicated separately. Your manager and most stakeholders will want to see the budget in two formats—by cost center and by month—to assess cash flow and cost allocations.

Types of Budgeting Methods

There are two established methods for budgeting: top-down and bottom-up. Which is best for your project depends more on your organization's standard approach to decision making. Does management dictate most mandates or is the staff expected to produce ideas and decisions that percolate up to management for final analysis.

Bottom-Up Budgeting

In bottom-up budgeting, staff get together and attempt to hammer out a budget from the task level detail. As a group, they can speak frankly. One member might have a solution superior to another's. It's also a good way to avoid missing a subtask. If one group member forgets it, another (hopefully) will remember it. This helps avoid budget gobbling tasks appearing mid-project and throwing everything off down the line.

Top-Down Budgeting

More difficult than bottom-up management, the top-down approach has senior managers estimating budgets from their experience and then allocating funds to lower level managers for execution. Top-down budgeting works *if* managers are carefully allocating costs and possess significant project management experience.

Refining the Budget

When the budget numbers are in, although subject to correction, the next step is to fine-tune the numbers. You might have to go through this process several times as new estimates arrive and are revised, or as tasks enter the project that were forgotten or ignored in the initial estimating pass.

Here are the steps (all required) in refining the estimates:

1. *A rough cut.* This is a number pulled out of a hat and might have little to do with the final number. "Ed, I think we're looking at $50,000 for the *Forbin Project.*" (If you missed this movie, keep it that way.) "Tammy, will $200,000 open the new office?" On a megaproject with subprojects, "Sally, Interchange 195, how much will that cost with the art deco toll booths?"

   Rough cuts should never become the actual budget numbers. This will kill a project manager and project faster than anything. Rough cuts are remembered as real budget quotations. Run like hell if you're asked to stop budgeting at this step.

2. *A second cut.* Each task estimate is reviewed carefully. This might demand the use of outside providers or require more than one take as a complex subset of work is reliably broken down.

3. *Getting it right.* The third pass is the one in which you do the fine tuning. For example, you might reveal that your initial $2,400 guesstimate is more realistic at $15,243.23. This process accomplishes two things: it turns guesstimates into something close to reality and provides an overall estimate of the project's real scope. This might not please the bill payer, but it must be done.

Time Is Money

Are you assembling a budget using a spreadsheet program, such as Excel? Don't accept the final numbers without calculating them separately using a calculator. Otherwise, an error in an underlying formula might be invisible until the money prematurely runs out. Or, the numbers might come in so high that management scraps it as impossibly expensive.

High Water!

You must understand that once a budget is established it becomes sacrosanct. You are stuck with it. Changing an *entrenched* (note this word) project budget is like trying to modify the Ten Commandments—*if* you could find the original stones and do a little chisel (again, note the word) work.

4. *Wrapping it up.* If the budget appears workable (that is, affordable), then it gets wrapped into the project plan while simultaneously heading for the front office for approval or at least groans. (Bring a bottle of aspirin to such meetings.)

5. *Presentation for approval.* The budget is presented for approval. You may be asked to find ways to cut it, or the project is scrapped as not worth the money (more common than you would think), or, if you're lucky, it gets approved right there. If not, continue to revise and present until you get consensus and signatures on the bottom line.

> **Project Lingo**
> *Padding* means adding extra money to a budget for overruns. This is a standard project management tactic (also known as a contingency plan) used to combat sloppy estimating or unexpected cost overruns.

Stuffing the Pillow with Money

Are you uncertain of the level of risk in a project? Want to provide a buffer of extra money? Add 10 to 100 percent to the budget to ensure completion and treat it as an insurance policy. Padding is a standard procedure in managing any project. There's no way that every risk can be fully calculated or anticipated. Everything from lightning blowing out your computer network to an outbreak of Legionnaire's disease might increase the budget as progress decreases.

A U.S. Coast Guard Idea Perfect for Projects

Consider using the Coast Guard's two-thirds rule for boaters when accessing funding needs. The Coast Guard states that when procuring fuel for a voyage, assume one third will be used for heading out and one third for the return voyage. That way, due to weather havoc or miscalculation, you still have one third of a tank to reach port. This rule works just as well on projects. By automatically assuming that your project might run one third over budget, you have a comfortable buffer zone or cushion against unexpected incidents, cost overruns, and Father Time.

> **Words from the Wise**
> They hired the money, didn't they?
> —Calvin Coolidge, referring to European war debts, 1925

Master Budget Control

Who holds the purse strings? You? Your management? Or a combination of both? Whatever the arrangement, you want as easy access to the money as possible. That way you can pay bills and purchase supplies in a timely manner. In one kind of arrangement, you theoretically own the budget, but must get multiple signatures from senior management each time you need to spend a chunk of it. This slows projects to a crawl because some members of the executive suite might be out of town and unable to sign. Besides, executives often let authorizations requiring their signatures sit in their in-boxes because they're too busy with their own projects.

Removing the Lid from the Pressure Cooker

Here are two techniques that won't make the problem go away, but at least might ease the pressure:

➤ Get as much signing authority for yourself as possible, anywhere from $500 to $5,000 is appropriate. This allows you to pay the majority of expenses without the multiple signature process.

➤ Establish (and closely monitor) a $500 petty cash box. It's a resource for quick payoffs for small parts, day laborers, or taking the gang out to pizza after reaching a major milestone. All cash that comes from the box must be replaced with a receipt. Replenish the petty cash when it reaches the $100 level. Regularly, count the remaining cash and receipts to ensure that no 20 dollar bills have grown legs and walked out the door.

The Bottom Line

All in all, if you estimate carefully and document your assumptions thoroughly, you'll get a good budget approved—one that gives you enough to get things done on time.

The Least You Need to Know

➤ Establishing a reliable budget is likely the most difficult task a project manager faces—for political as well as logistic reasons.

➤ Management will rarely accept your budget as reasonable; they will attempt to squeeze money from it, even if it means putting the project at risk. You'll need to document and negotiate what you really need.

➤ Your budgeting skills will improve after successful completion of several projects.

➤ You want as much direct control of your budget as possible if you're going to be held accountable for the project outcome.

Chapter 15

Putting It All Together: The Approved Plan

In This Chapter

➤ Recalling the importance of planning in project management

➤ Putting the whole plan together

➤ Why project plans fail

➤ Analyzing the risk in a plan

➤ Cross-checking the plan for accuracy

➤ Selling the plan to management and getting it approved

Okay. You've assembled a work breakdown structure (WBS), network diagram, schedule, team, and budget. You understand the tasks for the plan and the resources required. After all this effort, you may feel too tired to start working on the project, but don't throw in the towel. Besides, you haven't even finished the plan. You still need to integrate, evaluate, and get approval for the fruits of your planning labors. Yes, it's nearing ground zero in your plan, but you need your plan approved before you can start working on your project.

This chapter reminds you of all the good reasons for planning in the first place and provides advice for getting your project plan approved so you can get to work. Don't fret. D-Day is almost here! With an approved plan in hand, you'll be ready to start working on the project. Finally.

Reasons to Plan in the First Place

Sometimes people complain that plans take too much time. People would rather start working on the project than thinking about the plan. Other plans are created only because other people want to see the plan. Your boss asks for a plan and you write one. The customers want a plan so you draft something to make them happy. Plans prepared slavishly rather than thoughtfully are a waste of time for the reader as well as the writer. And plans written only for the benefit of someone else rarely meet their goals of guiding the project to a successful conclusion.

If you're not going to take planning seriously, don't bother. Without a good plan, you're like a surgeon who decides to remove his appendix with a can opener. You'll likely get the offending organ out, but you'll also make a mess of things in the process.

If a plan is not perceived as valuable, it will be of little use in achieving project objectives. Plans that get stuck in a drawer after approval will not help you or anyone else. But a thoughtful plan that guides a project from start to finish will help you reach your goals.

Don't let the sometimes monumental process of producing tasks, resource lists, network diagrams, and budgets cloud the value of doing the planning in the first place. Always keep in mind that the plan for your project is good for three very important things:

➤ Knowing where you are now

➤ Understanding where you want to go

➤ Defining the most likely path and resources required to get from where you are to where you want to go

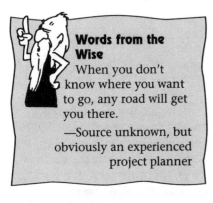

Words from the Wise

When you don't know where you want to go, any road will get you there.

—Source unknown, but obviously an experienced project planner

A good plan can help avoid most problems (but not all). Even so, you should know that no amount of planning will make your project go exactly as planned. Your plan will go off course because of things you didn't know in advance—and every project will encounter some things that cause you to deviate from the plan. Of course, if there are too many deviations, you might never reach your destination. So, the better the plan, the more likely you'll get where you want to go. And the better you keep the plan up to date, the more likely you'll be able to make the best adjustments to keep the project on course.

Putting It All Together

The diagram shows how all the pieces of the plan you've learned about in the book thus far are interrelated. Ultimately, all of these pieces should be put together in an integrated document, called "the plan."

Project plans can vary from fairly simple documents that list the tasks, budget, and resources on a single page with a cover memo to detailed books with overwhelmingly intricate levels of detail. Typically the plan will include additional narrative and organizing information to help readers (and team members) understand how the entire project fits together. The complete project plan for a large project might include a table of contents like the following:

1. Executive Summary of the Project (or Project Overview)
2. Project Objectives
3. Project Assumptions and Risks
4. Project Milestones
5. Work Breakdown Structure
6. Network Diagram
7. Resource Details

   Human Resources

   Equipment

   Materials and Supplies

8. Budget Details
9. Project Organization
10. Operating Procedures
11. Assessment and Review Standards
12. Contact Points and Information Sources (if relevant)
13. Project Approvals

There is no magic formula for the right level of detail in the plan. We use this rule of thumb in our own planning efforts: never spend more time on the plan that it would take to fix the project if there were no plan. Thus, if your project is only a week in length, it doesn't make sense to spend two weeks on the plan. On the other hand, if your project involves hundreds of people and millions of dollars, you'll want to put detail in the plan that allows the myriad resources to be coordinated.

The project planning stage dominates almost one third of this book, but the actual time required to complete the plan (including work plan, resource assignments, schedule, and budget) might only be a few hours for a very short project. It might take a month or more for a very large project. But it is the quality and thought that goes into a plan—not the time—that determines its value in the project management process, which is why it's so important to understand the issues in creating each component of the plan as we've explained them in previous chapters.

The project plan-ning documents are interrelated. Make a change to one and you need to adapt the rest. If you don't keep the plan up to date, it doesn't matter how good the initial plan was. An out-of-date plan is a statement of what didn't hap-pen—not a guide for the future.

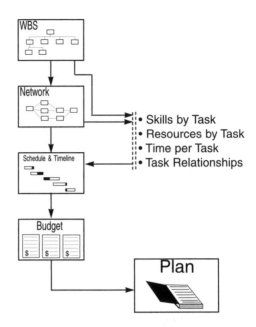

Who Should Write the Project Plan?

When you have completed a WBS, a network diagram, a resource list, a schedule, and a budget, you have all the elements necessary to put together the plan. But who does all this work? And who should put the plan together in final form?

You generally have three alternatives in preparing the final plan. Your choice of approach will depend on your organization, your personal experience and expertise, and the complexity of the project.

Create the Plan Yourself and Have It Reviewed

Creating the plan on your own is a good approach for small projects that have only a few participants, or if you have expertise in a project that makes you especially well-qualified to draft the major sections of the plan. Also, if you are basing your project on a plan used successfully for a previous project, this approach can work because you will only be making adjustments to an existing plan that has worked before.

The downsides of completing the final plan on your own include:

➤ It is more difficult to identify errors in the logic of a network diagram or WBS.

➤ You might not identify missing tasks or incomplete activities.

➤ You might not have all the information you need to create an accurate schedule or budget.

➤ It is often difficult to see your plan objectively when you do it yourself. Even when other people review it, they might not be familiar enough with the logic of your plan to offer alternatives.

➤ In a complex project, it is rare for one person to have the expertise and experience to detail all the tasks at the same level with great accuracy.

➤ People might feel left out, thus creating a negative political environment that affects your ability to manage the project through the next stages.

There are two primary advantages of doing the plan on your own:

➤ It is faster. If you are familiar with the steps and logic in a project, you can usually create a WBS and network diagram with little input. It takes less time than asking opinions and having meetings to discuss the options.

➤ You can complete a plan on your own before the team members are identified. Of course, when you do identify other people who will be working on the project, they will need to review your work and offer suggestions for modifying the work sequences and tasks.

In a project with a short deadline, these advantages can be critical to getting a plan done on time—but the disadvantages usually outweigh using this approach.

Construct the Plan with the Key Players

Getting the key players and stakeholders involved in project planning requires one or more structured meetings and advance preparation by each of the team members. Of course, if you haven't yet identified the key players in the project, this is not practical. Instead, you might identify a team of people who have had similar responsibilities to those on your project to help you create the plan, even though these people won't necessarily be involved in your project. In any case, it always helps if you provide some initial planning information (such as a milestone network) and some overall project objectives to get the planning started in the right direction.

The disadvantages of the team approach to detailed planning include:

➤ It can be time consuming. Meetings take time and a complex project might take multiple meetings to plan to the task level.

➤ Unless you hand-pick the participants, different levels of planning expertise will be evident, making it difficult to establish consistency in each component of the plan.

➤ Conflicts will need to be resolved and compromises in the plan might be necessary to keep the project team cohesive and focused on the project goals.

➤ To be successful using this approach, the project manager will need to spend a significant amount of time in pre-planning activities to coordinate, structure, and lead the meetings.

The potential benefits of the team approach include:

➤ It can create shared responsibility among team members for planning the project.

➤ Team members will benefit from a better understanding of the work required of others.

➤ It can identify potential conflicts and inconsistencies early in the project planning cycle, so they can be dealt with before they affect the project outcome.

➤ It can be used to create camaraderie among team members who have not worked together before.

➤ The process provides a way to verify and clarify the team's understanding of the project scope and goals.

For completing the plan for an entire project, this approach works bests if there are 10 people or less on the project team and the total project network involves 200 tasks or less. Otherwise, bring the team members in after some of the planning has been done.

Break the Project Into Subprojects and Plan Accordingly

For large projects, you can assign small groups to develop the subplans for the individual subprojects and then meet to put all the subplans together. Then, a few selected people from each of the groups will be assigned to integrate the subplans into a project plan, using a methodology similar to the team approach described earlier.

The disadvantages of this approach include:

➤ The coordination of the various groups can be difficult and time-consuming.

➤ The different groups might define tasks with inconsistent levels of complexity. This can be minimized if the project manager is involved with each of the groups to help assure consistency.

➤ Each group must have a manager trained in project management techniques. This is not necessarily a disadvantage, but it can be a constraint in some organizations.

For a large or complex project, this approach can have all the advantages of the team approach, and for an extremely large project, it is mandatory. No single project manager can define the work for something large and complex without making mistakes or omissions in the plan.

No matter which of the alternatives you choose to develop the plan, you will need to have the plan approved and reviewed by the appropriate people in your organization. And even after the plan is approved, as you bring new people into a project later in implementation, changes might be necessary if the new team members offer better or more appropriate alternatives for completing their assigned tasks and reaching milestones. (When you start thinking about changing and modifying a network diagram with hundreds of activities during the life of a project and communicating these changes to multiple people, the rationale behind using computerized project management tools becomes apparent.)

From Plan to Approval

In the real world, the plan for a large project (or even for a small one) will go through multiple versions on its way to approval. First, project objectives are established. Next, a rough work plan, schedule, and budget will be produced. These will be debated, discussed, enhanced, expanded, and revised until the project plan is complete and approved.

When the Planning Phase Terminates a Project

Of course, some projects collapse before the project plan gets approved. Here are some standard scenarios for projects that never make it out of the planning stage:

➤ *Inadequate planning.* You rush a plan together and it's tearing at its seams under the weight of reality. If the stakeholders see the plan as inadequate, it's not going to get the go-ahead.

➤ *Incomplete plans.* You or your team provide uncertain estimates for scheduling and budgeting, or fail to bring in the expertise to quantify the technical tasks.

➤ *The mission of the organization changes during the planning process.* Many organizations change their priorities like people change clothes. A project must fit into the current political, economic, and business priorities of the company to gain approval. The truth is that many organizations are trying to react to a rapidly changing marketplace—this is more of a reality than a fault.

➤ *The project is no longer relevant, seems too risky, or has little chance of completion before the target date.* Who wants to support a project going down in flames in front of their management peers? After all, part of your work as project manager is to evaluate and present the feasibility of a project to stakeholders and senior management. You are helping management decide whether to proceed with the project as defined.

High Water! While you work on a plan, your project might change in relevance and you might be plugging away at something currently as important as yesterday's newspaper. Avoid this problem by continually feeding progress reports to management and other stakeholders during planning. And learn to take the company's pulse on a regular basis to see how the political health might be changing.

Sometimes the plan demonstrates that the project is not viable. If you get stuck with one of these, just be happy that the project got stopped at the planning stage before you got stuck with trying to manage an impossible feat.

Other Issues That Can Sink a Plan

Upon integrating the various components of the project plan, you might find issues that have not been addressed in your other planning efforts. Not all of these are worthy of a task in the plan, but if you ignore them or don't address them somewhere in the schedule, the project will suffer. Typical things that get left out of the plan (but shouldn't) include:

➤ *Space and facilities.* Do you have basic office, manufacturing, and sleeping accommodations arranged that are suitable for your team. Do these costs appear in the budget?

➤ *Transportation.* Should your team need transportation above and beyond their normal commuting, you must locate effective transport and budget for it.

➤ *Permissions.* Do you require written or at least verbal permission to use specialized equipment, trespass on private property, cross international borders, or similar?

➤ *Licenses, permits, and clearances.* Do you need official permission to use hazardous chemicals, to block access to a structure or roadway, to enter restricted government facilities, to move confidential equipment or materials, or similar?

➤ *Insurance.* Is your team and other resources underwritten for accidents and infringements that might occur? If insurance is required, what existing policies protect you and how can you fill the gaps with additional coverage?

➤ *Weather.* How will the weather impact your plan? Can you hold the dates together if rain or snow delay construction, hinder delivery of materials and equipment, or impact team member performance.

➤ *Unavailable resources.* Is a strike possible within your organization or that of a major vendor? Is a key material in short supply? How will you meet with the problem and resolve it?

These are just some of the more common risk factors that might impact your project's timely completion. When reviewing your plan, you might find others that must also be addressed with contingency plans or specific tasks and schedules.

Uncertainty and Risk—What Level Is Acceptable?

When you submit your plan for approval and discuss it in review meetings, the reviewing managers or stakeholders will judge the risk factors associated with each aspect of your plan.

Remember (from Chapter 7) that tasks with less than 50 percent certainty reflect a need for better planning or the assumption that the plan is more a guideline than a real project plan. In many projects, pivotal points with low certainty become high risks. Designing a new appliance? What happens if during a too-brief testing prior to production, the sample units catch fire and melt?

Words from the Wise

Take calculated risks. That is quite different from being rash.

—George S. Patton, letter to his son, 1944

Most projects have important but potentially weak points. You should study your plan to identify each one if you want to get the plan approved. If you don't want to be blamed for your failure to predict the future when things don't go "as planned," be honest about the risks by documenting them in the plan.

The Reality Check Before Approval

Before submitting the plan for final approval, you need to perform one last cross-check of your planning efforts. This involves a line-by-line matching up of the WBS, schedule, budget, and network diagram, assuming you created these pieces. Computer-based planning software can help by finding impossible dates and durations on the critical path, missing network links (only if they're obvious), and missing task data. But even when you use a computer, you should check the logistics and flow of your project personally and by hand.

Here are the steps for cross-checking a project plan:

1. From the network diagram, match the tasks, durations, and dates to the scheduling worksheet.

2. From the network diagram, match the resources to the scheduling worksheet.

3. From the network diagram, match the task to the activities shown in the WBS.

4. Verify the numbers on the budgeting worksheet and re-total them to ensure they match your existing estimate.

5. Study the tasks on the critical path. Is the right path selected? Are there any tasks that require more time? Have you separated the labor required from the duration on each task?

Project Lingo

One of the best tests of completion, for doors in an airliner or for the workability of a project plan is to *cross-check* it. To cross-check a plan, one person lists a procedure and another verifies it. With two independent bodies carefully verifying the plan, chances for error greatly diminish.

Time Is Money
All steps of the plan should be run past your core team members before approval. The final fine-tuning of the project plan is no exception. After all, if you missed something, they might be able to fill in the gaps. If you asked the impossible of a team member, you'll have an opportunity to hear about it before the work starts.

6. Verify that the milestones (if you chose any) make sense as a means of summarizing the main activities in a project.

7. Check that the start date and finish date are still reasonable. Also verify that you have accounted for all holidays and vacations in the schedule.

If you didn't assemble either a network diagram or a WBS, it's almost impossible to cross-check a project. Reread earlier chapters on why the components are important. If you're unwilling to prepare this level of detail in plans, whether formal or informal, consider another type of job. A plan is an absolute requirement of success in project management.

Checking It Twice

Inevitably, discrepancies will appear in the cross-checking process. As you might expect, larger projects tend to have more mistakes than small, simple ones. After finding the errors, you must modify the plan to correct them. If more than three percent of the plan requires modifications due to your changes, perform the cross-check from scratch, one more time, after the changes are made. It's always possible to "fix" errors by introducing new ones. For that reason, review your notes from the previous procedure and do it again.

One way to encourage review is to have a dedicated wall or cubicle where the latest project data is displayed. Team members can check it and flag changes or problems. Team meetings take up a lot of time, and should be limited. In today's networked world, you might consider additional "groupware" tools to share project information. But don't let tools replace your involvement as project manager.

A plan that changes more than 10 percent during the cross-check demonstrates a plan that needs further work. Look at the errors to establish where they lie: schedule, budget, resources? If a definite pattern to the mistakes appears mostly in one part of the plan, consider redoing that part of the plan from the beginning.

"Let's Synchronize Our Watches..."

Now, with all tasks and amounts verified, it's time to verify resource availability one last time before the plan goes to management or customers for approval. You might have had to modify your plan due to errors or a slipping start date. Check with all resources that, based on the revised plan or even one with no changes, all resources will be available in the right timeframe. If the planning and approval cycle have been lengthy, people, vendors, and equipment might no longer be ready when you need them: people might have been reassigned or vendors might have gone out of business.

Should a vital resource become unavailable, you will have to find a suitable replacement, modify the project (if possible) to accommodate actual availability, or change the project's scope so you don't need the missing resource.

Getting the Plan Approved

The final step, before the ship sails, so to speak, is getting the project and its cross-checked plan approved by those who are paying the bills. Those who approve the plan will vary by company, project, and assignment. Make sure you know who will approve the work and the budget for the project. Sometimes multiple departments will be involved. Sometimes you'll get to sign the approval sheet on your own. In any case, the most important aspect of the approval is getting the money freed up (the budget) so you can start work on the project.

You'll need to package a large plan in an organized way. Using tabbed dividers is a good idea. Don't forget to put in summary sheets and narrative explanations about the assumptions you made when planning the project as part of the appendices.

Most projects require a presentation by you to sell the project to the people with the money (manager, customer, VP of Finance, or whoever is "it" for your project). Your presentation might be little more than a brief chalk-talk with a whiteboard, or, for a large, big budget project, the presentation of the plan might be a project in its own right involving an interactive multimedia extravaganza that wows and amazes the stakeholders into utter submission.

A Presentation of Project Priorities

Before you present your project for final approval, study the presentation of the plan from an outsider's viewpoint. Do the tasks explain themselves or is additional notation required? Are the tasks equal in scope (or almost)? Is the presentation clear and organized? Is the level of presentation appropriate for the scope of the project?

If you present your plan to a manager, customer, or review committee, you must be prepared to justify your choices, dates, and budgets. You'll need a compelling reason why each task is required and the associated budget justified. (Even if the reviewers don't ask, you should be prepared.) You also need to be prepared to talk about risks and contingencies if things go wrong.

Use judgment in what you present from the plan. Always start with an overview of the plan and then move on to details. Remember, the people who approve the plan will have a copy of the complete document to review anyway; you don't need to go over every detail in the presentation. The goal of the presentation is to present the overall structure and objectives of the project, answer questions, and establish your credibility as the project planner (and project manager).

Too much detail in the presentation can be as devastating as too little. With too many tasks in your presentation, you'll be bombarded with questions and arguments from management about the details. Managers might grandstand their opinions and try to save money on things they don't really understand. Avoid this by using milestone summaries of the tasks so managers don't fail to see the big picture during your presentation. Keep the meeting short (one hour) and focused. Senior Managers dislike meeting longer than an hour. So keep it crisp, but make time for their searching questions and time to get their approval.

The result of your presentation will either be the approval (by signature) of the project (which is unlikely on a first presentation of a large project) or a request to make revisions. Changes should be made to the general plan (scope and strategy) first; then to the details of the plan (the tasks, network, resources, and so on). Remember, you must change both.

You can't just adapt the schedule because the stakeholders don't like it. If you've done a good job of planning, you'll have to communicate this fact to the people who approve (and sign off on) the plans.

> **Time Is Money**
> An efficient way to present a plan is with a summary presentation backed up by hard copies of the plan's WBS, worksheets, and network diagram. Presenting a management overview hopefully will avoid a line item review of each task, its schedule, and budget. But if it comes to that, the back-up data you've provided will do the trick.

If real objections crop up, stop the presentation and re-schedule the meeting after the plan has been modified. Should more than three revision meetings be required, then your plan has serious problems, or the political agenda of those approving it is likely to prove impossible to circumvent. Without full management commitment to your project, successful completion is unlikely at best.

If you get caught in a political situation, have one-on-one discussions with individual stakeholders to understand their concerns and then come up with a strategy for circumventing (or reducing) the politics from the process so you can go forward with the plan.

Presenting Your Plan as an Outsider

As an outside project management consultant or vendor, you might be required to present your plan and sell it in a competitive bid. Although management will be focusing on costs, try to emphasize the quality of your proposal, as well. If you're not the lowest bidder, convince the potential customer that your organization delivers consistently high quality work, on time and within budget. (Hopefully, this will be the truth.) As for a group sold solely on schedule and/or budgetary concerns that turns down your carefully honed estimates, you probably wouldn't have liked working for them anyway.

Approval at Last

Finally, there's great news: your plan is approved. They've signed on the dotted line. The accounting department has assigned a budget number and account codes for the project. You're ready to go.

The plan you created and got approved is not the only plan you'll use during your project. In a project, you'll typically have three or more versions of the plan active at one time. First, there is the original approved plan. This is sometimes called the *baseline plan*. Second, there is the actual plan, which reflects the actual work done to date. Third, there is the future schedule based on work done to date. Finally, there could be a number of contingency plans developed for a complex project over time.

Just remember to keep the plans numbered and keep them up to date. A big filing cabinet is a good idea if you'll be managing big or frequent projects.

Bringing a Delayed Plan Back to Life

In too many organizations, your carefully constructed project plan might be shelved if organizational and market changes alter management priorities. Then, vampire-like, the project rises from its grave to haunt you.

Before you seek the approval of such a plan, make sure you verify all the tasks, assumptions, and budgets. Don't just blow the dust off yellowing pages. Make sure the old plan still makes sense.

If a plan slips a month past its starting date, a new schedule is mandated. If it slips more than one month, the entire plan must be scrutinized. A new schedule is in order, but you must also verify resource availability and make changes to the plan to reflect management dictates. Even equipment and supply lists must be updated. Last year's order of 48 top-of-the-line computers might be superseded by newer, cheaper models. Suppliers might have closed up shop or moved, or be unable to deliver a brand they carried 365 days ago. You'll have to modify the budget to reflect the improvements in technology, market changes, and the effects of time.

> **Words from the Wise**
>
> When the company archives your plan because it's so important, it's a goner. You won't ever see it again. And it will never ever serve its purpose as a plan.
>
> —A project manager for a multinational company

> **Words from the Wise**
>
> The longer a project's duration, the less likely that changes in organizational priorities and happenstance will allow it to reach completion.
>
> —A standard project manager's axiom

From Plan to Action, Finally

After getting a plan approved, it might seem like you've done an awful lot of work and still not gotten anything done.

The central role of the plan in the project management process often leads people to the mistaken conclusion that the creation of the plan *is* project management. It's not. Most of the time spent in project management involves management. As you've already surmised, project management involves much more than just a plan.

Still, don't be surprised if people identify your project management skills with your ability to create a nifty network diagram and an impressive looking planning binder. Worse things could happen, and as long as they pay you for it, well, you don't have to tell them that it wasn't really that hard.

You'll soon get to work and to put your approved plan into action. Forward and onward! The executing phase is about to begin. In the next phase, you'll learn how to take the baseline and create plans that reflect work done, and schedules for remaining work. But that's to come. For now, just enjoy your completion of a demanding phase of project management.

The Least You Need to Know

> ➤ You need to cover all bases in planning. A brilliantly scheduled research project in Switzerland will come in over budget if you don't remember to include the team's travel, food, and lodging expenses.

> ➤ Projects with a degree of significant risk might require a second look, from the bottom to the top.

> ➤ Risky tasks should be analyzed. If a less risky approach is possible, the plan should be modified to accommodate it if possible.

> ➤ All planning documents from the WBS to the network diagram should be scrutinized to ensure they match and work together.

> ➤ Aging or delayed project plans require revamping before going for approval.

> ➤ You'll probably have to present your plan to management and customers before it gets approved. And it probably won't get approved the first time around.

> ➤ You must sell your plan to management and get their commitment to the plan, its schedule, and its budget before starting work on the project.

Part 4
The Executing Phase

Well you've done it now—you've initiated a project and have the plan approved. You're ready to begin, and the beginning is a very delicate time in any project. How you begin the executing phase of the project will establish your likelihood for success— or failure.

To start toward the finish line of a project, you start by establishing your leadership, organizing the team for optimum performance, instituting operating guidelines, and yes, figuring out what kind of reports and other paperwork you'll need to get things going and keep them headed in the right direction.

These are the things you'll learn how to do in this section. Always remember that the right direction is spelled out in the plan—but only if you keep the plan up to date will this direction continue to be the right one. But keeping things on track is part of the controlling phase. You can't start controlling until you get started. So, let's do just that.

Chapter 16

Getting Started on the Right Track

In This Chapter

➤ Project kickoff activities

➤ The first project meeting

➤ Getting project members in synch and enthused

➤ Avoiding the floating start date

At this point, you have an approved project plan in hand. You have identified most of the key team members, sought permission to use them, and established a budget and a source of funds to pay them. You're ready to get started. Or are you? How will anyone know what to do? What's the first step? Who's on first?

For most projects, these questions are answered at the project kickoff event and the first project meetings with the group and individuals. These activities are the first steps in the executing phase of any project. The "big kickoff event" (or at least a small one) serves to get everyone in synch with each other and build a feeling of camaraderie. The project kickoff is like the locker-room rally before a big game. It gets the juices flowing and reinforces the goals for the project. The first project meeting is like the initial huddle in the Super Bowl. This is where you actually agree on your first play on the project and get the team lined up to win the prize.

In this chapter, you'll learn how to hold a project kickoff that motivates the troops and gets everyone moving in the same direction—toward the project finish. You'll also see how to make the first project meetings part of the key strategy in your project game plan.

The Great Leap Forward

With the complete, approved project plan in hand, you are ready to get started on the actual work of the project. For small projects, getting started might involve simply sending a memo to the staff announcing the approved plan and reviewing key dates. This note and a few calls or personal visits to the team participants are all that is necessary to get people started on their objectives. For larger projects, a project initiation or formal kickoff event is usually desirable (which we'll describe in detail in a bit).

If you're working on a really large project, you will have a cycle of execution phases, where plans, guidelines, and operating procedures are re-established as each new milestone begins. That's because some large projects are really a succession of smaller projects linked together. In such large projects, you'll have a series of "first" meetings, as each new milestone of the project gets underway.

Always Get Your Own Act Together First!

Before you have the kickoff event, you'll need to consider both your leadership style and your management tactics—the two are intertwined and central to the implementation of projects. Your leadership skills and the appropriateness of the management tactics you adopt for each of the various people on your project team are of paramount importance in achieving project goals. The first time you get to try out these strategies and tactics will be at the kickoff event.

In Chapter 17, you'll learn a lot more about becoming a leader on your project. We mention it now only because, to get a project kicked off, you must be both a manager and a leader. You can use the project kickoff to gain the trust and respect of the project team, so people feel comfortable taking your direction. You can also use the kickoff to explain the reports and administrative procedures you'll use to help people get work done on time and within budget.

Are You Ready?

Before you schedule the project kickoff event, make sure you're comfortable with the plan dates, the budget, and resources available. It may be better to hold off the official project kickoff until you are comfortable with all components and have all the round pegs in the round holes.

Of course, delaying the project kickoff is a double-edged sword. Jump in too fast, when all elements are not adequately quantified, and the project may unravel. Delay until everything is firmly in place and the project window may elude you because you failed to beat the competition to market.

Do It Now and Do It Right

Once you've decided that you're really ready, you need to decide how to kick off your project. Whether handled formally or informally, the kickoff events of the project or subproject need to accomplish the following objectives:

➤ Communicate the goals of the project to all team members to assure that everyone is crystal clear on their own objectives and responsibilities to the project.

➤ Attain the commitment you need for the project and get people enthusiastic about making things happen.

➤ Establish the leadership milieu for the project and get the team ready to follow you.

➤ Identify critical deadlines and phases of the project.

➤ Review the overall schedule and work plan with the appropriate team members.

➤ Explain basic operating procedures including required reports, meetings, and other on-going communications necessary between you and other team members.

➤ Explicitly give the people responsible for the initial tasks the go ahead to begin work on the project.

If you add all these objectives together, you'll see that the overall goal of the executing phase is to establish a set of conditions so work can get done. These conditions start with clear communications about the plan and procedures associated with your project. The project kickoff is the first step in opening up the channels.

The Formal Kickoff

Although some projects don't require more than a small meeting and a memo to get started, when a formal project kickoff event is appropriate, the event should be both celebratory and informative. Some common formal kickoff events include:

➤ A slide-show or multimedia presentation of the project in an auditorium with buffet lunch or snacks served afterward.

➤ A sit-down dinner with motivational speakers, formal introductions of key project personnel, and a spectacular multimedia display of project goals and objectives.

➤ A pizza and beer party at a local pub, where you talk enthusiastically about the project and introduce the various team members to each other. Here you'll also review the documents that describe the project.

➤ A meeting of all key project supervisors in the board room with coffee and a presentation on the overhead projector led by the project manager. A formal summary of the project plan is provided to all the attendees.

The type of event will depend on the size, importance, organization, and budget for the project. Use your judgment. Look at the kinds of events given in your company for similar projects—and ask about the events that worked and the ones that didn't. And if a customer is paying the bill, keep the event simple and economical.

It's a Go

Regardless of the sophistication or format of the kickoff event, the event should put team members on notice that the project is a "go." The event should emphasize that each

167

individual's contribution is vital to the success of the project. The kickoff event can also help individuals relate their goals and work within the overall project to the efforts of other team members. This is a first step in establishing a "team" spirit.

In most cases, a formal kickoff for a large project should include stakeholders, customers (if appropriate), managers, and most of the key team members, even if their contributions won't be required for weeks or months down the road.

The kickoff event should also establish priorities, tone, and energy for the project. The kickoff should avoid too many individual details; leave those for the first project meetings and one-on-one sessions with key project players. Those meetings should take place during the first week after the project kickoff event.

Between Kickoff and Team Meeting: Use the Time Wisely

The time between the project kickoff and the first formal project meeting (usually three days to a week is recommended) gives team members time to reflect on their roles.

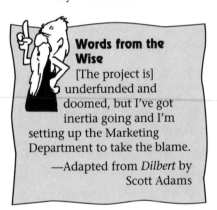

Words from the Wise

[The project is] underfunded and doomed, but I've got inertia going and I'm setting up the Marketing Department to take the blame.

—Adapted from *Dilbert* by Scott Adams

Feedback after the kickoff event is invaluable to plugging up holes in the project plan. During the period before D-Day (the day of the first project meeting), you may have team members approaching you with questions or problems.

Based on the feedback, you can fine-tune your project plan and look into problems that team members throw at you. Issues and problems can also be run by senior management to level out the small molehills before they turn into major mountains. Gathering feedback allows you to come to the project meeting prepared with answers to objections and explanations of issues that were inadequately addressed in the plan.

The First Project Meeting

After the kickoff event you're finally underway! You'll need to schedule the first team meeting in about a week (or less for a small, short project). This meeting will be the first true test of your leadership skills as the project manager.

All working members of the project team should be invited. (Customers and the executive management team should *not* be invited.) This is a meeting for getting work started. The first team project review meeting should accomplish the following:

➤ Establish a model for future meetings:
  1. Start on time.
  2. Develop and distribute an agenda of objectives *before* the meeting.
  3. Conduct one agenda item at a time and conclude it before moving on to the next (and avoid getting hung up on the order of topics).

4. Encourage open communication; meetings give individuals a chance to express suppressed ideas.

5. Take notes.

6. Establish the time and place for the next project team review meeting.

7. Agree on and reiterate any follow-up activities or action items required. Be sure to assign people to these tasks and get their commitment to complete them.

8. End the meeting on time.

9. Distribute (brief) minutes to all attendees within 2 days of the meeting.

10. Make sure the action items and responsibilities are indicated in the minutes (so people don't conveniently forget what they agreed to do in the meeting).

➤ Introduce the members of the team and their project roles.

➤ Review the first priorities for the project and repeat/reiterate briefly the other objectives and overall schedule.

➤ Review individual plans for getting work started.

➤ Discuss methods and tools to be used to manage, control, and operate the project.

➤ Deal with objections to the current project plan and work them out if possible.

➤ If decisions need to be made by the group, follow these steps:

1. Discuss the problems and seek opinions from all.

2. Don't allow one person to dominate the discussion.

3. Test for readiness to make a decision.

4. Make the decision.

5. Assign roles and responsibilities.

One-on-Ones: The Individual Starting Events

In addition to the kickoff and first project meeting, you'll need to meet with key individuals at the beginning of the project to make sure they have all the information they need to get to work. These initial meetings with new players may continue throughout the project as different aspects of the project get underway.

Formal meetings with project team members, known as one-on-ones, should be used to clarify priorities and discuss schedules and plans. Many of the people will have worked with you on the project plan already, so you won't need to go over all the details with these folks. However, you will need to turn their focus away from planning and start delegating work to these people so things start happening.

One-on-ones with key players should also be scheduled on a regular basis throughout the project. For a short project, the one-on-ones might happen daily or weekly with key personnel. For a longer project with more players, the formal one-on-ones might be monthly or even less frequent depending on your other level of interactions.

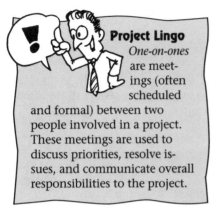

Project Lingo
One-on-ones are meetings (often scheduled and formal) between two people involved in a project. These meetings are used to discuss priorities, resolve issues, and communicate overall responsibilities to the project.

In the first one-on-one meetings, these things should be clarified and reviewed with the individual:

➤ Why he or she was selected

➤ Performance expectations

➤ Individual priorities, tasks, and milestones

➤ Administrative procedures and project management methods and tools in use

➤ Challenges and issues

➤ Processes for solving problems

➤ A schedule for future one-on-one meetings

➤ Action items for future meetings

Always take notes in these meetings. Suggest that the other participant do the same.

Step Up or Flub Up?

Your ability to organize and control the first team meetings will be a major step in establishing your leadership of the project team. If you do it well, the meetings will serve as a model for subsequent project meetings, as well as set a tone of open communication and professionalism that will make managing your project a lot easier. If you flub up the meetings, you'll not only waste the time used on the meetings, but also lose credibility as the project manager. Preparation, organization, and focus are critical to making the first team meetings a success.

Words from the Wise
If you go into battle, it's better to win the first time.
—Gen. George S. Patton

Information Everyone Needs to Get Started

The purpose of the kickoff and initial meetings is to inform people and to get people in synch with the project plan. From the beginning, those who work on the project need access to relevant information in the plan so they can do their jobs. Tasks and schedules should never be a secret (although budget and other financial information may be held confidential when people aren't responsible for the costs). The project plan should generally be an open book to help guide people to the promised land.

Provide every member of the team with a summary of the plan during the initial stages of the project. This could be done before the kickoff event, in a team meeting, or during a one-on-one at the very start of the project. For team members who will remain with the project from the beginning, we recommend presenting these documents prior to the kickoff event, and then discussing them in the first project meeting and one-on-one sessions. As new team members join the project during later stages, you'll need to make sure that they get the information as well.

Here are the pieces of information from the project plan that every team member needs in order to be able to contribute appropriately to the project:

➤ *A summary of the overall project goals.* The project summary explains the purpose of the project, its goals, and outlines the overall schedule.

➤ *The team member's role and task assignments.* The specific tasks and milestones for each team member (or sub-team) should be laid out in writing. At the beginning, the milestones and task overview might be general, with specific tasks being introduced by you or other supervisors and managers at a later date.

➤ *A list of who's who on the project.* The directory or list of key project team members should include a description of each team member, his or her role (and title) in the project, and contact information (telephone numbers, office location, and E-mail addresses).

More Things People Need to Know

In addition to information about the project plan, every team member needs to be informed of the administrative procedures that will affect his or her life. These include reports, forms, legal documents, etc. Don't drown them in paper. If your reports to them are crisp and timely, their reports will hopefully be on time and accurate. For a large project, you may want to provide a "Project Administration Handbook," which assembles examples of all the forms, reports, and other documents required from project personnel, along with other relevant documentation of the project plan. For small projects, a simple list and an example report will probably do the job.

You should also let team members know that regular status reports are required and explain why the reports are essential to tracking the project and keeping it on time and within budget. Set the report intervals for weekly, biweekly, or monthly intervals, depending on the nature of the project. Present people with sample reports and completed forms that set the expectations for their reports. (We offer more recommendations on reporting frequencies and formats in Chapter 20.)

If confidentiality or other legal agreements are required for your project, now is the time to get them signed. If your organization contracts with the military or other government agencies, rules may be more strict and you should look into the proper forms of agreement and reporting that are required and make sure the requirements are understood by the appropriate team members at the beginning of the project.

Avoid the Floating Start Date

Getting a project started is key to finishing a project successfully. The right information in the right hands goes a long way to making things happen. But a project with a floating start date never goes anywhere. If you kick off a project and then fail to follow through with clear delegation of the work to get it started, you may have a good plan, but you won't have a project.

Never rev up your team to tackle mountains unless you're really ready to reach the summit. If a project fails to happen as announced, you'll likely find the team has lost interest by the time you decide you're ready to begin work. Team members may even find something else to do that precludes their participation. Delays also mean adjusting the dates in your carefully honed project plan and getting things approved all over again.

Information Every Team Member Needs for Every Project

➤ Summary of project objectives and milestones

➤ An organization chart of the project (large projects only)

➤ A description of key personnel on the project and their roles

➤ Personal task list

➤ Enough authority to do the job and an understanding of the limits of that authority

➤ The schedule

➤ Due dates for reports, meetings, and other recurring activities

➤ Samples of required reports, forms, and other documents

➤ Procedures for reporting problems and suggesting changes to the project

➤ Contact information for key project personnel and vendors

If you kick the project off, be sure to follow through with the next play. If you start as planned, you'll have a lot better chance of finishing as scheduled.

The Least You Need to Know

➤ Getting a project started right involves communication.

➤ All projects need starting events which clarify project goals, responsibilities, and operating procedures. These events can be simple or elaborate, but should always be commensurate with the size and importance of the project.

➤ Prior to the first project team meeting, a review of the project by team members may point out holes in your plan that need patching.

➤ At the beginning, all (or at least most) major problems, whether financial or political, should be satisfied in the plan.

➤ Focused, productive, informative team and individual meetings are the best way to get things started on the right track.

Chapter 17

Leadership and You: Taking the Bull by the Horns

In This Chapter

➤ Your role (and as James Thurber said, "Welcome to It")

➤ Establishing your role as leader and manager

➤ MBWA (Management by Walking Around)

➤ The leader in times of crisis

Regardless of the words, charts, and spreadsheets, a project plan is useless without a project manager to put ideas into action. Since *people* will complete the work specified in the plan, you, as the project manager, must employ appropriate methods to motivate, coordinate, facilitate, and administer your project team. If you don't, the work may never get done.

As a project manager, you must also identify and implement the appropriate leadership style for keeping the team motivated. In Chapter 4 we talked about the traits of successful project managers. Now, it's time to put those traits together with your trusty project plan in hand and guide your project team to victory. We're going to talk about ways to do that in this chapter.

Going from Planner to Project Manager

Consider Jack, the specialist in the finance department who is responsible for assuring the smooth implementation of a new sales-order system designed to reduce shipment times to customers and provide better accounting information for financial reports. Jack needs to lead a team of people from the sales department, the data processing department, the production department, and the accounting section of the finance department in order to develop and implement an improved sales-order system.

Jack has taken on the responsibility for meeting this objective and, as result, is the "project manager," even though he was never given a title as such. Jack has already coordinated the development of the plan. Now he must get the work started and track progress to assure that the project is completed as specified. He must also communicate progress to the departments that will be affected by the new sales-order system and keep the other project participants motivated to meet deadlines. In addition, the managers Jack reports to must be kept informed of the status of the project. Thus, both horizontal and vertical communication must be maintained.

If Jack uses project management techniques, including the planning, tracking, and reporting methodologies presented in this book, this horizontal and vertical communication will become easier, and tracking the progress against the planned objectives will be relatively simple. But all that good communication will count for little if Jack doesn't assume the role of leader (even without a title). Without establishing his leadership, he may never get the support he needs to make things happen. Jack may find that the project suffers from poorly defined performance criteria, unclear and unspecified responsibilities, burdensome and poorly coordinated communications (both internal and external to the department), relatively slow implementation, and a lack of cost and schedule data that makes it virtually impossible to keep things on track. Without leadership, the other departments may become frustrated as well, because things simply don't get done as planned. So how can Jack make sure things get done as planned?

The Importance of Establishing Your Leadership

Whether managing the remodeling of the Empire State Building or the installation of a projection TV in a restaurant, you must take command in order to lead your project to success. You can use every technique in this book, but without assuming leadership of the project, you'll get nowhere. You must become the leader *and* manager of the project if you want to succeed.

As a leader, you will command authority and take responsibility for guiding the project. You will also be a trusted and reliable source of information on the project. As a leader, you will be expected, by your team, to be honest, competent, and inspirational.

As a manager, you will monitor and control the project through to completion, using specific techniques and procedures that establish the framework and structure of the project. You'll review the plan, complete reports, balance the budget, update the plan, fix the schedule, update the plan again, then report on the updates to the plan, and, yes, then update it again. You'll also do a lot of other administrative stuff that will drive you crazy.

Some people get so caught up in the management, that they forget about the leadership. It's possible to complete the management part of the project and not attain the status and influence of a leader. That's why we've written this chapter—to make sure all those good project management traits get transformed into leadership skills as well.

Time Is Money
Managing the work does not mean you do the work. The victory charge of a successful project manager is always, "Delegate, delegate, delegate!"

Wearing the BIG Shoes

You *must* be a leader who provides strong guidance but at the same time offers a receptive ear to those with problems. Your team members may not always fill the big shoes you've offered them. The well-known Murphy's Law often assures that anything can go wrong on projects from the tiniest to the most colossal.

As a leader, you should also know the plan inside and out and be able to talk to the team about priorities without sounding frustrated or rushed. If a team member has a problem that requires discussion, as a leader, you should always be seen as a resource to seek out, rather than as an obstacle to avoid.

Also, remember from Chapter 4 that, as a successful project manager, you must be both a manager and a leader. Managers go to meetings and complete paperwork. Leaders must gain the trust and respect of the project team. People must feel comfortable taking your directions or they'll make up their own. Yes, as a manager, you must also develop protocol and administrative procedures for assuring that work is getting done on time and within budget. But establishing yourself as a leader is more important than any report or process.

Leadership style and your management tactics are intertwined and central to the successful implementation of the project. Your skills and the appropriateness of the management tactics you adopt for each of the various people on your project team are of paramount importance in achieving project goals. There are lots of hard-nosed books on becoming a leader, but we favor a simple, soft approach involving only eight things:

➤ Listen to the people.

➤ Ask lots of questions.

➤ Observe what is going on and take notes.

➤ Know enough to know that you don't know everything.

➤ Be available when people need you.

➤ Make decisions when called upon to make decisions.

➤ Delegate the work that needs to be delegated.

➤ Don't micromanage. You manage the project; they manage their work.

A Style That Gets the Job Done

Business writers have described a wide range of effective leadership styles that can be adapted to meet the needs of different people, organizations, and projects. You'll need to choose among three basic styles to lead your project:

➤ *Task-oriented leadership* emphasizes getting the job done and concentrating on methods for assigning and organizing work, making decisions, and evaluating performance.

➤ *Employee-oriented or people-oriented leadership* concentrates on open communication, the development of rapport with team members, and an on-going direct concern for the needs of subordinates.

Project Lingo
The approach of matching management style to the specific needs of a situation is often called *situational management* or *contingency theory*. Project managers must effectively apply the best style for the job—whether task-oriented, employee-oriented, or reward-oriented leadership—in order to meet the needs of individual team members.

➤ *Reward-based leadership* ties positive feedback and other rewards directly to the work accomplished. The reward-based style assumes that a high level of performance will be maintained if work results in meaningful rewards that correlate directly with the quality of the person's efforts. Rewards include pay and promotion, but also encompass support, encouragement, security, and respect from the project manager.

As you try to implement a style, don't assume that because you like something done a certain way that your team members will have the same preferences. Individuals differ from one another by experience and personality. Each person has a different conception of how the job should be done, who should get credit for the effort, and how each individual should be rewarded for his or her work. For these reasons, different leadership styles and management methods must be used to monitor and coordinate different projects.

How to Be a Leader

There are two components to project leadership: visibility *and* communication. First, you must be visible in the role as project manager. Second, you must communicate your intentions and the progress of the project to team members on a regular basis.

Taking the Reins Through Communication

Communication and leadership go hand in hand. The project managers who consistently succeed in bringing their projects in on time and within budget are those who effectively manage the interfaces and communications between people and organizations. The people working on your project, and other members of the project team, need to be comfortable with bringing issues to your attention. This goes for people who report directly to you, their managers, and your managers as well.

There are three types of communications that must occur for a project to be managed effectively:

1. *Vertical communications.* These are the up-and-down organizational communications based on the hierarchical relationships established on an organization chart.

2. *Horizontal communications.* Horizontal or lateral communications involve communicating and coordinating activities with peers.

3. *Diagonal communications.* The diagonal relationships are rarely shown on organization charts, but they are almost always important to the success of a project. Diagonal communications involve upward relationships with managers and officers from other areas and with subordinate groups in other departments. They also include downward diagonal communications with third parties such as contractors, suppliers, or consultants.

Words from the Wise
The greatest mistake an executive can make is to be afraid of making a mistake.

—John Capozzi, *If You Want the Rainbow You Gotta Put Up with the Rain* (1997)

If you have established the requisite communications in all three dimensions before conflicts occur, when the inevitable conflicts *do* arise between organizations, styles, procedures, or priorities, there will be an established channel available for resolving issues. If you have established the basis for discussion before the conflicts arise, the resolution process will usually be easier.

Meeting regularly with team members; reporting to them on team accomplishments and success (or lack thereof) in meeting objectives; and becoming a resource of project knowledge, suggestions, and conflict resolution also make you the leader. Your team members will look toward you as a central clearing house of knowledge and praise (and you should provide plenty of the latter).

This is not to say that some team members won't be uncooperative, but much of this eases once a project is underway and your—for lack of a better word—charm builds a cohesive team bent on meeting schedule dates and making you and them look good!

Good Communication from a Real Leader

If you want to be a really good communicator and a leader as well, here are some guidelines to follow:

➤ *Hold regular meetings with team members—and don't cancel them.* Effective meetings should start with the project kickoff, described in Chapter 16, and continue throughout the life of the project.

➤ *Meet both in groups and individually.* Some things won't be said in front of other team members in meetings, but may come out in one-on-one sessions. In groups, simmering conflicts, which won't be mentioned in private, may rear their heads.

➤ *Provide your team with constant feedback on the project's status.* Be available, friendly, and willing to discuss anything that team members are burdened with—from project problems to personal problems. Include outside vendors in relevant project conversations as you deem appropriate.

➤ *Keep meetings short and to the point.* Team members respect leaders who don't waste their time. Have meetings over lunch (you buy). That way, you have the benefit of a congenial conversation coupled with time required for the project. And, everyone likes a free lunch.

➤ *Save major parties and celebrations for important mile-stones and accomplishments.* Members of your team, especially those with life commitments such as small children, may resent too much time spent on work-related dinners. Many people regard evening "get-togethers" as extensions to their work day.

➤ *Use written messages like golden bullets.* Written communications are important, but fire off very few, and make them count.

THIS WAY

Along the Critical Path

Good leaders know how to prepare effective messages. Here are some guidelines to help your messages achieve your best intentions:

➤ Always think through the politics before you communicate. Before you send any message (oral or written), consider the potential effects the message may have after it is received.

➤ Be aware of all those who will receive your message, even if they're not on the address line or at the meeting. Consider the people who will be copied, given the cover sheet, or told about the message over coffee in the cafeteria.

➤ Decide on both the format for the message (letter, e-mail, fax, telephone, face-to-face) and the timing. Writing is permanent and not soon forgotten— so always make written messages something you won't mind being brought up again. Oral messages can be misconstrued—so if absolute clarity over time is required, put it in writing as well.

➤ Make sure the content, tone, vocabulary, style, length, and grammar are exactly what you want to say.

➤ Always follow up on the message to see if it was received and understood. Note reactions and ramifications, so you can do better next time—or change the approach if the message didn't accomplish what you expected.

➤ When in doubt, don't send the message.

➤ *Keep written communication brief and to the point, unless complex technical instructions are involved.* No written communication should exceed one or two pages, or almost no one will plod through it.

High Water! If someone will lie for you, expect that they'll also lie to you.

Taking the Reins Through Visibility

The project manager's classic mistake is to climb into an ivory tower and effectively disappear. The disappearing act may be accidental as you get buried in a project problem, management dispute, paperwork, or just a lot of busy days. But, the results are the same. When you're invisible, the project team assumes:

➤ You don't care about the project or them.

➤ The project is unimportant to the organization.

➤ You are an ineffective project manager/team leader who should be replaced.

Also note that if team members perceive you to be invisible, they may feel they are free to make decisions and act on their own, sometimes to the detriment of the project. Worse, if you're invisible and team members perceive they are working on a doomed project, they may work actively to save their own reputations (and point fingers at you), rather than pull together to make the project succeed.

For these reasons, you must become a Visible (with a capital V) member of the project team as well as a leader. Avoid the ivory tower routine and rendezvous regularly with the troops. Pitch in. When a body is needed for anything from draining the castle swamp to stapling 500 copies of the agenda for the frenzied user conference, be there, if possible. Role up your sleeves and become an in-the-trench hard worker who inspires the team as well as leads it. You'll make friends, make your workers appreciate you as a comrade, and get a little project-related work done at the same time.

Use MBWA (Management by Walking Around)

Remember, the channels of communication are best opened by you being physically visible. When supervising a project, just walking around the project and chatting with the participants improve both the quality and timeliness of the work underway, and also give you essential information on project progress. Building a 200-foot condo complex? On the phone, the foreman may claim progress on the tenth story. But, on-site, you may see that only nine stories are in place. By using MBWA, you get a real-life assessment of project progress, some exercise, and the chance to work out problems team members are experiencing. At the same time, you are building visibility as project leader, establishing and strengthening communications channels, and making sure that everyone knows you care about the project. It helps if you appear that you love working on it too!

Avoid Management Fads

About once a week, a new management fad claims ultimate results in the business press. You may be pressured as a leader to adopt one and then have to make it work. Most of these management systems are like fad diets. They work briefly as people embrace the idea and then fail as the starving bodies go into survival mode. Before adopting odd project management practices, make sure they have some practical relevance to your project.

Leading a Technical Project When You Don't Have Expertise

You don't have to be technical to provide leadership to a technical project or supervise engineers working in a discipline you know little or nothing about. Instead, you need be an efficient project manager capable of listening intelligently and of understanding and handling the human and business issues at hand. Yes, it's possible that technical people may try to "snow" you with jargon, but you can work around these efforts to stall the project.

Always talk regularly to each member of the technical team, insist on periodic updates, and ask (with genuine enthusiasm) to see results, no matter how small. At the same time, never allow a single team member to be the only repository of key project data. Instead, insist that more than one member of the technical team understand (or at least be involved in) key technical areas. Keep copies of work descriptions on paper or back-up tapes/disks, and archive them regularly (off-site!) as additional backup and protection from acts of God (and disgruntled workers).

Being All Things to All People

As project manager, you change roles from day to day. One day you may feel like a hands-on manager in charge of a group of productive, motivated employees. The next day you may be relegated to a position that's really little more than that of petty bureaucrat, shuffling papers and dull appointments all day.

The role of project manager also changes as the project proceeds. At the beginning, during the initiation and planning phases, your roles focus on creating a vision for a project and working with stakeholders (managers, customers, other project beneficiaries) to reach consensus on the goals and objectives of a project. Then, as the project proceeds into the executing phase, your role involves supporting, coaching, and otherwise guiding people to the promised land of project completion. And, you'll have to spend time communicating the project status to the stakeholders, to make sure they remain happy with the results you are achieving as the project proceeds.

In all these roles, you will be expected to excel. Obviously, you can't be all things to all people—but as a project manager who is also a leader, you better be—at the very least—a lot of the right things to most of project team.

The Leader in Times of Crisis

To be the authority when things don't go right is the toughest challenge of all. You may have done 699 things right, but blown it accidentally on number 700. Sadly, no one will look at the 699. Instead, they'll focus on—well you can guess!

Avoiding problems is the obvious approach, but what can you do when 500 red bricks accidentally smash through your new glass ceiling? Before considering a long trip to Katmandu where no one can find you, consider these alternatives:

➤ Study the mishap, be it failure to deliver or a public relations nightmare. Get a firm grasp on all aspects of the problem and focus on how it impacts project objectives, budget, and schedule.

➤ Call the team or team managers to an emergency meeting. Ask for suggestions and recommendations. Weigh each recommendation carefully and consider the cost and time for implementation.

➤ Adjourn to your office, home, or other quiet haven and pour over the suggestions to see which will cost the least and can be implemented the fastest with the least damage to project outcomes.

➤ Act to salvage the project. Be up-front and honest with management, customers, and team members. Quick response, decisive decisions, and team spirit must be used to pull the project out of the hole. If you need 24 hours to revise the project schedule, then have a couple of cups of coffee and do it. Most importantly, communicate the schedule fix and any new elements to bridge the gap causing the problem.

➤ Never let a project get the best of you. Eat well, get enough sleep, and work hard while taking care of your team members *and* yourself.

If you can do all of the things we've talked about in this chapter, and still keep your spirits up and your focus on the project goals, you'll become the leader the project needs to make it to the finish line.

The Least You Need to Know

➤ To lead any project, visibility and appropriate communications are essential.

➤ Your team members look to you for problem resolution, team management, and feedback, both positive and negative. Make sure you give them what they need in appropriate doses.

➤ No project is an island. Your dedication is central to maintaining the schedule and controlling the budget to bring the project to successful fruition.

➤ Anyone with a good plan, dedication, and basic people skills can lead a project. The trick is really the people skills.

➤ A true leader can fix almost any project problem by adjusting objectives and realigning the project team and stakeholders.

What an Organization!

Go team! That's the spirit! Onward and upward. Let's review the plan and make things happen. Most projects begin on these positive cries. And as project manager, you should strive to sustain this positive "we can do it" attitude among the team members.

Unfortunately, it's not as easy as it sounds. Building the team and keeping it together is one of the most difficult tasks for any project manager. Whether through neglect or confusion, it's easy to let the team spirit slip away. And a spiritless project comes in with a bang and leaves with a whimper. Don't let that happen to you and *your* project! Read this chapter and learn how to organize your team to reap project success.

Whose Team Is This?

Composed of all the people you met in Chapters 8 and 11—a mix of concerned stake-holders, organization insiders, external vendors, and various suppliers—the working team is more than just people on an "org" chart. The team is a living, breathing group of people that must be organized and managed in the right manner—and "right" is different for every project. If you organize these people effectively during the executing phase, you'll help them become a team—and help them get their work done.

But how can you know what the right organization is for your project team? How do you get people to move where you want them to go? Who should lead the work and who should follow orders? In this chapter, we look at some of the pros, cons, and alternatives so you can organize your players for maximum impact.

No Easy Task, but Someone Has to Organize These Guys

Creating a productive project organization is no easy task, even in a small project. Politics get in the way, people get sick, and your boxcar load of widgets from Mexico fails to materialize—and someone always gets blamed. As on *Jeopardy,* the answer is, "build an adaptive structure coupled with personnel contingency plans." The question is: How do I organize my project team correctly?

The Three Cs in Successful Project Organizations

Communication

Cooperation

Coordination

Making Sure Everyone Is on the Same Train

Structuring a project organization is more than just choosing team members and committing outside vendors to specific tasks. To function effectively, your project team requires clear reporting responsibilities and a roadmap to their location in the project. On top of this, your core team may require ancillary support such as administrative assistants, computer installers, technical help, and others who are trained, ready, available, and prepared for secondary but vital duties.

Words from the Wise

There are two ways of being creative. One can sing and dance. Or one can create an environment in which singers and dancers flourish.

—Warren Bennis

Turning all these people into a viable project team involves cementing relationships, making the right resources available in a timely manner to the right people, implementing reporting relationships, and establishing a schedule that works. Because people are involved, it sounds easier than it is.

The Human Drama—Personality, Politics, and Corporate Culture

To help you understand ways to organize the people in your project, you can compare your project team to the cast members in a play or a movie. You have the producers and backers of the project (managers and other stakeholders), the director (the project manager), the main actors (the workers who play a role throughout all or most of the project), the bit players (those people who do one important task and then disappear from the scene), and the cameo players (the important people, such as consultants or advisors, who may add value to the project but don't necessarily stick around through the entire undertaking). You also have the special-effects folks and the production crew, who have special skills but aren't as visible as other members of the cast. You may have prima donnas and stars in your project team, and these people need special care and attention.

As you consider the organization of your cast, you'll need to develop a structure to get things done—with lead players, bit players, and cameo players possibly being directed (supervised) by assistant directors (other managers), and the production crew working for lead crew or assistant producers.

Sometimes after you design your ideal project organization, you'll find that the first choice for a team member in a particular role is not even a possibility. For example, a person you would like to use in the project may not be available because of commitments to other, higher-priority projects. Or, you may ask to use one person from an organization and the manager from the group assigns a different person to your project. Thus, you may not get the experience you want and will have to adjust the schedule to accommodate for the slow learning curve.

If you say you need a person with a particular skill for your project and the line manager (middle manager) assigns a person to you, then you usually must accept this person's judgment, unless you can make a good case for someone you have more direct experience with. If you find out later that the assigned person lacks the required skills, you can negotiate or look at other alternatives.

High Water!
On large projects that may affect many departments within a company, line managers may indicate that their organizations don't need to be involved. At first, you can accept this view and proceed with the project—but we recommend that you still return to these people periodically and provide an update on the project and invite their participation again.

Project managers often need to make these kinds of concessions to other managers to get people for a project. It's like signing up Sean Connery to star in your movie and finding out that Eddie Murphy was assigned the role instead. Obviously the script and direction will require some adaptations.

The Proud, The Few, The Project Team

When talented athletes play on a basketball team they all share and support the same goal (to win the game). To this end, the team members generally follow the lead of the coach, and each player does his or her best possible to fulfill the specific role assigned in each play. And even the stars, like Michael Jordan, must follow the rules of the game. People on your project need to play their positions in the same way.

In order for the people working on your project to become a real team, some specific things need to happen with your coaching and leadership as project manager. Project members need to:

1. Realize that they'll be working on tasks that involve more than one person. Therefore, communicate and cooperate with each other to get things done.

2. Share common methods and tools for assessing and communicating the status of the project.

3. Identify and solve problems together—and then live with the results (together).

4. Accept the fact that if one person messes up, the entire team suffers. Therefore, help each other avoid as many mess-ups as possible.

5. Realize that new people will be joining and other people will be leaving the project as time goes on, but that the overall team structure and project goals will remain the same until the project reaches fruition.

High Water!
There are times when an individual has a unique technical skill and must be given a supervisory or leadership role, regardless of how difficult this person is to work with. Then, you (and the rest of the team) just have to learn to work with the difficult personality to get the job done. This is one of the standard challenges project managers must handle with aplomb.

When other organizations or departments are involved, positive interaction among the project manager and these organizations is also critical to creating a good team. The relationships among line, staff, vendor, customer, and project personnel must be tempered with mutual trust.

On Becoming a Team—The Basic Ways to Organize People

Even though there are infinite possible combinations of people involved, there are only a few basic ways you can structure the organization of a project. These include functional (or line) organizations, pure-project structures, matrix organizations, or mixed organizational structures. And as you'd expect, each organization has its pros and cons.

The Functional Project Organization

In a project that uses people from the same organization, the existing line organization can be used to manage the project. This organizational structure is appropriate when the project is clearly the responsibility of one department. Many small projects use the functional organization as the project organization. A functional project is assigned to the functional department or division in a company that has the most interest and technical ability to complete the project. Almost all tasks in a project organized as part of a functional organization will be completed within the one functional area. Existing managers in the department double as project managers.

> **Words from the Wise**
>
> One of the many reasons for the bewildering and tragic character of human existence is the fact that social organization is at once necessary and fatal. Men are forever creating such organizations for their own convenience and forever finding themselves the victims of their home-made monsters.
>
> —Aldous Huxley, *Themes and Variations* (1950)

The advantages of using a functional organization to complete a project include:

➤ *Familiarity of the team.* The team members are already familiar with each other and the skill levels of the staff are clearly understood.

➤ *Established administrative system.* The general administrative policies and procedures are already understood by the team and cost centers.

➤ *Staff availability.* The staff is readily available to the project because the line managers control the staff assignments. Thus, there are few, if any, interdepartmental conflicts over the use of resources.

➤ *Scheduling efficiency.* The scheduling of staff can be highly efficient. As a staff member is required, the person can be immediately assigned to a task and then return to routine work without serious logistical interruptions.

➤ *Clear authority.* The lines of authority and communication are understood. Thus, the conflicts between project authority and line authority are minimized.

The disadvantages of a functional organization include:

➤ *Project isolation.* The project may be completed in isolation from other parts of the company and fail to realize larger strategic goals as a result.

➤ *Limited resources.* The project is limited to the technical resources within the department, which may not be adequate to complete the tasks required. Of course, outside vendors and consultants can be hired, but expertise within other departments of the company is not readily available. This may lead to inefficiencies or redundancies in the project organization.

➤ *Bureaucratic procedures.* There may be more levels of approval than really necessary for the project because of the established bureaucracy in the line organization. This may impede progress and slow decision-making.

➤ *Lack of project focus.* The project may lack focus or priority in a functional organization because it is not the only work being done. Thus, routine departmental work may interfere with project work. In addition, motivation for project work may suffer because the project is considered "additional" or "optional" work, as opposed to a clear responsibility.

➤ *Department orientation.* The project may suffer from "department-think." This is where the priorities of the department become the project priorities, regardless of the actual goals for the project. Work outside the department's normal concerns is given little attention, and the "finished" project may not be complete or may suffer quality problems as a result.

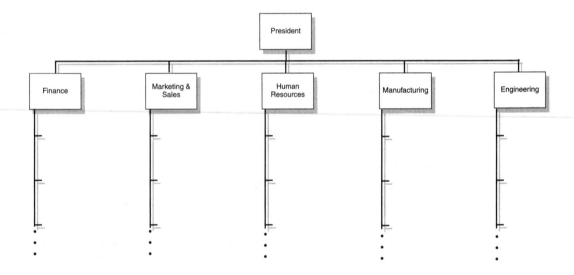

A Functional Organization

The Pure-Project Organization

In a pure-project structure, a team or "task force" is put together to accomplish the project's goals. In such an organization, all the team members report to the project manager during the course of the project. The team members do not have responsibility to other managers or jobs during the course of their work on the project. When a team member's responsibility for the project is complete, this person returns to another job or is assigned to another project. Only one project and one job are assigned at a time.

In the direct version of the pure-project structure, every project team member reports directly to the project manager. This is appropriate in small projects with 15 or fewer people involved. In the indirect version of the pure-project structure, suitable for larger projects, the project manager may have assistant managers or supervisors to manage sub-projects or functional areas within the project. As in an ordinary line organization, the supervisors and assistants report directly to the project manager, and the various functional teams within the project report to the second level managers. Extremely large projects may have multiple management levels, just like a corporation.

Pure-project organizations are found in companies fulfilling large government projects or in some engineering-driven companies that produce predictable model updates for their products. Large construction projects often employ a pure-project organization, as well. If work on a complex, priority project spans a year or more, then a pure-project organization is often an advantage.

The advantages of the pure-project organization include:

➤ *Clear project authority.* The project manager has true line authority over the entire project. Thus, there is always a clear channel for resolving project conflicts and determining priorities. The unity of command in a pure-project organization results in each subordinate having one and only one direct boss—a clear advantage in most situations.

➤ *Simplified project communications.* Communication and decision-making within the project is simplified, because everyone reports to the same project manager and is focused on the attainment of the same project goals.

➤ *Access to special expertise.* If similar projects will be completed by the company on a cyclic basis, specific expertise in the components of the project will be developed over time. It simply becomes a matter of transferring the experts to the right project at the right time.

➤ *Project focus and priority.* The pure-project organization supports a total view of the project and a strong, separate identity on the part of the participants. This helps keeps the project focused and integrated.

There are distinct disadvantages to the pure-project approach, however, including:

➤ *Duplication of efforts.* If a company has multiple projects with important goals in progress at the same time, some efforts may be duplicated, making the overall cost of the projects higher than necessary.

➤ *Unclear loyalties and motivations.* Project members form strong attachments to the project and each other, which is good. However, when the project is terminated, the team must be disbanded, and this leads to uncertainty and conflict. Team members fear layoffs or anticipate assignments in undesirable projects in the future. Thus, keeping the technically qualified people happy over the long haul becomes a major challenge.

➤ *Intracompany rivalry.* Rivalry and competition may become strong between projects in a company that uses pure-project organization for its major projects. This results in a company that competes with itself instead of with the competition—an ugly state of affairs.

➤ *Uncertain reintegration of resources.* Integrating a pure-project group back into the functional organization can be fraught with problems. People who were involved in the project may be considered "outsiders" when they return to their original jobs or the jobs may have changed during the course of the project.

A Pure Project Organization

The Matrix Organization

Implementing project management techniques sets in motion a significant change in the culture of an organization. One of the more common results of using project management in business is the introduction of "matrix management"—a situation where people report to multiple managers. Matrix management involves coordinating a web of relationships that come about when people join the project team and are subject to the resulting multiple authority-responsibility-accountability relationships in the organization.

The matrix organization is an attempt to take advantage of the benefits of a pure-project organization while maintaining the advantages of the functional organization. It is rare to find pure-project or pure-functional organizations in business any more. Matrix organizations are typical today, even when other project management tools aren't involved.

In a matrix organization, a clear project team is established that crosses organizational boundaries. Thus, team members may come from various departments. A project manager for this project is clearly defined and the project is managed as a separate and focused activity. The project manager may report to a higher-level executive or to one of the functional managers with the most interest in the project. However, the specific team members still report to their functional departments and maintain responsibilities for routine departmental work in their functional areas. In addition, people may be assigned to multiple project teams with different responsibilities. The problem of coordination that plagues other project structures is minimized because the most important personnel for a project work together as a defined team within the matrix project structure.

The management responsibilities in these projects are temporary—and a supervisor on one project may be a worker on another project, depending on the skills required. If project managers in a matrix situation do not have good relationships with line managers in the organization, conflicts may arise over authority over employees' work and priorities. Not everyone adapts well to the matrix structure for this and other related reasons.

The complexity a matrix organization causes is clear: people have multiple managers, multiple priorities, and multiple role identities. Because of these complexities, before an organization enters into matrix organizational structures, at least two of the following criteria for the project or the enterprise should be met:

➤ A need to share scarce or unique resources that are required in more than one project or functional area.

➤ A requirement for management to provide high levels of information processing and communication in order to complete the project.

➤ Pressure from the outside by customers or agencies to have one person or group centralize control of the project even though the project may be carried out by other groups in the organization.

In cases where projects meet these criteria, the matrix organization has distinct advantages:

➤ *Clear project focus.* The project has clear focus and priority because it has its own separate organization and management. Most of the planning and control advantages of a pure-project structure are realized in a matrix organization.

➤ *Flexible staffing.* Staffing is relatively flexible in matrix organizations because resources from various line organizations are available without job reassignment. Scarce technical resources are available to a wide range of projects in a company that regularly employs matrix-organized projects.

➤ *Adaptability to management needs and skills.* The authority of the project manager can be expansive or limited, depending on the priority of the project. If a project manager has strong authority, this person has command authority over most of the project. If a project manager has weak authority, then the line managers have a strong influence on project activities. Thus, the matrix organization can be adapted to a wide range of projects—some that need strong support from line managers and some that require independent management.

➤ *Staff development opportunities.* People can be given new challenges and responsibilities that are not as likely to be offered in a purely functional organization. People can gain exposure to new technical areas, develop management skills, and have new experiences that maintain their interest and motivation at work. Ultimately these new experiences can lead to more effective employees with high degrees of independence and flexibility. And because people tend to be more responsible for the quality of their own work in project-oriented groups, overall corporate productivity can improve.

➤ *Adaptable to business changes.* Matrix organizations can adapt more quickly to changing technological and market conditions than traditional, purely functional organizations. This is largely because of the high people-to-people contact in these organizations. In addition, matrix-organized projects encourage entrepreneurship and creative thinking that crosses functional responsibilities.

The disadvantages and potential conflicts within a matrix organization must be understood and dealt with in order to take advantage of the benefits of matrix management. The more frequently reported problems in matrix managed organizations include:

➤ *Built-in conflicts.* Conflict between line management priorities and project management priorities are inevitable. The question of who is in charge affects both the project and the routine departmental work. The division of authority and responsibility relationships in matrix organizations is inherently complex. Matrix organizations are no place for intractable, autocratic managers with narrow views of organizational responsibilities.

➤ *Resistance to termination.* As in pure-project organizations, team members may prefer their project roles over their line responsibilities, creating interesting motivational challenges for managers. Because the team members have unique identities and relationships in their project roles, matrixed projects often resist termination.

➤ *Complex command and authority relationships.* There is no unity of command in a matrix organization—a clear violation of traditional management principles. The team member is often caught between conflicting demands of the line manager and the project manager. The discomfort and uncertainty of having more than one boss at the same time cannot be adequately described to someone who has never experienced the situation. Of course, if the two bosses are adequately trained and open in their communications, many of these difficulties can be resolved or eliminated.

➤ *Complex employee recognition systems.* In a matrix organization, which manager should complete the employee's performance reviews or make recommendations for raises? If the reward responsibilities and authorities of the project manager and the line manager are not clearly identified, the employee may feel unrecognized. It is imperative that both line responsibilities and project responsibilities are accounted for in the employee's performance review process. And some form of reward system needs to be established for team members within the project—whether this is just public acknowledgment of a job well done or formal monetary rewards, depending on the project and your budget.

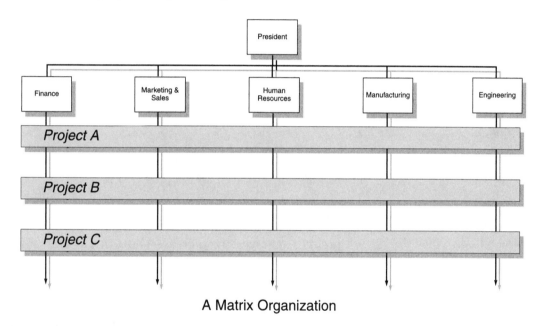

A Matrix Organization

The Mixed Organization

There are some organizations that employ a mixture of functional, matrix, and pure-project organizations to accomplish enterprise goals. In companies with a wide range of projects, a project office may be set up to help administer projects as well. The people in this office provide expertise and assistance in planning and tracking projects. In other companies, the project office may become a division in its own right, with full-time project managers and staff responsible for project-oriented activities.

When a project has more than one purpose, mixed organizational structures are usually the norm. The space shuttle missions are a perfect example. Getting the astronauts ready for a flight is one project. Building and installing a new robot arm is another. Although someone is responsible for coordinating all the projects to get done at the same time so the launch can happen as planned, the people are organized on a subproject basis. The subprojects require a completely different set of team members and organizational structures.

Mixed organizations are not distinguishable from most matrix organizations because of the complexity of relationships, and most of the strengths and weaknesses of a matrix organization apply to a mixed organizational structure. The unique problem in mixed organizations is one caused by the extreme flexibility in the way the organization adapts to project work. This leads to potential incompatibilities, confusion, conflicts, and duplications of effort if the managers are not adequately trained to deal with these complexities.

Which Structure Should You Use?

The organization you choose for most ordinary business projects will probably be an adaptation of a matrix or functional organization. If multiple departments must be involved and the project is outside normal functional responsibilities, then a matrix organization is appropriate. If the project is relatively simple and uses people from one primary department, then a functional organization can work.

High Water! Be aware that the combination of team players on a task always makes a difference. The combination will either work for you or against you. The personalities as well as the skills need to be complementary, especially on long project tasks where people are in close proximity. It's important that the sum of the people should always equal more than the total of the individuals.

Project size, project length, the experience of the team members, the location of the project, and factors unique to the project all have influence on the selection of a project organizational form. For example, in a small, short-term project for creating a newsletter the organization of the project might be along functional lines that already exist, with the involvement of a few outside resources and key vendors to complete specific tasks. In a larger project to design and build the prototypes for next year's luxury car model, however, a matrix organization might be more appropriate because of the wide range of involvement and on-going communication required across departments of manufacturing, marketing, engineering, and services.

What If You Need Someone Else?

Sometimes you don't have or can't find who you really need to build your project team—even if you've done all the people-planning suggested in Chapters 8 and 11. Other times you'll find that the team simply isn't working out because the people aren't as skilled as they'd have you believe. In these situations, don't underestimate the role that training can play in solving your people needs. Also, it may take time for people who aren't used to working together to build a relationship toward maximum efficiency. Here training can hasten the process (and possibly avoid conflicts).

When organizing a team for a project, it may be possible to train or retrain existing people instead of hiring new ones. Existing employees are already familiar with the project policies and culture, a distinct advantage. Existing employees are also known quantities, so you avoid the risk of hiring someone who doesn't fit in. Besides, training people is often cheaper than hiring new folks when all the costs and time are added together. And if you encourage the development of existing staff, the entire organization will benefit from the resultant knowledge gain and atmosphere of support and encouragement. If people are given an opportunity to advance they are much more likely to be consistently productive and loyal. When considering training as an option to meeting organizational requirements, the following choices are available:

➤ *Mentoring relationships with existing experts in the organization.* Mentoring programs are excellent for developing management skills. There are books on mentoring available in the business sections of most well-stocked bookstores.

➤ *The programs are best for general technical training or basic skills training.* Because these programs can be costly, check their quality before you enroll people.

➤ *Internal training programs developed by in-house specialists.* These programs are good for company-specific technologies and procedures. Internal training programs may be time-consuming to produce, but if there is continual need for new skills in specific topics, then a project to create these training programs is in order.

Working with the Outsiders

We've already discussed working with outside vendors of all sorts in Chapter 11. But, when assembling your organization, it's important to remember to tightly bind outsiders into the tangled web you weave for your project organization. Most key vendors should be included in the planning phases and updated regularly on the project's status. This will help you avoid bills for time not worked but committed because your project ran late. Outside vendors should also be made clear on reporting relationships, invoicing requirements, and terms of payment.

Managing Outside Resources

Don't forget that outside resources require careful tracking and management, even though the people you work with may be paid by other companies. You must ensure that the work is being completed on schedule and that your "outsiders" don't take on more than they can complete—be it your task, the company's workload, or client projects.

The Care and Feeding of the Off-Site Team

Many projects require resources available only off site. Whether essential personnel are working in the building next door or in manufacturing plants in Singapore, these groups require extra care. Without the MBWA (Management by Walking Around, which we discussed in Chapter 16) technique at your disposal, its easy for project workers to assume that if you're out of sight, the project is okay to put out of mind.

The best solution for keeping team members in multiple locations on track usually involves regular visits and phone calls. If the locations are far removed, a trusted assistant project manager is often the answer. Teleconferencing and electronic mail (e-mail) are also important tools in keeping long-distance projects in synch; but you should still make yourself or a surrogate manager available on-site on occasion to ensure all is well and stays that way.

THIS WAY

Along the Critical Path

Who's an outsider? Anyone not on salary with the project organization. You may be any one of the following people depending on your role in the project. Most "outsider's" roles are just that. It's like being a non-Japanese in Japan. You are a Gaijin (an outsider) and the rules and roles of traditional Japanese society may be ignored. Of course, you will also be treated with the courtesy of any outsider as a welcome guest. (And, your bill will be paid.) With projects, the same is true. You will be considered an external party, get paid more, and possibly treated better than the staff insiders. Your time will be more respected and your billable hours treated likewise because the people inside don't want to foot your $500-per-hour charges.

The Problem of Imposed Team Organizations

Even if you know better, you won't always have the advantage of being able to choose and organize your own team for your project. The team and its structure may be imposed on you by other managers within your own organization. Sometimes people are selected because they are available and not because of their skills or talent. Imposed teams are common in every business for a variety of practical and not-so-practical reasons.

Before you decide that your team is incompetent, give them a chance. People can often do more than you think. Remember the self-fulfilling prophecy. If you believe people have talent, they will exhibit talent. If you believe they will fail, that's likely to happen. Be realistic about your team's ability, but don't charge the project with unnecessary negative energy before it even starts.

We talked about ways to avoid the imposed team in Chapter 8, but when this is not possible, there are a number of alternatives you can consider to make things work:

➤ Do the best you can with the people you have, but make sure resulting problems are documented as they occur (otherwise known as covering your rear end).

➤ If your team doesn't have all the skills necessary, build training into the project.

➤ If your team is not qualified in all required skills, and training takes too long, consider hiring a consultant or outside vendor to fill in the gaps (if you have budget to do this).

➤ Compromise and negotiate for the team members you really need. Don't just complain—be constructive. If some of the team members are not appropriate, suggest a different team to the people who made the original selections. Always discuss the alternatives with the appropriate decision makers. These people may be able to offer explanations for the staff selections that you never considered, making the choices more reasonable than you thought. If you have documented your own case with task requirements and skill inventories as suggested earlier in this book, a rational manager will usually listen. You may not get everyone you want, but if you identify the priorities, you might be able to negotiate for the people you really need.

As an alternative, you may attempt to approach the manager with specific alternatives in mind and convincing argument why your proposed changes would result in a more efficient project team better able to deliver the project on time and on budget.

➤ Suggest an alternative team-selection process for the next project. Though this may not help this time, it may be that the other managers never considered having you involved in the selection process. Explain the advantages of having the project manager involved and offer a structured approach to the staff-selection process. You may meet with political resistance if people are afraid of giving up their authority for making project decisions, but you can explain to your bosses that they can make the final selections—you just want to be involved.

There are many reasons why the project manager should be involved in personnel selection, such as becoming familiar with the strengths and weaknesses of the team as early as possible. This insight leads to better schedules and the development of monitoring and control systems that are geared toward the needs of the various staff abilities.

Focus on the Launch

As with the space shuttle missions, the complexities in project organization multiply as the project goals become more complicated. But whether your project is large or small, the team members need to know who they work for, how to communicate project status, and where to go when there's a problem. As project manager, you must balance the workload, skills, and reporting structure of the organization to achieve its goals of on-time, within-budget delivery. If you do this, it really doesn't matter how you structure the team—as long as the people make it to the blast off at the same time.

The Least You Need to Know

➤ In addition to the right team members, the correct organizational structure (functional, project, matrix, or mixed) is key to managing a successful project.

➤ Smaller teams are usually more efficient, but sometimes this isn't an option. Therefore, organizing the team into smaller groups is often an option to make things manageable.

➤ If people don't have exactly the right skills, training is often a better option than hiring other people.

➤ Off-site teams need special care and feeding to ensure they're on time and within budget.

➤ You must make organizational responsibilities and communication channels clear to all resources.

➤ As project manager, you're the coach for the team. If you don't make the rules clear and assign people to specific roles, the team won't know how to work together to win the game.

Chapter 19

Operating Guidelines: Setting Up to Get Things Done

Before you get your project team together to start work on their respective objectives, you need do some thinking about the way you will manage the general day-to-day project activities. So, at about the same time you open the floodgates to get your project moving, you'll need to let your project team know just how you plan to get things done.

The general operating procedures for your project should help you guide people to work on the right tasks at the right time. Operating procedures also help you stay abreast of the status of every activity and cost associated with your project. You need to delegate the work and gather information without de-motivating the team with too much administration, paperwork, and redundant communications. In other words, your operating procedures should help you manage the project but not keep you from getting the project done.

Operating procedures should also allow you to gather the information necessary to make changes in a timely fashion, thereby maintaining control of the schedule, resources, and the costs—and ultimately guiding your project to completion on time and within budget. In this chapter, we're going to talk about the general operating guidelines that every project needs to get started on a positive note.

The Things That Need to Get Done

Getting work done on the project should always be the first priority. To get the actual work started you'll need to delegate all the work that isn't your own responsibility. You should do this in meetings, written communications, and through reviewing the project plan with team members. But as you start the project, you'll also need to develop a process or work schedule for the many activities that won't be found on the work plan or task list for the project. Those required tasks include:

Time Is Money

The supervisory role may not appear to be a task, but project management is about managing projects, so you should treat the operations side of any project as a set of tasks and list them out as such.

➤ *Coordinating activities among groups and vendors involved in your project.* Coordination is one of the major uses of a project manager's time in large projects. This involves managing the interfaces between people, vendors, managers, and clients who are involved with a project, as well as controlling schedules.

➤ *Monitoring progress on the project.* Managers must compare the time, cost, and performance of the project to the budget, the schedule, and the tasks defined in the approved project plan. This must be done in an integrated manner at regular intervals, not in a haphazard, arbitrary way. Any significant departures from the budget and the schedule must be reported immediately, because these anomalies affect the viability and the success of the entire project.

➤ *Adapting the project schedule, budget, and work plan as necessary to keep the project on track.* As the project progresses, changes in the original plan may be required for a number of reasons. It is the project manager's responsibility to make sure that these changes are appropriate, valid, and approved.

➤ *Documenting project progress and changes and communicating them to team members.* The quality and level of detail of your reports and communications needs to be consistent, reliable, and appropriate for each level of the project team.

To do all these things you'll need operating procedures and policies. Necessary guidelines start with the general approach of working together as a team and go on to include formal and informal communications and procedures for doing the coordinating, tracking, adapting, and documenting necessary to keep the project pointed in the right direction.

Formal and Informal Ways to Tell What's Going On

Every project should have both formal and informal monitoring and reporting activities. The larger and more complex the project, the more monitoring and administration is required. Regardless of the type of administration, the goal is to keep your team working toward the final deadline, within the budget, and in line with the goals specified for the project.

Formal monitoring includes reports, audits, and project review meetings. Informal monitoring includes general conversations with the team, ongoing interactions with stakeholders, and observations during MBWA (Management by Walking Around, which is discussed in Chapter 16) sessions. The size and complexity of the project, along with the culture of the organization, determine the extent and type of monitoring to use.

Time Is Money

When distributing project status reports, ensure that they are being received, read, and understood by all team members. You may want to create two versions: one for those who need details and a summary or simple format for the less technical or less involved members of the team (such as customers or managers).

Keep in Touch

If any of your vendors or project participants are at a different location, a phone call now and then just to see how things are going is vital. This is also a good time to provide positive feedback about accomplishments to date.

And never be a pest in your MBWA program. You want to be encouraging and motivating. If you are perceived as a spy, then the results of your monitoring efforts will backfire. People don't want you standing over their shoulders, especially if they have creative or thought-intensive work to complete. Think how you would feel if your boss came over two or three times an hour and asked you how you were doing. For best results, make the visits unpredictable, spontaneous, and sincere.

Start with the Open Door Policy

Your operating and monitoring activities should start with the informal guidelines—and the most important of these is the "open door policy" (ODP). The ODP should be the premise of everyday life on the project. Every organization claims to offer such a policy in which employees can discuss a difficult problem with their boss or boss's boss; but few people would actually take advantage of this "opportunity" for fear of retribution. You must make sure that your team actually believes in the open door policy, otherwise all the communications, tracking, and other procedures are of limited value. ODP is not just a "gripe line," it's also a way to keep good ideas flowing and a key aspect of identifying issues before they turn into problems. To repair project pitfalls quickly or minimize their impact, you must be available to all team members regardless of rank, location, or job. The open door policy must be real.

The advantage of the ODP approach is simple. When people have little experience working together, communication can become a bottleneck, especially if someone tries to conceal a problem in order to save face. Team members who are aware of the problem must feel comfortable presenting the project manager with their concerns. That's where the open door policy comes in. If you are a trusted leader, you'll be told about predicaments before they become disasters.

If people know that your door is usually open they'll learn to respect the times when you need to close it for private meetings or intensive work sessions. Sometimes you may want to use a closed door as a filter for trivia. The occasional closed door informs people to make minor decisions on their own today and invites them to depend on themselves to answer ordinary questions. When the closed door is used with sensitivity and in contrast to the ODP, it can be a powerful tool for getting things done.

Establish an Environment of Motivation

Beyond the ODP, you need to cultivate an environment of motivation around your project. People often refer to the working environment as the "culture" of the organization, and you want your policies and actions to establish a positive culture for getting things done. Here are some things you can do as project manager to ensure the culture you nurture is one of motivation (as opposed to frustration):

➤ Lead by example. Arrive at work on time and work hard. Get things done as promised, be respectful of others' time, be knowledgeable about the project, and ask good questions when you don't have answers.

➤ Adopt a positive attitude and others will do the same.

➤ Respect your leaders and the staff will respect you. Never criticize management in public. Be considerate of others, even if you disagree with them.

➤ Never make promises that you know can't be kept.

➤ Don't be secretive about the project. Let people see the things they need to see, such as reports, customer requests, and letters of appreciation.

➤ Don't try to conceal problems when you encounter them. Instead, seek advice from more senior or experienced people.

➤ Give people the attention they require. Initiate MBWA from Day One and schedule (and keep) one-on-one meetings on a regular basis.

➤ Offer assignments that provide challenges, but don't challenge people to the point of exhaustion.

➤ Clearly define performance expectations before people start their tasks.

➤ Make all team members aware that their efforts are important and have a direct impact on the outcome of the project.

As the project progresses, remember to always acknowledge work well done, but never reward mediocrity or you'll end up with a mediocre project. We discourage monetary bonuses and exclusively individual awards. The results of such "incentives" are often counterproductive. Instead, offer public acknowledgment of good work at meetings or in status reports and provide group rewards for meeting milestones in the form of group events or tokens of appreciation that everyone on the team gets at the same time.

It is also important to have some fun on projects. This is an important part of creating a motivated team and a positive project culture. Here are some ideas to get you started:

➤ *Use jokes (sparingly) to loosen up tense situations.* Sometimes a bit of humor can break the ice so people can get on with solving the problem.

➤ *Circulate cartoons that relate to projects.* The Dilbert strip is a rich source, but there are others. Encourage team members to do the same.

➤ *Copy articles on project disasters and circulate them.* These are usually educational and help team members to see their own problems as pale by comparison.

➤ *Have pizza parties for team successes (or for solving problems).* A little bribery never hurts, especially if you need to ask people to stay overtime or work weekends.

Informal Meetings and One-on-Ones

Not all operations, reports, and meetings need to be formal and planned to be effective. Just inviting a team member or a few people who are working on the project to your office to sit and chat over coffee may be appropriate. Another useful technique is to schedule regular one-on-one meetings with staff members so they can go over their own concerns, not just yours. Giving team members an opportunity to tell you about the project from their point of view can be very enlightening. People will often let you know about particular problems and concerns in a one-on-one situation that they would never reveal in a meeting or report.

Administrative Procedures That Won't Hurt

Eventually, in spite of your good attitude and informal chats with people, you'll have to ask people to do administrative stuff like writing reports and reconciling expenses. Most people won't like it, but if you have a positive culture, they'll comply with your guidelines (most of the time and as long as you make the requirements clear in advance).

As you develop administrative procedures, be sure to collect only the information you'll use. At the beginning you may collect more information in the form of reports and updates than you really need. As you realize you're gathering too much data, make sure you give the troops a break and tell them to simplify or shorten their reports. For the data that you really need, make sure the information is stored for ready access and that it is easy to retrieve when you need to analyze it.

If your project is one of many similar projects in your organization there are probably established operating and administrative procedures in place already to help you complete your ongoing responsibilities to the project. These include report formats, timeframes for project review, and other tracking procedures.

If review procedures and administrative reports are not already well established in your organization, you need to develop basic administrative procedures before you begin work on your project. To establish the things you'll need, you must answer all of the following questions:

➤ *How will you assign the work?* If team members are already clear on "who is going to do what" because of their involvement in the planning process, how will you coordinate these efforts?

➤ *How will you measure progress on the project?* Will you ask for formal updates or just walk around, or both?

➤ *What kind of information do you need to assess progress?* Make sure you let people know exactly what you need or they won't give it to you.

➤ *What standards will be used for evaluating the quality of project deliverables?* People like to know these things in advance, as do customers paying for the project. People will try to achieve standards they know about—they will do what they think is best, and sometimes that isn't as good as you'd like.

➤ *How many project meetings will you have?* Which people need to attend? Be specific. Put it in writing. And don't have too many meetings or you'll never get any work done.

➤ *How often will you update the project plan?* We recommend as often as necessary, and that means every time a major change is made to objectives, schedule, budget, or sequences. And don't forget to date the plans, so you know which plan is current and which should be sent to the archives.

Words from the Wise

Bureaucracy, the rule of no one, has become the modern form of despotism.

—Mary McCarthy, "The Vita Activa," in *The New Yorker* (1958)

Time Is Money

It's better to do the paperwork now than to put it off. The longer you wait, the harder it gets to remember what really happened.

➤ *How will you determine what has been spent on the project?* And how will you verify the accuracy of these amounts? Maintaining control over expenditures is key to project success. Know how to get financial information before any money has been spent, and don't forget to have the accounting folks send copies of the invoices to you to review *before* outside vendors are paid.

➤ *How often will reports on the project be made and to whom?* The number, frequency, and detail of the reports and procedures you use will depend on the management requirements for your project, your manager's preferences, and your own need for ongoing information on the project. At a minimum, a formal status report should be distributed once a month on a long project, weekly on a shorter project.

Reports & Administrative Guidelines
for Small and Large Projects

ACTION	DAILY	WEEKLY	MONTHLY	QUARTERLY
Informal Discussions with Team	S	L		
Staff Meetings with Managers		B		
Project Review Meeting with Team		S	L	
Status Report		S	L	
Project Audit (optional)				L
Team Building Activity			B	
Report to Management			B	

S = **Small Project**
L = **Large Project**
B = **Both Small and Large Projects**

There's *always* an excuse to produce too many paper and e-mail messages. Like advertising, too many "communications" degrades their impact. (Ever notice how, on the most boring freeway journey, you tune out the billboards after the first twenty?) This means that your vital project status report gets the same attention of a project newsletter you never saw prior to publication. Since the newsletter has several strawberry jam recipes that aren't germane to the project, your report is ignored. That's why the paper trail must be carefully controlled.

The Reports You May Need

Your team, stakeholders, managers, and customers deserve informed communication about their project on a timely basis. In addition to the regular status report—which contains information on current progress, schedule changes, and the budgets—other reports may be required to both inform and motivate team members. In large projects, there may be cost-variance reports, load-leveling reports, supply inventories, and other formal documentation to track specific aspects of the project.

In addition to general status reports, a daily or weekly update report on large projects may be a good idea. The update report is a document that is distributed to all team members to emphasize important priorities, issues, or deadlines. The purpose of the update report is to convey information that might otherwise fall through the cracks. (If a major snag crops up, the update form provides information to keep troops focused on their own work while you deal with the problem.)

Simple Forms to Create Useful Reports

Reports allow your team to follow the project "roadmap" and stay on track, but the reports need to be easy to produce. We suggest using a good project management program (see Chapter 28) or simple forms for gathering regular report information. Here are forms we often use on our projects that may be useful for you:

Schedule Update Form. You will need to update the schedule as the project progresses and evolves. Team members should be notified each time the "map" changes, for whatever reason, so they can review the master chart and adjust their duties to match.

Supply and Equipment Request Forms. Team members will require supplies and possibly equipment you haven't thought of. Give them a simple worksheet to complete so they can tell you what they need before they need it.

Status Reporting Forms. If you don't use a groupware reporting system on a computer network that reminds people of status reports and other administrative requirements, paper systems can accomplish the same goals. Simply give each team member a stack of forms for reporting their weekly and monthly progress. Add a section specifically for them to report problems and roadblocks that are getting in their way. You're more likely to get completed status updates when you provide the blank forms in advance and have an assigned person go around to pick them up at a specified date or time. The status forms should include blanks for providing the following kinds of information which should be included on every formal status report:

➤ Tasks completed since the last status report with dates completed

➤ Tasks in progress with forecasted completion dates

➤ Tasks planned with expected completion dates

➤ Budget expenditures

➤ Issues that need attention

➤ Recommendations for project improvements or changes

➤ Questions or items that require other people's approval or input

When everyone uses the same forms, it becomes easier to summarize, synthesize, and analyze the status information for the formal status report you'll write as the project manager.

Every Report Needs a Purpose

For each report (or form) you choose to use on your project, the following should be documented:

➤ How often is the report produced? Some reports are produced weekly. Others are submitted monthly or quarterly.

➤ What is contained in the report?

➤ Who is responsible for producing the report?

➤ What is the objective of the report?

➤ Who will follow up on action items identified in the report?

➤ Who is the intended audience for the report? For example, there are three potential audiences for status reports—the team members on the project, company management, and customers or stakeholders (if there are any involved). The report to management and customers is typically more formal, but less detailed, than the report made to the team members. The reports that team members send to you (as project manager) probably have the most information; but some of this information is for your eyes only, so you need to filter what you summarize for other staff and managers.

Writing the status reports for the various audiences allows you to synthesize the formal and informal monitoring you've been doing. It allows you to relate your progress to the original project plan and understand any risks to meeting your planned goals.

Ask One Final Question Before You Start

Before any report or procedure becomes part of the bureaucratic process associated with your project, ask yourself the following question:

Is this report or procedure the best way to communicate this information, or is there some other form of communication or action that would be more expedient and just as useful? (Read Chapter 20 before you answer that question.)

Every Report Needs an Audience

In other words, is the report or procedure really necessary? Some reports are produced because they have always been required, not because they are really necessary for a specific project. This kind of mindless bureaucracy wastes time and energy. If a report is redundant, too frequent, or too long, don't be afraid to ask for it to be changed or eliminated altogether.

Overdoing It

It's common to be too structured in organizing a project. While this sounds improbable at first, when you look at all the tasks and people that need coordinating, watch for the following problems as you proceed with the project to see if you're going overboard with paperwork and control:

➤ *Do you feel isolated from the rest of the team because you always have reports due?* If so, you probably have too many reports or other administrative procedures to do. Try simplifying and combining reports to keep the volume under control.

➤ *Are the team members complaining of being micro-managed?* You must achieve a balance between task assignments and task management. Some team members will need more structure than others. You must decide which approach best suits individual personalities and the project. Err on the side of trust and loose control as you begin the project. You can usually tighten things up later (unless the schedule is a cruncher).

➤ *Are status reports always late from your team members?* Either they don't regard them as important (which you can resolve by talking to the people) or perhaps your report is too complex or detailed. Remember that every hour spent on forms and reports is an hour taken away from getting project tasks completed. Again, simplify and consolidate to keep administration in balance.

Dear Diary—Do You Need One?

In addition to taking notes at meetings, gathering information from project participants, and making general reports, a prudent project manager makes a personal project diary

> **Time Is Money**
> Document each project-day's events as they come and go. Putting it off "for a few days" may find you at the end of a project without enough data or notes to write a report or defend yourself should something beyond your control go astray. Your project diary will have little value if it's incomplete.

part of standard operating procedure. The daily diary should include notes on progress, problems, and any issues that impact the project in a positive or negative light. Unlike a young girl's "Dear Diary" entries, this notebook resembles a Captain's log from a ship. Entries are to the point, dated (by page) and contain as much or as little information as required to document project progress and issues. Use a computer if that's convenient, but back up your entries so this vital document doesn't suffer from disk or power failure.

The diary contains information on the outcome of key meetings, accomplishments, conflicts, and extraordinary events affecting the project's health and well-being. (Not to mention your own.)

The purpose of the project diary is four-fold:

1. It tracks your progress and can be inspected by all parties concerned with project status. The diary may pinpoint project sinkholes that are hard to identify by reading a pile of status reports. Long-term problems, such as a failing team member, become easily visible as you flip through the book. Unloading the team member is easier when you can document his or her non-performance through the written record.

2. Future project managers can use your experiences to better understand their role as project managers and the ins and outs of the organization.

3. Should management complain about a problem such as budget overages or tardy delivery, your meticulously kept diary serves as the perfect memory of what really happened so you can explain the situation.

4. Your diary is an excellent tool for doing a better job next time. Review it occasionally to see what worked or failed last time, and employ the positive and reject the negative. A good project is fuel for laughs years down the road.

Before heading home for the night, always update your project diary. This process gives swirling thoughts and worries a place to rest and acts as the formal termination of your workday. The diary also keeps the "fossil" record intact for later review and writing the final report. With work done, reports completed, and diary done, you can go home and watch *Gilligan's Island* without a pinch of guilt.

Keeping People Up-to-Date

One of the most important operating procedures you need to develop is a way to make progress visible to team members as work progresses on the project. Seeing movement toward the finish line of the project is vital to maintaining morale and keeping people focused on their contributions to the project. Here are some things you can do to make project progress visible from the onset:

➤ *Display a large map of the project-network diagram and post it where everyone can see it.* Fill in the shapes or highlight the activities on the list as they are completed. If remote sites participate, then each site should have a chart so they can see what the other sites are doing.

➤ *Use a whiteboard or other display to show current tasks and schedule assignments.* (This puts pressure on lagging team members to get with the program.)

➤ *Display samples (where appropriate) of the team's progress.* These might include brochures printed for a product launch, a sample of a new product or its prototype, or anything tangible that represents team progress. Change this display frequently to keep people interested and motivated.

➤ *Regularly publish a project newsletter.* This is a good communication tool if the contents are relevant. Articles can be used to describe team accomplishments. Include a list and photos of team members who contributed to the accomplishments if possible and relevant. Be careful not to leave anyone out. Focus the articles on group accomplishments. (But if you don't intend to keep the newsletter going, don't start one.)

Remember, recognition rewards don't have to be large to be effective. But they do have to be part of the operating procedures if you want to create an environment of motivation. A laser-printed (but signed) certificate congratulating team members on special-project success and work above and beyond the call of duty can make a big difference in making people feel appreciated. A coupon for a pleasant dinner out for two makes these awards more fun. Be careful not to overlook the unsung team members who are located at a remote site or those who work quietly with little day-to-day visibility to the rest of the team.

The Bottom Line

In implementing all the operating aspects and creating the administrative guidelines for your project, you should remember that it's the management and leadership of the project that make the difference in your success, not the forms or the paperwork. You must act as a manager and leader, not just an administrator. With that in mind, we're ready to attack some of the best ways to keep all the "adminis-trivia" under control and make communications more effective.

The Least You Need to Know

➤ Every project needs administrative procedures to delegate work, track progress, and report status—but no project needs long-winded reports with irrelevant details or meetings without objectives.

➤ Recognition for work done well and open communications are the two most important operating procedures any project manager can initiate.

➤ Leading a project by example and keeping a project diary are things that every project manager should do as a matter of policy.

➤ Leadership is always more important than paperwork in getting any project done—but paperwork gets noticed, so you'll need to do it anyway.

Chapter 20

Making Your Communications Count

In This Chapter

➤ The various ways to distribute information on a project

➤ How to choose the medium for your message

➤ How to get your message across

➤ Why limiting formal communications is a good idea

Consider the United States government paperwork-reduction act in which an additional piece of paper is printed to explain the paper reduction. Projects typically generate too much paper and too little information. Even using computer technology, the plans, status reports, and action item lists (to name but a few) use significant cellulose-related resources. Fortunately most of this paper is recyclable and large project management firms regularly recover significant sums of money from the piles of paper they recycle. They even lock down their dumpsters so no one steals the bulk of recyclables. It's a good thing, too, since reusing the paper saves both trees and money!

We noted in Chapter 19 that good administration is central to a project. But that doesn't mean you have to have lots of paperwork. Yes, in theory, you *can* use a computer and whiteboard (for communication purposes) but all too often people opt for the paper-only approach in order to cover their posteriors. We think this is a bad idea for most project managers.

In the modern world there are many options to the traditional memo and written report. You can communicate in person, both formally and informally. You can use the telephone for long conversations or leave short messages via voice mail. When you choose to use the written form for your messages, you can write casual notes by hand, send e-mail, transmit a fax, or, when necessary, publish a formal document or dazzle people with a multimedia presentation.

In this chapter we look at some techniques to make your project communications more effective (whether written, e-mailed, faxed, or phoned). These tips should help you improve your overall control of the project as well as the impact of your communications.

The Advantages and Disadvantages of Various Communications

By considering the format of your message, the time of day, and the job of the recipients, you can predict with a fair degree of accuracy whether a message will reach the intended receiver. But before you deliver any message, always consider the impact of the message if it gets into the wrong hands, because it might.

To paraphrase Marshall McLuhan's wisdom: On projects, the medium is often as important as the message. Or, in other words, the means of communication can have a greater influence on people than the information you're sending. With that in mind, the following tables present some general advantages and disadvantages of using various kinds of communication formats.

Table 20.1   Telephone Calls

Advantages	Disadvantages
Good for short, focused communications that need a personal touch or that would be best if not put into the permanent, written record.	Possible to play phone tag for days. Chance of actually reaching someone on first call is about 25%.
Possible to combine personal approach while reaching people in remote locations at relatively low cost.	Can be disruptive to the receiver if the call is not expected in advance.

Table 20.2   Voice Mail

Advantages	Disadvantages
Great for getting short messages that aren't sensitive or personal in nature.	Long messages can be lost, scrambled, or deleted without the receiver knowing there is a problem.
Quick way to contact people in remote locations.	People may not pick up their messages on a regular basis.

Table 20.3   Electronic Mail (E-Mail)

Advantages	Disadvantages
Provides a written record without sending paper and allows you to attach other documents to your message.	People may forget to save important messages or fail to realize that other materials are attached to the e-mail.
Quick way to send messages to people in distributed locations.	Can seem impersonal if not worded properly. Not good for sensitive issues because it's so easy to forward messages to others without thinking about the long-term ramifications.
Most of the time you can find out if the mail has been read.	People may not read their e-mail messages on a regular basis.
High credibility, because people perceive it as being written by the sender (not an administrative assistant).	Requires a good, precise title so people take the messages seriously and read them.
Good for precise details that can be conveyed in one screen.	Long messages are considered bad form and may alienate the reader.
Messages can be forwarded to other people who need to know.	Risky because of permanence of the message and lack of privacy (it can be forwarded to almost anyone).

Table 20.4   Handwritten, Short Notes

Advantages	Disadvantages
Great for kudos and thanks. A personal approach that contrasts positively with computerized communications.	Might be overlooked if the note is small.
Quick, simple, friendly, cheap.	Limited to short, concise messages and best when people are in the same general location.

Table 20.5   Informal Visits and Management by Walking Around

Advantages	Disadvantages
Great way to see things in action. Gives a real impression of the tone and productivity of the team.	You might be perceived as nosy or disruptive if you aren't genuine in your interest or if you visit too often.
Can discuss a wide range of topics and issues in detail.	Discussions can be forgotten or misinterpreted at a later date. Keep the discussions focused to avoid wasting the team's time.

Table 20.6   Formal Meetings

Advantages	Disadvantages
Allows multiple people to express opinions and issues.	Can degrade into time-wasting and confrontations if not managed effectively.
Can discuss and resolve a wide range of topics and issues in detail.	Some people may feel uncomfortable offering their opinions in public.

Table 20.7   Formal Reports and Memos

Advantages	Disadvantages
Used sparingly, good for communicating updates and important procedures.	Easily misunderstood, especially if the message is negative.
Provides a permanent record.	Can't be taken back and isn't easily forgotten if the message is poorly conveyed.

Table 20.8   Faxed Messages

Advantages	Disadvantages
Good for getting reports and messages to people in diverse locations.	Too easily seen by others, so not a good idea for sensitive messages.
Quick way to get important written documents to people.	Refer to the cons for messages in general—they all apply to faxes as well.
	If no one is expecting your fax, or if the fax machine is not regularly checked, your fax can languish, thus defeating the purpose of a fax.

Table 20.9   Formal Presentations

Advantages	Disadvantages
Great for presenting complex status to audiences of various sizes.	Requires considerable planning and skill to achieve a positive impression.
Allows effective use of graphics and other display methods.	Time consuming for production and attendance. An expensive alternative.
If done professionally, can have a lasting positive impression on the audience.	Poorly presented material can negatively affect attitudes toward an otherwise successful project.

There are other media you can use as well. Many people have pagers and beepers—although contacting people through these devices is generally annoying unless you really have an emergency to convey. You may use groupware (software that lets people talk together through a computer network) for keeping status reports and general project information up to date. You may create a project Web site for a really large project to keep people informed of objectives, accomplishments, and project plans.

Regardless of the medium you choose, you need to employ common sense. You can never ignore the unexpected impact of your messages. You need to select the medium wisely and with intention. Even the a casual disparaging remark to a team member can come back to haunt you later in the project.

> **Words from the Wise**
>
> Speak less... No one ever put their foot in their mouth when they were not speaking. Worse, if you are speaking, you can't be listening, and we always learn much more from listening.
>
> —Mark H. McCormack

Selecting the Best Medium for Your Message

To help you select the best medium for delivering your project information, consider these guidelines that we've come to appreciate through trial and error. You can avoid many of our mistakes if you take these truisms to heart.

➤ *When you have real issues to resolve, have the discussions in person.* People are reluctant to commit their opinions on controversial issues in writing.

➤ *Never use meetings to berate people or make personal attacks.* If you must discuss performance problems, limit the meetings to the people involved and keep the discussions confidential.

➤ *Use e-mail for routine messages and day-to-day work on the project, but limit the number of messages.* Don't send everything to everybody. Too much e-mail can actually waste time and distract people from more important project issues.

➤ *Let people know through fax, voice mail, or e-mail that a long report or other formal document is coming.* You'll have a better chance that the document will actually be read and taken seriously if you announce it in advance.

➤ *Limit your formal meetings to those that are absolutely necessary.* Have clear agendas for meetings or don't bother to have them. And limit the attendees to those who really need to be there. Distribute minutes of the meeting when other people need to know what was discussed.

> **Words from the Wise**
>
> You know, sometimes, when they say you're ahead of your time, it's just a polite way of saying you have a real bad sense of timing.
>
> —George McGovern

➤ *Consider the culture of your team.* For a number of reasons, some teams require more communication than others. Some teams are simply more or less cohesive than others. Some team members have only limited contact together. Other team members may have established relationships. Less cohesive groups need more ongoing communication and support from the project manager. More cohesive groups will generally be more self-directed and require less direct communications from you. Consider the individual and group issues as you choose and construct each communication.

Developing Effective Messages

Communicating on a project is an art. The better you get at it, the smoother your project will flow from beginning to end. You must provide enough information to keep team members informed without boring them out of their socks or stockings. Every word counts. What you send, who you send it to, and when you send it are always issues. If in doubt about a message, always wait. But, when you decide you need to say something, here are some guidelines to help you decide exactly what you want to say (regardless of the medium you choose):

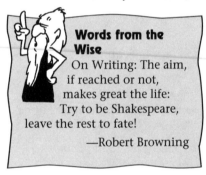

Words from the Wise

On Writing: The aim, if reached or not, makes great the life: Try to be Shakespeare, leave the rest to fate!

—Robert Browning

➤ Always outline the message before you deliver it. This will help when you feel the urge to send something nasty and negative. If you wait, you'll probably realize that sending such a message is a bad idea.

➤ Think about the audience expectation for the message, any actions required as a result of the message, and your expectations after the message is delivered.

➤ Justify your choice of delivery medium for the message and the timing of the message.

➤ Start the message with an introduction that identifies the issue, context, or opportunity of interest.

➤ Make any required actions clear and specific in the message.

➤ Be as concise as possible without seeming insensitive or rude.

Listening Is Part of Communicating

In addition to the ability to construct powerful, appropriate messages, the ability to listen is one of the most important communication skills a project manager can possess. Only through listening you can determine if your messages are understood. Focused listening also helps keep you abreast of project progress better than any status report. Observant listening can also help you foresee political issues, before they start bogging down the project.

Here are some hints to make you a better listener:

➤ Stop talking and let others tell you what they want to say.

➤ Let people finish what they are saying. Try not to interrupt, because you'll never hear the complete intent of the person if you do. If there is a brief pause in the discussion, don't jump in prematurely. Make sure the other person has finished before you take your turn.

➤ Eliminate distractions, such as telephone calls or people coming in and out of the office. Give the person your full attention.

> **Words from the Wise**
> …Just as a wise man can say a foolish thing, a fool can say something wise once in a while.
>
> —John Capozzi, *If You Want the Rainbow You Gotta Put Up with the Rain* (1997)

➤ Listen with purpose and intent. Try to hear between the words for the underlying meaning of the message. Notice body language and facial expressions as people talk. These are often the clues to dissatisfaction or issues that are not being addressed. If you see something wrong in the faces, ask some probing questions to get at the real concerns.

➤ Restate what you heard people say to make sure you got the message right. You must receive *and* understand the message for communication to occur.

You Are Responsible for What Other People Hear

If you really listen and find out that a message doesn't accomplish its goals or causes problems you didn't have before the message was sent, you've failed as a communicator. The reasons for most message failures are simple:

➤ The message was misinterpreted. This means your tone, vocabulary, medium, or timing (or any combination of these) were deficient.

➤ The message was considered unimportant or was ignored.

➤ The message arrived too late to be effective.

➤ The message ended up in the hands (or ears) of the wrong person.

Regardless of the reason for your message's failure, you need to take responsibility for the problem and work harder to improve your communications. We always recommend being hard on yourself and being forgiving to others. You must constantly strive to become a better communicator and learn to make better interpretations of the ways that receivers will interpret and act on your messages. And, once you learn to deliver messages that get noticed in the right way, you'll have achieved one of the most important skills in leading your project to a successful conclusion—the skill of effective communication.

The Least You Need to Know

➤ Because you're in charge, everything you say or write counts toward helping or hindering your project.

➤ Never underestimate the importance of personal communications or the risk of putting things in writing.

➤ Carefully plan, assess, and construct every formal communication you make.

➤ Only through careful, focused, sensitive listening will you find out what's really going on.

➤ Never send a message that has more negative than positive potential to motivate people.

Part 5
The Controlling Phase

Like any good driver, to maintain your lead over the project, you need to exercise control. As a project manager, you need to adjust your speed on the curves and compensate for the condition of the road. Control of a project starts with a detailed plan, good communications, and clear administrative procedures you've developed for the project. But to actually have some control, you need to deal with change, problems, and unexpected circumstances. You need to compare the time, cost, and performance of your project at every stage—and then make adjustments to the activities, resources, and plan to keep things on track. Sometimes you may need to slam on the brakes to slow things down or to avoid catastrophe. Other times you'll need to step on the accelerator to keep pace with the traffic.

Learning how to use information to keep the project under control is the theme of this section. Just focus on the plan and keep your eyes on the prize, and you'll reach the project finish in first place.

Chapter 21

Monitoring and Control: Keeping on Top of Schedules and Expenses

In This Chapter

➤ Why control is a good thing

➤ The criteria for establishing positive control over the project

➤ How to use status information to help control the objectives, schedule, and budget

➤ Keeping the plan up to date to help keep the project on track

Once a project is underway and you've established the operating procedures and started working on perfecting your leadership style, your key responsibility is to keep things going on time and within budget. After meticulously planning your project, you might assume that team members will simply stick to your plan and get things done as specified. Unfortunately, this almost never happens. In practice, like using the autopilot on a modern airliner, when faced with an uncharted mountain, you need the intervention of a real person who can take the controls and guide the project safely to its destination.

In this chapter, you're going to learn about the basic control techniques that can help you.

Taking Charge and Getting Control

High Water!
Never make the mistake of confusing activity with progress.

Words from the Wise
Trouble has no necessary connection with discouragement—discouragement has a germ of its own, as different from trouble as arthritis is different from a stiff joint.
—F. Scott Fitzgerald, "Handle with Care" (1936)

Once a project is underway, it takes on a life of its own. You know the company's future depends on getting the projects done on time and within budget. Your job and your reputation are on the line. But you feel out of control. How can you keep it together? How will you know if people are doing what they promised to do? How can you meet your objectives and still get everything else done? It's all too overwhelming.

Don't give up yet. You've just started. Getting a handle on your project isn't really that hard. You have a plan, and now is the time to use it. Your plan is your main tool for maintaining control of the project through its lifetime. This requires your careful management of both the plan and its resources—including the people—to move forward and keep everything in gear and well lubricated. While change *is* an inevitable consequence of moving through time (see Chapter 23), you must measure and manage its effects. Otherwise, you won't meet the goals established at the project's outset. The schedule, budget, and procedures you've put together to this point provide you with the structure you need to evaluate where you are at any time.

Control Is a Good Thing

The word "control" may have a pejorative connotation to you. Control can imply domination, headstrong authority, or excessive power. Because of these negative connotations, people new to project management may be reluctant to implement project control. But the controlling phase is not about domination—it's about gathering information so you can measure, monitor, and adjust progress toward your project goals. That's a good thing, because otherwise you'll never know if your project is on the right course.

Success Criteria for Project Control

How you use your reports and communications (from the last chapter) to control your project will directly affect the end results your project will achieve. Here are some guidelines for using reports and communications that can help you achieve positive control of your project:

> ➤ *Use the project plan as the primary guide for coordinating your project.* A major portion of this book is devoted to the preparation of the plan because of its centrality in the project management discipline. If you diligently follow the steps laid out in previous chapters, your plan is likely a good one—and thus something worth following.

➤ *Consistently monitor and update the plan.* A plan that stays in the top drawer of your desk will not help you guide your project to a successful conclusion. Instead, it must be updated regularly to be useful. It must also reflect the current status of the project and any changes that become necessary because of new information, budget constraints, or schedule or product modifications.

➤ *Remember that quality communication is a key to control.* Never provide too much information. Never offer too little. Every person on your project org chart requires ongoing communication at various levels of detail. Higher-level management requires summary reports on the project. Operational members of the team require more detailed information. Some communication will be formal and some will be informal. The objective of communications is to keep people informed, on track, and involved in the project.

➤ *Monitor progress on the project against the plan on a regular basis.* Managers must compare the time, cost, and performance of the project to the budget, schedule, and tasks defined in the approved project plan. This should be done in an integrated manner at regular intervals, not in a haphazard, arbitrary way. Any significant departures from the budget and the schedule must be reported immediately, as these anomalies affect the viability and success of the entire project.

➤ *Get involved.* You won't have time to sit in your ivory tower waiting for results and accolades from the big boss. Instead, you'll need to roll up your sleeves and get down in the trenches with the team. That way, you not only have a finger on the project's pulse, but you actually contribute to a workload that may otherwise weigh heavily on team members' shoulders.

➤ *Adapt the project schedule, budget, and work plan as necessary to keep the project on track.* As the project progresses, changes in the original plan may be required for several reasons. It is the project manager's responsibility to make sure that these changes are appropriate, valid, and approved.

➤ *Document project progress and changes and communicate them to team members.* The quality and level of detail for your reports and communications need to be consistent, reliable, and appropriate for each level of the project team.

High Water!
Be sure to gather status information from all members of the project team, even those low on the totem pole who don't report directly to you. More senior team members may whitewash or deliberately misrepresent problems in a misguided effort to present themselves in the best possible light.

What Should You Monitor?

In order to keep things running smoothly, the following must be monitored for every project, regardless of size or complexity:

➤ Status of work being performed compared to the plan

➤ Volume of work being completed

➤ Quality of work being performed

➤ Costs and expenditures compared to the plan

➤ Attitudes of people working on the project and others who are involved with the project, including customers and management

➤ Cohesiveness and cooperation of team members

Note that there is more to be monitored than just the tasks, schedule, and the budget. The level of communication and cooperation between team members and the quality of the work being performed are also obviously important aspects of the project. In addition, you must monitor the use and availability of equipment and machinery. For example, you may be responsible for the usage of computer equipment or heavy machinery in a large project. You also want to make sure the equipment doesn't "walk out the door," so to speak.

In a large, complex project, the effort required for monitoring and control may take more time than you actually spend working on the project. This is okay. It is your job as a project manager to guide the project to a successful conclusion. Of course, on smaller projects, the degree of monitoring and control should be much less time consuming.

Time Is Money

Here are three things you can do to make communications better: 1. Be sympathetic to others' problems. 2. Always make an extra effort to remember names and titles. 3. Make it easy for people to talk to you by being available and friendly.

One thing that helps minimize time spent in monitoring activities on both small and large projects is the use of simple reporting formats. Keeping reports clear and succinct is more important than getting hundreds of pages of narrative on each aspect of the project. In addition, the use of appropriate project management software that is adapted to your project needs helps reduce the time required to understand the impact of current activities and changes on the project plan. (See Chapter 28 for more on choosing an appropriate software program to help you track progress.)

What Monitoring Should Accomplish

The tasks, milestones, and budget you documented in the plan for your project are the starting point for project coordination and control. These tasks and milestones form the checkpoints to be used to monitor progress. Whether formal or informal, project monitoring should serve one or more of the following basic functions:

➤ Communicate project status and changes to other project team members

➤ Inform management (and clients or customers) about the status of the project

➤ Provide the justification for making project adjustments

➤ Document current project plans compared to the original project plan

Consistency is very important in the monitoring and control process. The project must be monitored from start to finish, because problems can occur anywhere along the way.

Inexperienced project managers may start out full of energy and monitor everything during the first few weeks. Then, when things seem to be going okay, the monitoring falls off. These managers often end up with big mess at the end of the project, because they've failed to keep track of progress and problems. Don't let it happen to you! Maintain your zeal throughout the project.

Getting a Handle on Project Status

Controlling a project takes time and effort, but it's not that difficult if you keep up with things. In the following sections we'll give you some tips to help you keep on top of the work flow.

Make Status Reports Useful

Status reports are more than nice documents that fill your filing cabinet—they are a fundamental monitoring tool to identify progress and problems.

> **High Water!**
> Project managers fall into three basic categories: those who watch what happens, those who make things happen, and those who wonder what happened.

You should encourage your team to take status reports seriously—and help them learn to write and interpret them. Whether you make formal or informal status reports, status updates should be completed by each team member (or supervisor) and then compiled and summarized by you, the project manager. You should add your own comments to the summary report, draw conclusions based on the data you've received from others, and make recommendations for actions and changes before you send your report on to other managers, executives, or customers who need to be kept apprised of project status.

Through a review of status reports and personal communications, you'll discover the discrepancies between where you are and where the plan says you should be. These discrepancies are always there, because no plan can predict the exact sequence you'll follow in getting from idea to finished project. But isn't it better to know about the discrepancies sooner than later? That's what project control is all about—being able to take action sooner so the project will still come in on time and within budget.

Compare, Compare, Compare

An easy way to monitor status is to use two columns to compare the current schedule and expenditures with the original project plan. The comparison allows you to understand the most immediate issues regarding your plan and can help prioritize your needs to adapt the plan or make further inquiries regarding the problem areas. Always keep in mind that monitoring is used to establish the project's current position compared to the planned position. You need to make this goal clear to your team, or they'll perceive your scrutiny of budget and schedule as actions of a Gestapo Sergeant with an insidious, covert mission.

The Project Review Meeting as a Control Process

Analyzing reports from your office chair will never be enough to help you guide your project to fruition. Resolving conflicts, problems, and staffing issues is almost impossible with reports, so meetings with people are always a necessary component of project control.

The project review meeting is an opportunity for key team members, not just managers and supervisors, to get together to resolve issues. It's also a time to discuss current project status and review performance toward meeting objectives. Project review meetings are often held at the completion of a major milestone, or before or after a key phase of the project. Some project review meetings are held on a periodic basis, in place of formal reports. For example, a short newsletter project is best handled with brief reports and regular meetings, because the project is of a short duration. A project to build a new sales office has less frequent meetings, until the end of the project, when more coordination is required.

> **Time Is Money**
> When working with outside vendors, suppliers, and agencies, strike up friendships with their support personnel. That way, if things start running off the rails for any reason, your friends can tip you off before your project skips the tracks.

If a project meeting is necessary to resolve issues, have one now, not later. It's best to take action as soon as you know of a problem, instead of waiting for a regularly scheduled meeting. And make the meeting short and focused. Long, drawn-out meetings with no clear focus dampen enthusiasm and obfuscate the problem. At the end of three hours, no one cares anymore.

The Project Audit

The most formal type of project monitoring (and the process most feared by project managers) is the audit. Sometimes audits are required as a point of contract; other times audits are necessary because the project is really off track and the source of the problems remains a mystery. The goal of a project audit is to get an accurate picture of the quality of work, current expenditures, and schedule of the project. (These are the goals of all monitoring activities; so the audit is really no different than putting together a big status report.)

Audits are commonly performed in large government projects, projects involving multiple companies and big budgets, and projects involving customers who need outside assurance that work on their project is proceeding as planned. Audits may be initiated both during and at the end of a project. Internal audits can also be performed by project managers and team members at key milestones in a large project.

In most cases, an audit is performed by (supposedly) objective outsiders who review progress, costs, and current plans. After discussions with team members, reviews of reports, and direct observations, the "objective" auditors (who usually work for the customer or the government) then report their conclusions on the current status of the project based on their audit to the project manager or to executive management. They often make strong recommendations about better ways things should be done to keep a large project under control.

If your projects ever get audited, you'll be okay if you've followed all the tips for monitoring and tracking progress that we've given you in this chapter. If you've done a good job of communicating and monitoring, the audit shouldn't reveal any surprises—but if it does, take them to heart and take action. Just because you didn't discover the problem is no reason to ignore the solution.

Monitoring and Controlling the Budget

Reports and meetings are great for tracking schedules and performance, but budgets and cash outlays require special monitoring techniques. The way the budget tracking is set up depends on the accounting systems already in place in your company. As you make expenditures or sign contracts with vendors, you need to establish some formal tracking method to measure your actual commitments.

To help control expenditures, you should initiate review procedures for any expenditures that were not in the original plan. Even if expenditures are in the plan, you may want to have approval or review of any purchases that exceed a certain amount (say, any expenditures that exceed $1,000).

In most companies, if you rely on expenditure reports from the accounting department to provide financial status on your project, you will likely go over budget or think you have more money than you actually have. Money is often "spent" in the form of contracts or agreements long before it is accounted for in the billing and invoice cycles of the corporation. Accounting reports typically report on invoices that have been "paid to date." Unfortunately, they don't usually report on invoices that have not been paid or have yet to be billed.

For this reason, you must track actual expenditures to date, in addition to reviewing the accounting reports. Ultimately, your expenditures and the accounting department documentation should match, but it might take as long as 90 days for the two systems to be reconciled.

(Amounts in $Thousands)	Lease (Broker & Deposit)	Build-Out	Phones	Furniture	Recruitment	Public Relations	Supplies	Equipment	Total
Planned	$87	$12	$6	$8	$31	$17	$14	$63	$238
Actual	$94	$21	$6	$6	$27	$16	$18	$58	$246
Variance	$7	$9	$0	($2)	($4)	($1)	$4	($5)	$8

Final Expenditures Report for a Sales Office Project

You, and each person on your project team who will be making financial commitments to vendors or suppliers, must account for all monetary commitments as they occur. At a minimum, all expenditures should appear on the formal status reports.

A simple way to keep track of the money is to have each person provide a photocopy of each contract, agreement, or order for your project as it is approved. These go into your "project expenditures file." The total of these expenditures then becomes a part of the actual expenses committed to your project. As vendors specify new prices or change their bids, these must be put into the file as well, and budget figures adjusted accordingly for the next status report and plan review.

When you get reports from accounting that do not match those in your budget file, you will have the documentation necessary to reconcile the differences. If you don't have such a file, you'll be at the mercy of your accountant or finance officer (not a desirable condition).

Why Status Reports Don't Tell the Whole Story

Never rely on written reports alone to assess progress on your project. People often leave problems out of reports because they don't want to put them in writing. Or, they fail to report schedule slips in meetings because they think time can be made up later. People often don't want to expose a problem in front of others, for fear of reprisal or embarrassment.

For example, John, the customer support manager, was late on writing the articles for the newsletter project. Still, in the weekly report he stated that the articles were "on schedule," even though they hadn't been started. John reported this way in good faith, fully believing he would be able to make up the time next week. Unfortunately, this kind of reporting causes many problems, especially if the person never does find the time to get back on schedule. If Sue, the project manager, fails to realize the problem until it is documented or reported, the entire newsletter project could be in jeopardy.

The quality of performance on a project is also subjective—so performance reported as outstanding by one group may really be substandard to another. In the sales office project, the contractors assembling the new office walls reported that everything was completed "to specifications." It wasn't until Roger, who was responsible for the project, actually visited the site, that he realized two of the offices had doors in the wrong place, and the baseboards in the conference room were missing altogether.

Words from the Wise

So much of what we call management consists in making it difficult for people to work.

—Peter Drucker

For reasons like this, you need to informally review progress on the project on your own, through direct observation and direct communication with the team members. Informal monitoring is completed by simply listening, observing, and communicating on an ongoing basis. The goal is to spot problems before they become unmanageable.

Using Information from the Project Team

The project team is your best source of ideas for keeping the project on track. The more you can allow people to adjust their own work and schedules to meet project goals, the easier it will be to keep the project on track. Thus, everyone on your project should be part of project control. People can do more than just tell you what they're up to, they can also provide ideas for speeding project progress or saving money. (Evaluate these ideas as you would any change to the plan.) In general, the best ideas come from informal sessions on the site of the team member, not from written status reports or scheduled meetings.

While visiting team members, not only do you get to observe people at work, but they have materials on hand to explain their progress and ideas. A similar meeting held in your space may find a team member without the requisite documentation, demonstration, or explanation at hand. By all means, take these opportunities to show your appreciation for a job well done, assuming it was.

Information from Other Sources

As part of your ear-to-the-rail approach to collecting information, other sources can provide useful information as well. Vendors involved in your project provide important feedback on the performance of the team member(s) they work with. Other managers may have thoughts or opinions on project progress, especially if yours is a high-visibility project. Take outsiders' comments, at least initially, with a grain of salt until you have had a chance to weigh them.

Employing a Guru for Guidance

We've already touched on the sensibility of using a project guru to help in the planning stages. You can also use such a person—either an experienced project manager or a person with technical knowledge you lack—to help control the project. This person does not replace your authority as project manager, but instead steps in on occasion to verify project progress and provide advice for making project adjustments. Your guru can be another manager who works for free, or an outside consultant "rented" for the occasion.

Choose your project guru wisely. It must be someone you can work with who won't step on your toes. The person must be affordable, if you have to pay for his or her services, and truly experienced. Before hiring someone, check references and ask for specific evidence of past results. Otherwise, your guru may lead you down the primrose path instead of the path to enlightenment!

Words from the Wise
From listening comes wisdom, from speaking repentance.

—Italian proverb

What's Really Going On?

Beyond gathering data on schedules, budgets, and outcomes, you must consider the emotional status of your team to control a project effectively. All projects involve a mix of people with different emotional requirements. Some are highly dedicated and committed, others aren't. Even though your team was carefully selected—whether by you, a previous manager, or senior management—once underway, a number of "strangers" may emerge where team members used to be. This is especially true when the pressure of missed dates puts a strain on personalities. Here are some of the folks you may encounter:

➤ *The overly ambitious team member,* who aims to please, but still doesn't get much done. (Their skill levels may vary.)

➤ *The middle of the roader,* who does competent work, on time, but has recently developed a thirst for project blood.

➤ *The procrastinator,* who promises results, but delays progress by piddling. This person may do excellent work, but deliver it late. He may also claim progress in expectation of completing the task later without you knowing about the inflated claims.

➤ *The industrialist,* who puts more effort and time into a task than it requires or deserves because he thinks you're wrong in specifying a lower quality for the outcome.

Time Is Money
When you collect data from your team, collect information on all aspects of the project at one time (tasks, budget, quality, and issues). If you keep going back to people for additional information, you'll irritate them and diminish productivity.

As you can see, each of these "new" employees requires a different management style to handle. While the ambitious team member may be hurt if you aren't overwhelmed by his or her progress, the procrastinator may require micromanagement to keep moving. Eventually, all four employees may produce equal results assuming their experience is also equal, but you'll get them to that point with different types of control. Some require kid gloves; others a kick in the pants.

Quality and Goal Assessment

When you're up to your rear in alligators, it's hard to remember that the objective was to drain the swamp. Anyway, as project manager, you will be constantly barraged with input, problem resolution, nonperforming vendors, and other issues. It's easy to get buried in day-to-day operations and forget about your real goals—to meet the project's goals with appropriate quality.

For that reason, you must make an ongoing review of project goals part of your project assessment and control activities. If the project is to repaint the Golden Gate Bridge, the project is a failure if the painters can only meet their dates if they use green paint instead of red. (For those of you who have never seen this monument, it's always been red, never gold.)

It may take a trained eye to see problems early in the project. On a technical project, you may need to bring in outside experts to check that quality, as well as timeliness and careful budget management, is in place. Otherwise, at the end of the project cycle, you may end up with egg on your face when you were expecting to pop corks from champagne bottles.

Putting It All Together

Once you have complete input from your team, you can analyze project status and decide on new actions to take (if any) to keep the project moving toward a successful conclusion. This includes two steps. The first one involves updating the project plan to reflect the current status. The second step is a review with the stakeholders and team to gain consensus on the revisions to the plan. We discuss this second step in detail in Chapter 23.

Updating the Project Plan

If you're comfortable with your cross-checking of project tasks, schedule, and budget, it's time to modify the plan to better predict what's going to happen from here on out. For large projects, this is most easily done with computerized tools (see Chapter 28). Plugging in the status data may predict required changes to the schedule, budget, and critical path. (Computerized tools allow you to see comparisons of the old versus the new by highlighting changed paths, dates, and budget variances.)

As you consider changes that may be necessary to adapt the plan, consider all ideas and their impact and decide whether the change is worthwhile or adds a serious element of risk to the plan. Changes you plan to avoid can be argued against by simply showing the "changee" how his or her idea or need, no matter how dumb or intelligent, can't be accommodated within the budget or schedule.

Once the new data has been used to project a new schedule and budget, you can look for problems that are causing the variances. If your critical path suddenly goes late, you can follow the lines back to see what tasks are late and who or what is responsible. If the critical path changes, that may or may not be a major flag. Again, study the flow to see what went wrong.

The budget is more difficult to track because it's less visual than the task network. But the process of comparing current to planned events expenditures is similar to matching work completed to the planned

Words from the Wise

There are many limits to authority; so project managers should learn how to wield influence.

—Milton D. Rosenau, Jr., *Successful Project Management* (1991)

task network. If the bottom line suddenly jumps $100,000 in your new projections, follow the money trail back to the point of discrepancy. Or look for an overall change, such as the carpenters' union getting a 35 percent pay raise. Such an event may mean cutting back on the project, asking for more money, or hopping a rusty steamer to Mandalay to look for another job. (Leave no forwarding address!)

The People Side of Things

High Water! If your managers feel that your project is doomed or seriously in jeopardy, they may take resources, including staff, from your project to work on other projects. The best way to avoid this problem is to keep everyone informed of positive results and keep the project on track through careful monitoring and control.

Once you are comfortable with the plan and the necessary changes, it's time to look at the people side of things. Who is performing well? Who is almost in burnout because a task has taken longer than expected and there's no extra time? This is an opportunity to review your notes from the on-site meetings and see how you can help your staff. A trip to the resource leveling chart may be required to study how to change task assignments.

If a task handled by a project team seems to be constantly late, study your notes to look for personality conflicts, procrastinators, work overload, lack of experience, or lousy equipment. You may find a mix of all four as team members struggle first with too much work, second with inadequate equipment, and finally take it out on each other. No wonder they're slow! Most people try to work hard—so never blame the people until you understand the issues.

Clue 'Em In...

The central tenet to controlling your temporary fiefdom is through monitoring and adjusting the plan. As schedules, tasks, or other assignments change, let the team members know as soon as possible—or better yet, let them be part of the decision to change the plan in the first place. Then, as Jean-Luc Picard implores, "Make it so!"

The Least You Need to Know

➤ Control requires knowledge of the project status, and since the status is constantly changing, you'll need to monitor the project and compare it to the plan in some way every day.

➤ If you keep the plan up-to-date to reflect changes and adjustments, your status can be more accurately determined.

➤ Reports are good tools for synthesizing information, but informal discussions often reveal a more accurate picture of the project.

➤ Always ask the team to offer suggestions when things are off track.

➤ If your project is in serious trouble, ask for expert advice before it's too late.

Chapter 22

Conflicts: Resolving and Benefiting from Them

In This Chapter

➤ Conflicts are inevitable but not always bad

➤ People are the source of most conflicts

➤ Conflicts are usually strongest at project initiation

➤ Not all conflicts have a negative impact

➤ Five ways to resolve conflicts

Conflicts are a way of life in projects. Just like families, all projects have them. Sometimes project managers are even described as "conflict managers." But conflicts don't have to bring your project to a halt. If you know something is going to exist, you can plan for dealing with it—and that's the way it should be for conflicts.

Recognizing the difference between negative and meaningful conflicts is vital. (Yes, some conflicts are a good thing because they bring ideas and energy to a project.) But getting control of the negative variety is necessary to reach your project goals.

It's possible for just two people to bog down a project through a clash of personality, ideas, or opinions. (Don't believe it? Consider the venerable institution of marriage!) In this chapter, you will learn what causes conflicts, what kinds of problems manifest themselves at what point in a project, and how to resolve them.

Most conflicts, short of reconciling the Russians and the Chinese, can be resolved, but not all conflicts are worth the effort to eliminate them. Some interpersonal problems are unlikely to be fixed. Some conflicts require more effort (and time) than a repair merits. Instead, a little creative thinking to invent a way to work around the problem that neutralizes the conflict may be just what the doctor ordered. In this chapter, you'll also learn where and when to draw this line.

Questions to Ask to Scope Out the Issue

As you read this chapter, especially if you're looking to this section for advice on resolving an immediate conflict, ask yourself the following questions:

Project Lingo
Sounding like something worked out via fisticuffs, a project *conflict* is one in which something—people, priorities, or problems (the three "Ps")—begin to interfere with completing a project on time and within budget.

1. Do I have enough information to understand the true source of the conflict?

2. Do I have the diplomatic skills to resolve it?

3. Will the conflict work itself out with a meeting between members?

4. Is it self-terminating? (Amazingly, some conflicts work themselves out or burn themselves up without your intervention.)

If the answer to the first two questions is "no," then who can you tap for the task? It must be someone with enough authority for the job, without overshadowing you in your role.

Conflicts Are Inevitable in Projects

As a project progresses, people conflicts enter into the picture. Properly identified in a timely manner, these conflicts can be mitigated without affecting the project's schedule. What causes conflicts? Essentially, any project, no matter how mundane it looks (digging a trough for a new phone cable, for example) is a creative project of sorts. Ideas may come from multiple players for planning the project. Once underway, better ways to accomplish the same objectives may appear. Team members may become out of synchronization with one another.

There are two schools of thought on why personnel or group conflicts occur. One is considered increasingly old-fashioned, but plays a role in many conflicts: failure or lack of leadership on the part of the management team. The other, considered more important today, recognizes conflicts as a part of the project process. Surprisingly, they can be beneficial, as you'll see later in the chapter.

In a commonplace project such as laying a phone cable, team members may disagree on the start date due to weather, how to route the cable, or how long the project will take. Once underway, the route may become perilous as an old concrete sewer main blocks the original plan. Part of the team may want to route the cable differently, while the other team may want to add time to the schedule and remove the offending concrete. This second option also requires approval from the sewer department. Further, the dig crew is late because they must work by hand near a gas main rather than rely on a backhoe, and the wiring specialists appear two days before they can actually start work. You may still have to pay them. Or worse, they may not be available to handle the wiring by the day you need it done.

> **Words from the Wise**
> There's trouble... right here in River City! ...and that starts with T and rhymes with P and that stands for project...
> —Adapted from lyrics for "Ya Got Trouble," from *The Music Man*

The Four Kinds of People Conflicts

Conflicts involving project team members manifest themselves in a number of ways. They are:

1. *Intrapersonnel.* A team member feels he or she isn't living up to expectations or is frustrated with something on the project.

2. *Interpersonal.* Two team members don't get along, or one member may not get along with the rest of the team.

3. *Intragroup.* Internal feuding and bickering among people working on the same part of the project.

4. *Intergroup.* Hostilities, rivalries, or competitions that appear between two different groups working on the project.

Any of these conflicts can have negative or positive consequences. Positive conflicts foster harder work, new ideas, or positive competition to excel at getting things done. Negative conflicts result in poor morale, decreased productivity, or even work stoppage.

Negative conflicts are resolvable, but in different fashions. But before you can resolve a conflict, you must know what led to the conflict in the first place. Keep in mind that more than one source of conflict may be at hand, and it takes careful evaluation to decide which one(s) you are dealing with. The general sources of conflict are covered in the following sections.

> **Time Is Money**
> Conventional wisdom is that no one is irreplaceable. But just try losing a couple of key team members in the middle of a project and see just how untrue this idea really is!

Goal Incompatibility

Not everyone in the organization may be functioning on the same wavelength regarding the project's goals. From a simple misunderstanding of the project's intended outcome to differences between the project manager's goals and team members' goals, conflict can arise. There might be a difference in perception or erroneous assumptions, or others might disagree on the precedence of tasks, dates, and performance criteria.

Lack of Task Focus

Tasks must be specific. You mustprovide detailed instructions instead of relying on brevity. For example, as part of an office remodeling project, you may plan on moving the office cubicles in a department to lay new carpet. An ambitious facilities manager and his laborers may assume, lacking specific instructions, that the entire 10,000 square building is involved and knock down *everyone's* cubicles over the weekend.

Administrative Procedures

Mentioned in Chapter 18, conflict can arise in a project with regard to the number of reports, their kinds, and who should receive what. In a project involving sensitive or even classified information, team members experience conflict at all levels. High-level personnel want to keep as much information secret as possible. Low-level members complain, "How can I complete my tasks correctly with so little information at hand?"

Role Uncertainty

A common kind of conflict is one of, "I'm not sure what I should be working on." Every team member, manager, and even the project management staff, if there are others besides yourself, must have a clear understanding of their roles. Not having this understanding is especially problematic if your project is structured using a matrix management approach. (See Chapter 18 for information on project organizations.)

Technical Uncertainty

If new technology is being developed, uncertainty and conflict are sure to arise. What's the best way to do it? What steps must we take to complete the project faster? Will it work at all? The Boeing 747 required an entirely new engine to actually get the monster off the ground. One team demanded the choice of manufacturer A's new engine. The other demanded engines from company B. B finally won out. Good thing too, because when A's engines were completed for sale to other companies, they did not provide nearly enough power for the 747!

Staffing and Resource Allocation

Staffing is a major source of conflict—from who will have to give up staff for use on a project, to those perceived as having the fun tasks versus those doing dull tasks or menial labor. Even within a multi-team project, managers can act like kids assembling a baseball team. Insist on getting the choice members for your team at the expense of the other team. Plenty of controversy is common, and even when a project is well underway, staff members may attempt to move up the ranks or undermine other team members for a variety of unpleasant reasons.

Budgets and Costs

Another point of conflict in every project is its budget. Conflict begins when those footing the bill for the project fail to allocate adequate funds. Then the project manager must allocate funds, with team members or groups squawking for a bigger piece of an already too-small pie. Even more conflict is generated if a group is seen as spending too freely at the expense of other less well-endowed groups. The process repeats itself if and when the project runs out of money and the project manager must go back to the well for more.

Schedules

The schedule is usually the main focus of conflicts. People never think they have enough time to do the work right. One team may want more time than the next in line perceives as necessary. Squabbles over scheduling lead to conflict. When upriver, the project goes late, and those downstream are often squeezed to make up for lost time. Anxiety and conflict result.

In resolving schedule or task difficulties, we've had good results by dragging the entire master plan into a conference room (or auditorium, if that's what it takes). Then we work through the network diagram and break down the structure with the staff to see where the plan has misstated the actual work requirements. As we adjust the tasks, we work through the schedule.

Comparing the work being done to the work that was projected in the plan, you'll eventually get the team to understand why the schedule or the objectives are derailed—and hopefully get some insights about what can be done to get back on track.

Personality Clashes

Personality clashes are almost inevitable when many people work together. Those with superior roles, training, and experience may look down their noses at team members perceived as less important. Sometimes people seem caustic or have different values about work and quality. Sometimes it's just a chemistry thing that can't be explained. You can minimize the negative affects of personality conflicts by building open communication and trust among the team members, but sometimes you'll just have to mediate to keep things on track.

> **Words from the Wise**
> When you add power, self-esteem, motivations, and status to the equation, you'll likely see fireworks where the project team used to be.
> —Sunny Baker, *On Time and Within Budget* (1992)

Conflicts Are Strongest at Project Initiation

Problems such as personality conflicts can pop up any time in the project cycle, but some conflicts are more common at specific times. During the project initiation phase, conflicts tend to swirl around goals, priorities, authority, and responsibility. At the beginning of the executing phase, conflicts over administrative procedures emerge, but soon fade as people get used to project operations. As the project gets into full swing, conflicts move from goals to schedules and technical issues. And as the project phases out, conflicts continue to involve the schedule, but may also have growing personality-related issues. Of course, the sequence of conflicts is not true of all projects, but predictable enough to help you plan for your resolutions before the problems emerge.

Ignore It or Solve It? What Should You Do?

Conflict resolution requires careful consideration. The conflicting parties may both have legitimate grievances. As project manager, your task is to sort out the real problems that may be buried in the hubris of personalities. On the other hand, the clash may be the problem itself. We recommend the time-honored technique of interviewing each person or team separately and taking careful notes. It helps to have a witness with you in case legal issues come up later. (This is unlikely, but not unheard of.) Then, after a period of time to reflect on the issues and a solution, present your resolution to both sides, either individually or together. Usually there is no perfect solution, but adjustments and compromise may mend the breach, at least until the project is complete.

Resolving Conflicts: The Five Options

Many people have studied conflicts and how managers resolve them. In general, these studies have identified five general ways that conflicts are resolved—and all of them are appropriate at one time or another:

1. *Withdrawing* means that the manager retreats (withdraws) from the disagreement. This is often an option if the conflict is petty, of inconsequential impact on the project, and not worth spending time to figure out.

2. *Smoothing is used to emphasize* areas of agreement to help minimize or avoid areas of disagreement. This is the preferred method when people can identify areas of agreement and the conflict is relatively unimportant. However, this is a weak approach and chances are the conflict will flare up again even though sparring parties shake hands and make up. Use it to get the project moving until a better solution can be found.

3. *Compromising* involves creating a negotiated solution that brings some source of satisfaction to each party in the conflict. Compromises are best made after each side has had time to cool down (if the conflict has escalated to the anger and hostility stage). The best compromise makes each party feel as though they "won." A well-constructed compromise will hold the project together. A poor or weak one will come apart in the future, and you should be ready for it. The solution to a collapsed

compromise is usually another compromise. This works best when people have a give-and-take attitude and a shared focus on the priorities of the project. (The delicate art of negotiation is described in Chapter 24.)

4. *Forcing* is used when someone exerts their position of power to resolve a conflict. This is usually done at the expense of someone else and is not recommended unless all other methods failed to resolve the conflict.

5. *Confronting* is not quite as strong as forcing, but is the most used form of conflict resolution. The goal of a confrontation (if handled professionally) is to get people to face their conflicts directly, thereby resolving the problem by working through the issues in the spirit of problem-solving.

Decide on the Best Approach

Almost any conflict can be ironed out, although resolution may impact the budget and schedule if the problem is complex or has been allowed to fester too long. Analyze the situation and choose the method of conflict resolution that makes the most sense and has the most chance of success. Of course, if you are trying to reconcile the Russians and the Chinese, the five methods of conflict resolution may be of little use. Instead, you'll just have to work around the conflict to get things done.

Provide What's Needed

Attempt to provide what each party wants if possible. We once saw a conflict over computer floppy disks (still expensive then) that brought a major software development project to a halt. One team thought another was taking more than their share of disks. Buying separate supplies of disks resolved this incredibly stupid source of hostilities in minutes!

Work It Out

Best saved for personality conflicts, getting the unhappy parties together in a room with you as mediator can work. From a mix of yelling and tears a new friendship can often grow, like a phoenix rising from the ashes. Beforehand, have each side prepare a list of grievances, so nothing is forgotten that can smolder later. Two meetings might be required to work out a complex problem. If the problem is a highly technical one on a topic in which you are not well versed, bring a third-party expert whose impeccable credentials are unassailable by either party.

Know When to Ignore It

Some problems fix themselves, such as a problem team member realizing he or she doesn't fit in and finding another job or fleeing the country. This approach is only applicable to projects in which the schedule is loose and the problem isn't vital to the project's success. Alternately, mature teams or team members may work things out themselves without your intervention. Lastly, if the conflict is tangential and doesn't affect the project, it can also be ignored, at least until it does affect the project.

Employ Brute Force

As a last resort, use the chain of command to order warring parties back to work, with or without compromise. This approach is best saved for situations in which the schedule is so tight that there's no time for forging a compromise. It can also be used when one side is adamant in its position and refuses to accept a compromise solution.

The toughest problem is one you can't fix—a fundamental weakness in the project that you can't easily remedy, such as an impossible schedule or a lack of resources, be it cash, personnel, equipment, or facilities. The only solution is either an ingenious workaround (more common in movies than real life) or to go up against management, fingers crossed, and explain the quandary and what is required to solve it.

Conflicts Aren't Always Negative

The conflict—what does it mean in the scheme of the universe? As project manager, you probably look at any conflict as troublesome. It slows the project, costs budget dollars, and reflects poorly on your abilities as team leader. But not all conflicts are negative in their impact. A conflict can point to real problems, lead to better ideas for the project, or serve as an attack on the entrenched thinking of the citadel.

When studying a conflict situation, look underneath the obvious motives to see if what's there may consist of a better way of accomplishing a task, a method for producing a better end product, or an imaginative team member constrained and confined to a lowly role. Stop, look, and listen. You may find something useful or important to the future of the project underlying any kind of conflict.

The Least You Need to Know

➤ Most conflicts can be resolved, but you may need to bring in an outside project expert to resolve a sticky conflict.

➤ To successfully resolve a conflict, you need to choose the right action for the job: withdrawing, smoothing, compromising, forcing, confronting, or using brute force.

➤ Conflicts are particularly common during the project initiation phase, and the schedule is almost always a candidate for conflict at any stage of the project.

➤ Not all conflicts are negative if you know how to manage them for positive impact on the project.

Chapter 23

Changes, Changes, and More Changes

In This Chapter

➤ It's true: Change is inevitable

➤ Making changes to keep on track

➤ Accommodating the unexpected

➤ Understanding the trade-offs and the options for change

➤ Handling resistance to necessary changes

As Sylvester Stallone would warn—"*Yo!*" Project manager, take note! Even the best-managed projects change, and you need to expect the unexpected.

You can't predict everything, and since noted psychic Jeanne Dixon died, you're out of luck if you want to see into the future as a way to eliminate changes to your project plan. Because you can't always predict changes, we recommend that you rely on ongoing monitoring, open communications, and careful analysis as ways to deal with unforeseen changes. Of course, there are always tarot cards and tea leaves if you want to guess your way through the project.

If you don't have a trusty soothsayer and want to get ahead of changes in your project, read on for some guidelines on managing change—so change doesn't manage *you*.

Managing Change Is Part of Control

Some projects get completed exactly as planned—but not many. Projects often change direction, shape, or size. Goals. Budget. Schedule. Work Plan. Priorities. Personnel. Any or all of these can change during the life of a project.

Some changes are under your control. For example, you might be able to shorten a schedule because you learn faster ways to do things as you proceed through the steps of the work plan. On the other hand, if it rains on the day you were going to pour cement, you'll have to change the schedule, like it or not. In both cases, you'll have to anticipate the impact of the change and adjust your project plan accordingly. Because change is inevitable, managing the impact of change is a key aspect of controlling your project.

The Battle Cry of Change: Flexibility

Yes there are project managers, often former military officers, who will tell you that the quickest way from Point A to Point B is a straight line. But, after managing a multitude of projects of all sizes, we've learned that only a flexible project manager can actually complete a project on time and within budget—and that often means taking a longer or more circuitous route to get things done. If you insist on the rigid attitude of getting things done exactly as planned, you'll only frustrate yourself and your project team. Remember, plans are guidelines, not bibles. And your project plan is a living document that should be designed to be changed.

High Water! When managing a project, you need to constantly monitor it. Today's purring project can become tomorrow's glitch-filled problem if you don't stay on top of things. Ongoing monitoring is always your first defense against the undesirable impacts of a changing world.

Planning for "likely, but undesirable possibilities" is an absolute requirement for any project manager. That's why we suggest that project plans include a best-case and worst-case schedule and budget. Flexibility is the rule for project managers, not the exception.

Changes to the schedule, the budget, and even the task order are necessary parts of keeping your project on track. Rigid scheduling or fixed budgets can work occasionally, but eventually you'll have to change the plan to get to where you really want to go.

The Marriage of Review and Change

Managing change and reviewing the project go hand in hand. As you monitor your project over time, you'll get feedback on the general issues, problems, and other factors that may be affecting your progress (positively or negatively) in completing the project. Lots of things enter the picture as the project proceeds, some desirable, others unpredictable, and once in a while, a disastrous event. The good ideas and the unpredictable problems will all result in the same thing: the need to change the project plan in some way.

Through project review, new ideas and new ways of doing things become apparent. The realities of what can and cannot be accomplished shift tasks and goals. Then there are the changes handed down from senior management or the customers.

All these things require that you update your plan for the project—and updating the plan means making changes to the goals, tasks, workflow, schedule, budget, or people.

Slacking Off and Padding the Fall

Some project managers build extra time or "slack" time into their schedules and also "pad" their budgets as a way of managing changes. Yes, extra time in a schedule can be used to accommodate some of the inevitable changes or problems in a project. And when tasks cost more than you had hoped, if you have a little extra in the budget, you can comfortably lean back and congratulate yourself for including the money for the changes.

But, if you build in too much slack and padding, it will be obvious to your managers and customers, and you'll get a reputation for being sloppy in your estimates, overpriced, or both. It's probably better to come up with the best plan you can at the beginning, and then negotiate the changes to the objectives, workflow, budget, and schedule as the project proceeds.

The Rules of Change

Now that you've accepted the inevitability of changes, here are four rules that will help you anticipate changes on your projects:

1. The longer the project runs, the more likely change will occur and the more shifts in direction the project will undergo.

2. Projects that lack firm political roots in your organization are the most likely to be extensively modified or done away with completely.

3. The project manager must negotiate, be assigned, or have the authority to make appropriate changes and to recommend against ill-advised ones. If the project manager lacks this authority, uninformed changes from those outside the project are more likely, and eventually the inability of the project manager to control change will doom the project.

4. Change is necessitated by external factors as well as poor planning. Weather, a shortage of materials and equipment, legal complications, labor stoppages, process failure, and many other factors can run any project off both the schedule and budget tracks. The trick is to minimize the changes due to incompetence and reduce the impact of changes that are beyond the control of mortals.

Time Is Money
The best way to deal with a runaway project is to get involved as soon as you suspect a problem. The longer you wait, the less you will be able to salvage your schedule and budget. But, before you jump in, ask what's really wrong. Determine what precipitated the problem so you don't end up in the same place next time.

Meddlers Beware!

There's always someone associated with your project who "knows" how to do things better than you're doing them. Sometimes you need to put your foot down and pinion these meddlers to keep them from getting in your way. Establish a clear process for suggesting and reviewing changes so people offer constructive advice instead of bothersome chatter. And (don't laugh), if you fail at a project because of outside meddling, guess who will get the blame? We bet it won't be the meddler with all those "good" ideas.

Communicate with Everyone!

Yes, you've heard it before, but when dealing with change, it's vital to get input from everyone on the team. Comments should also be solicited from other managers, senior management, and customers (where appropriate). Multiple inputs provide perspectives you may not have considered in your plan of change.

Change and Conflict Go Hand-in-Hand

In Chapter 22, we looked at ways to deal with conflicts. Many of the forces that cause conflict have to do with project changes. New ideas enter the project. Change is required. Schedules slip. Change is required. Jane and Joe are acting like children. Change is required. And when a task proves impossible as originally defined, you guessed it. Change again.

The list of potential change sources is a long one. Some changes you can see coming at you, and you can make a preemptive strike to minimize their impact. Others occur without warning. Project changes also vary in their impact on your project. Some are little more than a blip easily accommodated within the project flow. Others radically alter the budget, schedule, and scope of the project. Hope for the former, but prepare for the latter.

Here are some of the "typical" changes we've seen in our experience as project managers:

➤ *The organizational priorities are realigned and the priority of the project comes into question.* Sometimes you can salvage the project through careful planning, justification of the project, and skillful renegotiation; sometimes you just end up on the wrong side of the corporate priorities and have to look for another project to manage. Once a project has lost the support of the stakeholders, resign yourself to the inevitable and don't try to salvage it.

➤ *A company's restructuring or reorganization moves staff around, possibly depleting you of key team members.* Again, the first step is negotiation to get who you need. If that doesn't work, there are always outside vendors. And don't forget to consider some staff development for the people you have left.

➤ *An organization announces sweeping cuts in operational budgets.* This can have a profound impact on a project with a budget that's already on the slim side. Go back to your plan and look for ways to cut back on expenses. Just make sure that everyone knows that the results will likely be cut back along with the budget.

➤ *A competitor announces a product that is similar to yours.* You must get to market first, budget be damned. Now is the time to pull out all the stops and redraft the plan to get to market faster. You'll need more money as well as other resources, so expect to make a presentation to management that justifies your scheme.

➤ *The team committed to something impossible—like making a cow jump over the moon—and needs to put some reality into the plan.* As soon as you realize that your cow can't jump that high, you'll have to ask for more resources, scale back the project, or go back to the drawing table and draft a new plan. Should you accept an impossible mission even after you realize the goal is impossible, you and your Impossible Missions Force are simply doomed to failure. You'll need to negotiate another goal—or start updating your resume. The choice is yours.

Darwin and the Origin of Species

Charles Darwin had a brilliant theory of change that explained how species adapt over time to evolving circumstances. Fish developed legs (of sorts) in order to trek from the seas to sing blibbit in the swamps. Polar bears developed long necks to haul 400-pound seals over the ice to their family get-togethers.

Darwin's ideas apply to projects, too. Projects also evolve. If the project manager is in charge, the project evolves to be more adaptive to outside changes. The project survives. If the project manager lets things go on their own, things still evolve. The difference is in the animal you end up with.

Words from the Wise
If you leave a thing alone you leave it to a torrent of change.

—G.K. Chesterton

Understanding and Estimating the Impact of Changes

If you want to stay in control and help your project evolve in the right direction, a well-documented project plan is your first line of defense in managing change. If you want the results you expect, as opposed to the consequences that just happen, you need to keep your plan up to date. Period. With plan in hand, you can quickly assess the impact a change will have on the project budget, schedule, and resources. You can also use the plan to show why a new or different user requirement may have a negative impact on the final results of your project.

As you review your plan, you'll see that there are really only five major components in any project that can be changed. They are the same components that were used to create your project plan in the first place. Here they are again (in case you've forgotten):

1. **Goals** and specifications for the end results of the project

2. The **people** who work on the project

3. The **money** (budget) you have to spend on the project

4. The material and technical **resources** you have available to support your project

5. The **time** you have available to complete the project

Any change in your project plan will affect one or more of these project components. Most changes will affect all five in some way. If you want to keep changes under control, you'll need to address the impact of changes by updating your project plan and communicating the changes to everyone involved.

Sometimes you'll need to replan, reapprove, and replan again. That's why we drew the planning, executing, and controlling phases of the project management cycle in a circle. (Check out the diagram in Chapter 2.) As you execute your project, things change. You control things by adjusting the plan. As you execute the new plan, things change again. You repeat the cycle until the project is declared finished—and that means (finally) moving on to the closing phase.

Along the Critical Path

In Mel Brooks' comedy, *History of the World, Part One*, Brooks starts with the Twenty Commandments, drops one of the tablets, and ends up with the Ten Commandments. No, the idea isn't original, but we're talking about unpredictable changes to projects, not quality comedy.

The point is that sometimes the best way to get a project done is to scratch some of the work from the list. This can turn an impossible list of tasks into a doable (and scoped down) project. But before promising to do less as a way of dealing with change, make sure the downsized project is really worth doing and the stakeholders agree to the downsizing. If not, you'll need to negotiate what you really need—more time or resources, or a bigger budget—to get the project done right.

The Steps for Measuring and Accommodating Change

The best approach to accommodating change in a project starts with apprising your team members (or team leaders in a larger project) of the need for a change and then asking their opinions on ways to implement the changes.

This "town hall meeting" approach is vital because changes always impact people's work on a project. Occasionally, an inventive team member may even introduce a solution that accommodates the change with no hard feelings or frustrations. Rare—but it happens.

After discussing the options for change with the team, follow these steps to make sure the change has its desired impact on the project:

Time Is Money
Rather than waste time fighting a change dictated by your boss, ask questions and try to understand the rationale involved (if any). Then run the numbers to see what, if any, impact the change will have on your project. Communicate this impact clearly before you begin implementing the change. Chances are the imperative for the new idea will change if the numbers don't look too good.

➤ *Clearly define the expectations for the change.* You are not making changes for fun, but to improve something or fix a problem. Be sure you determine how you'll measure if the desired effect on the project is achieved. How will you know if the change is successful?

➤ *Plug the changes into the project plan to see what happens to schedule, budget, and resource requirements.* Never commit to a set of changes before assessing their impact on the project. Violators of this rule might find themselves with a failed project on their hands. Team review of the impacts is vital. Others may spot an impossible task dependency that you missed, and the technical folks may have knowledge of dependencies among tasks that you don't understand.

➤ *Always look for alternatives before you make a decision to change a major component of the plan.* One more time, consider the budget, staff skills, and the ability to meet the scheduled dates. Keep in mind that there is more than one way to accomplish almost anything.

➤ *Once the changes are determined, document changes on the original plan, date them, and get them approved as you would a new project plan.* It's important to always get approval for the revisions from the powers that be. Even if the disruption is minimal, managers and stakeholders should be fully cognizant of changes. For changes that impact delivery dates or the budget, written correspondence should accompany your request. Remember, if it's not in writing, agreements are easily forgotten.

➤ *After the new plan is approved, inform all team members of the changes to their tasks and delivery dates.* Make sure all team members are aware of *exactly* what will be expected of them and how the changes will impact the project. You'll also need to let team members know how the effect of the changes will be measured, so things don't end up going on just like before. This should be done through ongoing monitoring, reports, and communication. (And yes, you might need to change some of your project reports or procedures to make sure you get the new information you need.)

Along the Critical Path

Always remember that more people doesn't always mean more work gets done. Yes, naive managers often solve problems by throwing more resources (usually people) onto the project. But adding more people doesn't always improve productivity—especially when creative people are involved. Adding additional writers, designers, architects, or engineers may actually slow a project down.

When you add more personalities, people can lock horns in what is called a "creative conflict." This can bring work to a standstill until the mess sorts itself out or a creative team member stomps off for good in self-righteous disgust. Sad, but common.

Only add people if people will actually help get things done faster. Look for other means to improve productivity. If you scoped out the work and selected a good team in the first place, you may need to change objectives instead of the team.

Comparing Changes with Trade-Off Analysis

Trade-off analysis is one method of dealing with change that lets you evaluate the impact of various alternatives. "We can do this if we skip that. Which is more important?" Analyzing trade-offs is also a way to understand the pressure change is placing on the project. Understanding trade-offs clarifies the changes that affect later tasks and milestones. Here are some considerations for understanding the impact of various options (or trade-offs) when implementing a change to a project:

1. *Determine the underlying rationale for the change.* Are the changes motivated by rational thinking or a political agenda? Does the change really make sense?

2. *Are the project goals still appropriate or will the change also affect the eventual outcome of the project?* Imagine if God set out to make the eagle and due to project changes, created the dodo bird instead. Make sure your dodo will still be a desirable species—or figure out how to make the eagle you really wanted.

3. *Do the options affect the likelihood of completing the project successfully?* You should have already reviewed how the various options impact schedules, budgets, and team member availability. When changes increase the risk of failure, this needs to be carefully analyzed and then clearly communicated to all involved. Sometimes the risk is for good reasons, but sometimes it's just a plain mistake. Make sure you know which before you choose one change over another.

4. *Analyze the options at all levels.* Try to hold the budget and objectives constant and then evaluate how you can accommodate the changes. Look for alternatives, tasks that can be deleted or shortened, or dollars that can be moved around in the project. This is usually a team exercise. Be patient when trying to come up with alternatives. Don't always jump on the first ideas. It's often at 11:00 p.m., over a seventh cup of coffee, that a team member suggests the perfect compromise that hadn't occurred to you on first review of the problem. Only after looking at all options should you ask for more money or more time.

5. *Understand the skills of the team as you consider trade-off options.* If change forces a revamp of the project, consider surplusing team members and replacing them with others better suited to the new set of tasks. On some projects, you may be able to downsize the project due to changes.

6. *Consider scrapping or postponing part of the project as you review the change options.* If changes force the project over budget and beyond schedule deadlines, look for tasks or objectives to cut. For example, a project to build a large amusement park that is running over budget could be scaled back by reducing the number of less important attractions, or by changing the plan to finish the less important attractions after money starts coming in from admission ticket sales.

Time Is Money
Keep in mind that people get frustrated with endless rounds of picky changes. To avoid this frustration, limit the self-induced changes to those that are truly necessary and important.

High Water!
There's a dimension in many projects that you might call the Twilight Zone—the unreality between the actual time and resources available and the demands by the customer or senior managers in your company. Avoid entering the Twilight Zone by being firm and honest with those who attempt to pressure you into unrealistic goals, schedules, or budgets. Otherwise, say "Hi" to Rod Serling for us...

Use the Zero-Based Budget Approach

Sometimes you need to prioritize what really needs to be done in order to understand the things that should be changed on a project. If you're building a hot new computer system with many new multimedia features, for example, maybe some of the features could released in the next-year's model. To make this kind of decision, we often use the zero-based budget (ZBB) approach to establish the priorities and the bottom line for a changing project. ZBB is an approach that separates the *must do* from the *would like to do* work. (This is different than a trade-off analysis, which looks at one option for change compared to another.)

Assembling a ZBB is simple. Make a list of all the elements that you would like to see done at completion (see the following chart). Then rewrite the list according to priority. List the most important "must do" tasks or goals at the top, working down to the less important tasks toward the bottom.

Next, review your list. Rewrite it if necessary if you've made lots of notes, erasures, or arrows to move things around. When you have a prioritized list, starting from the top, write down the costs and schedule significance of each goal or task and weigh the time and budget required. As you work down the list, when you run out of resources, draw a line under the last goal or task you can accomplish within your budget (or schedule). Items above the line can be done. Items below the line should be scrubbed, since the resources required to complete them successfully are not currently available.

Haul your entire network diagram and schedule into the room and lay it across the boardroom table. Your convincing arguments to senior management may convince them that the change is *not* a good idea when you review the impact on the plan in detail. Often, simply telling them how much extra cash the change requires is a *very* persuasive tactic in managing expectations and change.

Sometimes Quitting Is the Only Choice

In spite of looking for reasonable options to keep your project on track, there are some changes that force only undesirable options. We're sorry we don't have better news. But as frustrating as such unforeseen problems are, sometimes no amount of planning or management will fix the problem. You'll just have to start over or quit the project. That's why it's always a good idea to have a contingency plan when opening a new business or bringing out a new product—along with some extra income sources in the background—just in case Murphy's Law prevails.

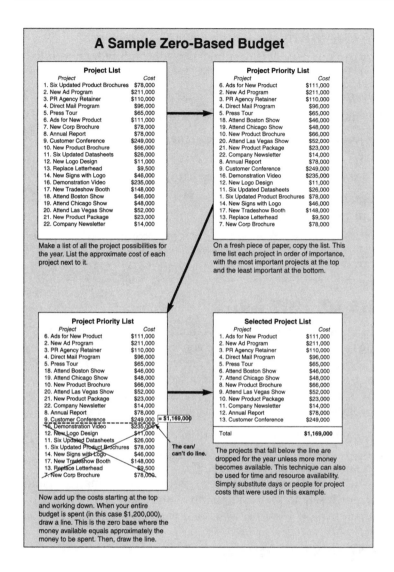

A zero-based budget is a simple tool for understanding and simplifying priorities based on the cost of getting things done.

Kerzner's Proverbs

Dr. Harold Kerzner included these project management proverbs of unknown origin in his comprehensive book, *Project Management: A Systems Approach to Planning, Scheduling, and Controlling* (Van Nostrand Reinhold, 1989). They add some perspective to the process of managing projects as well as change:

➤ You can't produce a baby in one month by impregnating nine women.

➤ The same work under the same conditions will be estimated differently by ten different estimators or by one estimator at ten different times.

➤ The most valuable and least used word in a project manager's vocabulary is "No!"

➤ You can con a sucker into an unreasonable deadline, but you can't bully him into meeting it.

➤ The more ridiculous a deadline, the more it costs to meet it.

➤ The more desperate the situation, the more optimistic the player.

➤ Too few people on a project can't solve problems. Too many people create more problems than they solve.

➤ You can freeze the user's specs but he won't stop expecting.

➤ Frozen specs and the abominable snowman are alike: They are both myth, and they both melt when sufficient heat is applied.

➤ The conditions attached to a promise are forgotten, and the promise remembered.

➤ What you don't know hurts you.

Changing Your Hours to Stay Sane

Has your project blown a tire? Does your family treat you like a boarder because they never see you? Do you eye the Geritol display every time you visit Walgreen's for yet another package of NoDoze? If this sounds familiar, it's time to get a life. Stop everything! Get a handle on the problems that are causing you to live at work and then use your leadership to fix the problems or choose to scale back or step down from the project. Your life is worth more than any project—even if your boss may express other sentiments.

After gaining some perspective, pick up the pieces (if possible), ramp the project back up in phases to maintain control, and eliminate the snarls that dogged it previously. The project workers? If they're freelancers, as little fun as it is, furlough them. If they're employees, either put them back on their regular jobs or ask for their help analyzing and reconstituting the project. Listen closely to their complaints. This might be the source of the problem—and your exhaustion!

People Predictably Resist Change

Change has predictable effects on the project team. Even changes for good reasons can have bad effects among the people on a project. Motivation-sapping resentment may build against the new bodies, management, schedules, or the project itself.

People may perceive that changes invalidate the work of team members. Imagine working 16 months developing an engineering process and having your work swept under the rug in less than a day when the changes to a project make the process unnecessary in the new plan!

If you anticipate that people will resist change, you'll have a better chance of getting their support—eventually. Never lie or pretend it's business as usual. Just tell it like it is, and then try to communicate the need for the changes. Take their concerns seriously and listen to their ideas. Don't let the project unravel.

Words from the Wise

A single lie destroys a whole reputation for integrity.

—Baltasar Gracián

In the following sections, we'll present some tactics for handling the effect of change on projects and project personnel that you should put into your "change management" arsenal. You may need to combine two or more of them for particularly sticky situations.

Frank and Open Discussion

When you know changes will involve people's jobs, talk to them *now* instead of waiting until the last minute. Even those forced into lesser or nonexistent roles will appreciate your empathy and candor. The earlier you let people know they'll have to go, the more time they'll have to look for another position inside or outside the organization.

Dwell on the Positive, But Don't Cover Up the Negative

Focus people on the positive aspects of the changes being made. (This is easier if there really are positive aspects!) If the news is bad, for example, cutbacks are at hand, be honest and forthright in explaining why they are happening. Above all, don't make the team feel it's all their fault, even if it really is.

Spell Out the Details

Clearly define or explain any new expectations, new organization chart (if there is one), new schedule, or new goals. Put changes in writing for distribution after your talk so that everyone is in sync with the changes, even if they don't remember everything you said. According to current management wisdom, if major and negative changes are imminent, schedule the big announcement for Monday. That way people can adapt without a weekend of inaction.

Assure Team Members of Your Support

Ensure that team members know that you are fully supportive of the changes and are putting your weight behind them. Don't allow individual team members to foment discontent that spreads like the flu among other workers. If people won't get with the program, spend one-on-one time with them discussing the issues. If that fails, dump them from the project before they do more damage to the morale. It's a last resort—but sometimes you have no choice.

The Least You Need to Know

➤ Changes are a natural and expected aspect of any project.

➤ Change is not a negative word; many changes on projects are made for positive reasons.

➤ Whether good or bad, change affects all team members, both inside and outside the organization.

➤ The original plan should be used as a benchmark to track the effects of changes.

➤ The end result of changes affects the budget, schedule, and goal outcomes—and this means the plan must be updated on a regular basis to reflect the impact of changes.

➤ Change should be resisted when unnecessary, frivolous, or obviously detrimental to the successful completion of the project.

➤ Changes should be communicated openly to team members at the earliest possible date.

Chapter 24

When Push Comes to Shove, You Can Always Negotiate

> **In This Chapter**
>
> ➤ The power of speech
>
> ➤ Putting the chips on the table
>
> ➤ Common approaches to win your case
>
> ➤ Steps to successful negotiation
>
> ➤ Knowing when to give in

You've certainly heard that talk is cheap (so what else is new, right?), but the fine art of negotiating requires years of practice to master. As in a card game when a player's facial muscles twitch slightly as he tries to maintain a sublime poker face, negotiation is prey to nuances and subtlety.

Negotiating skill is central to managing any project: How much will it cost? How much will you pay or will the other side charge? How many hours will it take? Can you do it in less time for less money? Do we need you/Do you need us? Asking yourself these and other questions is part of setting up and running all aspects of a project. Almost every resolution to every problem in your project takes negotiating prowess to keep your project as close to its original plan as possible.

You will be faced with negotiable issues throughout the project as problems and differences of opinion affect the budget, schedule, and even the team's morale. Unless you're approaching the negotiating table with white flag in hand like the losers on a battlefield, each party (you and the other side), will have something of value to put on the negotiating table. Even if the value is not totally equitable, terms can be worked out. And negotiating is much like playing poker. When you're holding four aces you can take a lot more risk than when you've got a hand with a four of hearts, a seven of diamonds, and a five, a three, and a deuce of clubs.

The Three Sides of the Negotiating Table

What makes negotiating in project management different is the three sides of the theoretical negotiating table. On one side is the customer being pitched to (your manager, for example) trying to unrealistically limit expense and hours. The second side is that of team members—be they inside your organization or outside vendors. The third and toughest side of the table is that of the middleman—that's you. Being a good, patient negotiator is a skill that takes time to develop. You as the pitchman of sorts must work on the budget, schedule, and would-be team members to sign on, work on the schedule, accept a realistic salary, and explain why you can't afford to send them to Aruba just for joining up.

The initial elements of negotiation happen long before the letters, discussions, meetings, and possible lawsuits. Before you negotiate, you must establish what you have to bring to the negotiating table.

What Will You Negotiate For?

The process of negotiating is one of reaching compromise. Your goals in the negotiation for your project will be to establish realistic pricing, prompt payment, appropriate resources, extended deadlines, or agreement on the terms of success for your project. Your positive spirit, high level of integrity, and fulfillment of promises motivate team members to say to each other, "Hey, I really like that approach! Let's do it!"

High Water!
Never say: "I have someone who will do it for half that price…" when the other side knows that no one else in town can do the job. You'll not only lose credibility, but may jeopardize the ability to get the project done at all.

But if you and your customer or you and a staff member have different opinions about any measure, task, or resource in your project, you need to negotiate. You negotiate up front before hiring a team member or consultant, signing a lease on equipment, or buying a 20,000-square-foot prefab tilt-up building that arrives as a "kit" on several tractor trailers.

Here are several examples of things you'll be asked to do as a project manager—and you'll need to negotiate a compromise if you can't give everything that's asked of you:

➤ *Reduce the cost.* Your compromise will involve changing the specifications of the project or coming up with less expensive staff to get things done.

➤ *Deliver things faster.* Your compromise will involve changing product specifications, extending the budget, or coming up with new sequences of tasks.

➤ *Add or change people on your team.* Your team is the central component (aside from you) in making the project a success. As project manager, the big boss may approach you with a list of people or vendors to use. You want the best team possible, and negotiating may take those obviously lacking the skills, stamina, and cooperation off your team, revise their dictated roles, or (hopefully) get better talent. Remember:

If you get lesser skills than desired, you'll probably have to compromise on the schedule or the quality of the project or both.

➤ *Deliver a different quality or product from that originally specified.* Stakeholders often change their mind about what they want in the middle of the project. You can negotiate to provide more or less quality—depending on your side of the table—but you'll also have to compromise on the budget, the schedule, and a lot of other things.

➤ *Accept the budget without looking at the details.* Stakeholders will try approaches like "I'll sign a contract *right now* if you can do it for $25,000 instead of $40,000." Don't be swayed until you understand the compromises you'll need to make if you take less than you asked for.

> **Time Is Money**
> When working out a schedule, you can negotiate too diligently for that better deal. The desperate employee, consultant, or vendor may cave and offer the sky at a reduced rate. You'll end up paying for overtime, project problems (or failure), and have a lot of unhappy employees because in the push-comes-to-shove, you squeezed a little too hard.

Negotiations of All Sizes

There are many kinds of negotiations. They involve a careful mix of power, money, skill, and prestige. Each negotiation for your project will have a different tone and priority. As you consider each situation, you should think about the approach to use during the negotiation to maximize your potential of getting the agreement you need to proceed. You may want to read up on negotiation in more depth than we can fit here (see *The Complete Idiot's Guide to Negotiation*), but here are some basic tactics to choose from in your negotiations:

➤ *Stress mutual self-interest.* You need a specific team member because you need a team. He wants your project's name on his resume and it adds to his credentials. You both get something you want and need.

> **Project Lingo**
> *Win-win* has a unique meaning in project management. Instead of simply a deal in which everyone gets a few bucks, other needs come into play. You may find a consultant more concerned about adding your organization's name to his list of credentials than about billable hours. Or you may have an employee more worried about job security than working on your project.

➤ *The appeal.* An employee about to be let go or a vendor in need of a contract would probably be very willing to join your project. In fact, they may outperform the rest of the staff just to have a job or stay in business. But if they're simply desperate, they may be the wrong party for the project.

➤ *A power play.* You can exert pressure on a lower-level employee or on a vendor who does a lot of business with you to join your team. This unhappy tactic makes for employees who don't perform and won't act with team spirit, but it's done every day in business. Use it as a last resort.

Centering

If you don't know what you really want—and what you can really do without—you'll never get what you really need. Before beginning even the first sparring steps in a negotiation for specific services or resources, be it for 12,000 pink pencil erasers, or ten temporary employees to support a telemarketing promotion, or the cheap carpet you need for the new cloakroom, you must nail down (in writing) exactly what you're looking for.

After understanding what you need, want, and would like in a negotiation, you need to understand the alternatives that would be bad, good, and better. This is a Zen-like process in which you must look at the negotiation from all known angles and decide on the most likely outcomes. After listing the alternatives, choose the five that are acceptable and also feasible. That doesn't mean you'll get the ones you want, but at least you have a center from which to begin negotiations.

If you find in this analysis that you're completely lost, you may need to bring in expert outsiders to help you assess value, isolate and analyze options, and study what the other side will likely bring to the table.

The Other Side

At the same time you are studying what you have to offer, you must also consider the other side. What have they got to "sell"? It could be a hot new technology effectively shielded by 2,000 patents and 5,000 attorneys. Or it may really be worth next to nothing as you further examine it under a financially equipped microscope.

Who Has What?

Build a chart of what you bring to the table and what the other offers. Carefully analyze each contribution. If possible, assess value. (Unfortunately, this is easier said than done for many items.) How much is an expert scientist going to cost? How much is he or she really worth? What about someone who answers the phone or a vendor that offers services at a rate so much lower than the competition that is scares you? (It should! See Chapter 14 on budgeting.)

You'll want to create a chart of your own. You'll need one with enough room to accommodate your project's needs, your way of working, or your computer's formats and compatibility. Create your form with enough space to address the number of issues you will deal with. Then add about 50 percent more space for the alternatives you forgot.

Us	Them	Analysis
We need more photos for newsletter.	Not enough time without extra charges.	We don't have the budget.
We could expand editorial.	They could recrop the pictures.	Should probably try both.
We could ask for more budget.	They could try using stock photos.	More budget is unlikely.

Looking At Who Has What for Negotiating Purposes

For example, when hiring a new employee for your project, you may have only a couple of items in your "must have" columns, such as salary level and specific skill requirements, but the person you want (the other side) may have many more requirements for you if you want to put him on the team. That's the purpose of the chart. Are you hiring a certain well-known Mr. Einstein, or someone lacking skills who is in need of a job and looking for (therefore, lacking) experience? How much compensation is required? In an in-house "hire," is this a project that will benefit the employee or a major compromise that will jeopardize the project in the name of the budget?

In a supplier negotiation, you always try to get the most for the least—but without compromising quality or bankrupting the vendor. This is not always an easy negotiation, because what you get may not match your needs. It may turn out to be an apples-to-oranges discussion in which you ordered apples but the supplier delivered oranges, or even potatoes for that matter.

Words from the Wise
The definition of a consultant: Someone who is unemployed but who has a watch *and* a briefcase.

—Anonymous

Time Is Money
If you're in a big hurry, you may get hit with sky-high prices and extra charges. If you aren't in a rush, prices tumble, billable hours decrease, and negotiations favor your side as sellers choose to go with you rather than risk losing the "deal." So, negotiating early in the project will get you a better price than waiting until the last minute.

What to Do

To negotiate successfully, we recommend some standard steps, outlined in the following section. Always let time be on *your* side. Go slowly and accommodate your people and suppliers, but don't pay too much or look rushed because this almost always affects your ability to work out an equitable arrangement. Try using that poker face you've been secretly rehearsing in the bathroom mirror.

Negotiating Step By Step

Here are some basic steps to get you started negotiating with potential employees, contractors, or vendors:

1. *Know your adversaries.* Find out as much as you can about their credentials, reputation, and ability to contribute to your project. This will also help you determine their worth if you have to pay them as an internal employee from your budget or as an outside vendor.

2. *Always be pleasant and avoid confrontation.* Listen to the other person, consider all arguments, and encourage discussion. Emphasize how you can work together. The last thing you want is to put him or her on the defensive.

3. *Make plans to "do lunch."* Breaking bread in a neutral, non-threatening environment is an ideal place to begin a working relationship.

4. *Be clear on your situation and status.* Everyone involved in the negotiation must be fully up to speed on the project and what your negotiation is about.

5. *Slow down if things go awry in early talks.* If the other side is particularly confrontational or completely impossible, try working it out, choosing someone else, or structure the negotiation so that you can do it in writing. Should someone's demands or attitude be outrageous, offer him the bottom line, and show him to the door if that fails. If you *must* have that person because he possesses skills not available elsewhere, you may have to meet his terms.

6. *Don't be forced into anything.* Take time to understand the ramifications of each proposal—but don't take too much time. You should have an idea about each alternative before you get into negotiating mode.

7. *Get back to her.* Your proposition will mean a lot more to someone who needs money or employment after two weeks of not hearing from you while you are both busy and studying possible alternatives.

8. *Accept only acceptable alternatives.* If this sounds obvious, just wait for your first project in which an employee fails to perform or a vendor delivers something that's

Time Is Money
On a project that's costing a lot of money, you need experts familiar with the field of the project to look over the contracts, work with you on the terms, and generally grease the skids to make things work. If the people funding the project won't pay for mandatory assistance and expertise, then the project won't come to fruition anyway.

useless and bills at the same time. The process of project management is fraught with people turning in work that's late, unsuitable, unacceptable, or simply incompetent. Occasionally it can also be too late to use. Avoid this problem by refusing substandard work and contributions. Why? Once you accept any kind of work, you have legally accepted it.(Ask an attorney for your state/provincial regulations!) Once "accepted," your bargaining power is limited—all you can do is withhold payment. (But this tactic gets noticed surprisingly fast.)

Get It in Writing!

Obviously all workable agreements need to be written, but you can also handle initial negotiations that way. Your people may provide potential contributors with a *Request for a Proposal* (RFP), or potential contributors may offer a proposal drafted from scratch without much input from your end. Regardless of who initiates the proposal, you will still need to negotiate the final document, unless the purchase is inexpensive or you're experienced and trusting of the provider.

Sometimes the proposal is simply a jumping-off point for price negotiations and hammering out terms. Read such documents carefully to understand their terms fully. Should things go wrong, the document could be used against your organization—that's why you want to provide a written response acknowledging terms and changes you agree on.

> **Words from the Wise**
>
> When a man is trying to sell you something, don't imagine that he is that polite all of the time.
>
> —Edgar Watson Howe, *Country Town Sayings* (1911)

A Room with a View

Choosing the right place to negotiate facilitates fruitful negotiations. Unfortunately, you may not be able to use the comfortable confines of your well-furnished office or similar environment. Instead, you may negotiate in a crowded room of the seller and be surrounded by managers from both sides. Or worse (at least until video phones actually happen), you may find yourself conducting a faceless interview over the phone with someone you've never laid eyes on. Here's an approach for each scenario, although a comfortable environment for everyone involved is superior to a 90° conference room packed with self-important people and noisy phones:

➤ In your office: Hold all calls—quiet should prevail. Relax and treat your guest to coffee, a snack, a cigar—whatever it takes to keep things calm. Work in Phoenix with the sun pouring in? Lower the blinds somewhat and keep the temperature as close to 70° as possible. Too hot or cold anyway? Take your guest elsewhere, such as a conference room or even a meal out on your tab.

Words from the Wise

The buyer needs a hundred eyes, the seller not one.

—George Herbert, *Jacula Prudentum* (1651)

➤ In a conference room with assorted managers from either or both sides: Have an agenda to pass out to stick to the topics. Set up a starting *and* an ending time. If you can't reach consensus in an hour or two, these may be the wrong people to work with. The exception would be a highly technical project, but laying groundwork before this critical agreement meeting saves time and frayed nerves on both sides.

Negotiating Over Lunch

Choose—if *you* are choosing and paying—a restaurant close by. It should be quiet and appeal to your guest's palette. Should your guest choose the place, you can learn a lot about her by the restaurant she picks.

Negotiating on the Phone

Get the other side's offer, assuming they didn't send it to you in writing already. Make copious notes during offer conversations. Then think about it and call them back with your counteroffer. If you've never met the other side in person, note that some people have an incredible phone manner but may not deliver in person. Ask for and check their references carefully before committing.

Negotiating Electronically

With fax and e-mail becoming so common, many such negotiations happen even without voice contact. This is fine, but if the project schedule is tight and the deal expensive, insist on a face-to-face meeting even if you have to fly somewhere. Otherwise…well, we don't need to tell you.

The Least You Need to Know

➤ Negotiation is skill you'll develop over time. We suggest reading a lot of books on the topic and watching the pros at work.

➤ You can negotiate for almost anything in a project, including better team members, lower prices, and a more realistic schedule.

➤ Know the needs and motivations of your opponent before opening any negotiation.

➤ Getting to a win-win compromise is always preferable to beating your opponent into the ground.

➤ Take a step back in any negotiation before committing to anything you don't totally understand.

we're broke...

Chapter 25

Common Project Problems: Get Them Before They Get You

In This Chapter

➤ A dozen or so common problems to expect on any project of any size

➤ Signs for identifying problems in the making before they undermine project objectives, schedules, or budgets

➤ Strategies to avoid or solve the most common project problems

Okay. You've read every chapter so far, and as hard as you try, some of your projects aren't getting done better. They're taking too long. They're not reaping results. Your team doesn't seem interested in meeting the deadlines. The boss keeps asking for changes. The customers want more results. Even Dogbert's advice and Dilbert's humor don't seem to help when deadlines are slipping and expenses are skyrocketing.

If you think that project management techniques will eliminate all your problems in getting things done on time and within budget, forget it. All projects have problems. In some ways, project management success depends on problem-solving techniques more than any other processes.

The good news is that most project problems are predictable. To help you anticipate problems in your projects, and thus minimize their impact, we describe some of the common project problems in this chapter. Like a Boy Scout, expect to encounter them and be prepared to minimize their impact.

The Floating Start Date

Some projects just never seem to get off the ground because other priorities keep getting in the way. Unfortunately, even though a project may start late, everyone expects it to finish on the original schedule. If you find that your project never gets started, consider these strategies for solving the problem:

➤ Reanalyze the priority for the project. Maybe the project really isn't that important after all.

➤ If the project really needs to be completed as scheduled, communicate the problem to management and get someone else to start the project, or adjust your own work habits to make time for it.

High Water!
Never assume that people will be available when dates slip. If you don't ask about the new schedule and people's availability, you may be the last to find out that you don't have who you need to get things done.

➤ If the project starts late, communicate (in writing as well as verbally) the new finish date to management and the project team. If you need to keep the original date, complete a trade-off analysis of project changes as described in Chapter 23.

➤ Analyze your daily activities and determine if you are wasting time on less important tasks. If you need time-management training, get some. There are many good books that offer guidelines for identifying the time traps in day-to-day work—get one and implement its advice.

There's Not Enough Time for Everything

Things always seem to take longer than we anticipate and there are always more things than we have time to do. In a search for solutions to the ubiquitous problem of finding more time for the project, look into the following alternatives:

➤ If the team is falling behind, don't try to catch up everything on your own. Delegate more of the activities and involve other people in the prioritization and assignment of work.

➤ Eliminate work that is not really necessary. Always question the necessity of each task on a project. Skip tasks that don't count.

➤ Learn to politely say, "No" (or if this isn't possible, at least, "I'll think about it") when someone asks you to add tasks that may interfere with more important project priorities.

➤ Change the priorities for the work. Some things may get done later than originally planned, but this is better than nothing getting done. Of course, you must communicate this change to the other people working on the project.

➤ Work longer hours when this is an option. But don't overdo it for too long, otherwise you and your team will become less productive and less motivated. All work and no play are ingredients for disgruntled project teams and poorly executed projects.

Too Many Reports and Not Enough Communication

Reports are not a substitute for one-on-one communication with your project team. Too many reports also bog projects down in unnecessary paperwork, and this affects quality, schedules, and motivation. To ensure that reports are not substituting for communication, do the following:

➤ Make a list of all the reports being produced for the project, the people responsible, and the content of each report. Then, critically review each report and make sure it is really necessary. Also, make sure that the reports are as simple as possible while still conveying the required information.

➤ Create a card file, or tickler file, reminding you to visit key team members on a regular basis. Note the last date you spoke with each person. Write a note to yourself in your calendar or organizer to talk to specific team members each week or day, as appropriate.

➤ Take people to lunch when you have time and ask them how things are going. Informal get-togethers often result in more open communications and more honest updates on progress.

➤ Keep your door open unless you're really in a private meeting. There is nothing more intimidating than a project manager who is always locked behind a closed door.

Time Is Money
You can avoid many costly problems by simply using the MBWA technique (Management by Walking Around) you learned about in Chapter 17 to keep in touch with project progress and team attitudes. Remember to be casual and interested, not threatening, as you cruise the cubicles, offices, and hallways to find out what's *really* going on.

They Always Need It Faster

Shortening the schedule is a frequent request because of predictable business demands, especially competitive pressures to get products out faster or to generate the revenue anticipated from the completion of a project. It's always good to *consider* faster alternatives for completing a project. However, implementing a "crash" schedule may cause your team to "crash and burn." You must consider the trade-offs in terms of other business priorities, the use of resources, and the costs of getting things done faster. The ways to do this were explained in Chapter 23.

> **Along the Critical Path**
>
> At least once a week, take 15 minutes to review your own work habits as they relate to the project. Are you keeping all stakeholders informed of progress? Have you been communicating clearly? Is the budget up to date? This simple self-reflection can help identify weak areas to focus on before they become structural problems that need immediate attention.

The 90-Percent-Done Syndrome

Many people are optimistic about their ability to make up for lost time. Others simply attempt to look good on paper. For these reasons, whenever we see the phrase "90 percent done" on a project status report, we know there's a big problem.

What is hiding behind that unfinished 10 percent that no one wants to admit? Why does it seem that 90 percent of the effort only takes 30 percent of the time, and the last 10 percent takes 200 percent of the original schedule?

If you see that 90 percent or some other large percentage of a complex task is completed very quickly, but then the work only inches up to 91 and 92 percent over the next couple of status reports, you need to figure out what is really going on by talking to the staff in an environment of support and understanding.

Here are some guidelines for getting at the root of the 90-percent-done syndrome:

➤ Investigate the scope of the remaining work through meetings or one-on-one sessions with key project members. Are there technical difficulties that the team doesn't want to let anyone know about? Should the task be broken down into smaller, more measurable tasks?

➤ Consider whether the remaining 10 percent of the work is really predictable. Creative tasks, such as inventions or coming up with ideas, are often difficult to schedule. In the development of a new technology or in other high-creativity situations, the breakthrough that is required to complete a project may not happen as scheduled. Creative tasks need to be more realistically assessed. You can't schedule spontaneity, so don't try. Just be honest about the creative blocks and document the schedule changes accordingly.

➤ Help the team be honest in their assessment of project status by encouraging open communication and pointing out the problems with being too optimistic about risky endeavors. They may be giving you the estimates they think you want to see—

not the real ones. Reward yourself and the team for honesty and effort rather than false statements of accomplishment or unrealistic commitments to impossible dreams.

The Never-Ending Story of the Reorganization

Possibly the hardest project to manage is the reorganization of people. In addition to the usual project hot spots, reassignments and changes make everyone uncomfortable. Such projects should be planned carefully and acted upon quickly. During the planning of a "reorg," word will often leak out with a subsequent shift in the performance of the people who may be moved around or lose their positions completely.

You can tell if the rumor mill is hard at work during the reorganization because the copy machine will be constantly in need of paper as folks copy their resumes. You'll also see more diligence than usual, as people try extra hard to prove their worth. You may even see employees jockeying into other jobs or departments that they perceive as safe, even if it means a cut in pay or stature.

If ol' Acme, Inc. is planning a shift in personnel and you're the project manager, you can follow one of two paths to get through the project with minimal problems:

1. If no layoffs or reductions in rank are anticipated, be frank with those involved and ensure them up front that nothing negative will occur. You can even solicit proposals for changes from the employees involved. Who knows? They might have better ideas than you do.

2. In a reorganization that reduces salaries or rank, or puts people on the street, the project plan is best executed in secret. It should also be done off site and as quickly as possible. Every moment you waste will undermine the work that needs to get done while the reorganization is in process.

Moving Target Objectives

Changes in project plans are valid for many reasons, as we discussed in Chapter 23. However, sometimes the changes in project goals and objectives seem to occur every time your manager walks into the office. Because there isn't time to plan and adjust for these daily or hourly changes, you just don't bother to update the current plan. This is a bad idea.

Words from the Wise
Now remember, the first step in avoiding a trap is knowing of its existence.

—From the movie *Dune*

Not adjusting the plan is just about the easiest way to end up with a project disaster that we know of. When changes are requested frequently and arbitrarily on a project, it is an indication of a lack of consensus regarding the original plan or some other political problem between your

Words from the Wise

I always figured that I've learned the most about projects from the ones that fell apart. It's a lot like taking the rings off a partly rotten onion. You can't tell what's worthy inside until you see the whole thing. Then you become a project leader: like it or not.

—A project manager with 30+ years experience

manager, the project, the stakeholders, and the organization. Here are some ways to save yourself in this situation:

➤ Make sure the authority for making project changes is clearly documented in the project plan.

➤ Don't start a project until the plan is approved by all appropriate levels of management and other appropriate stakeholders (customer or client).

➤ Don't promise to implement changes in a project until you have time to analyze and document the impact of the changes, and follow all the other rules for making project changes that are discussed in Chapter 23.

The Key Person Always Quits

Many projects depend on the special skills of a single person. If this person leaves, the project could be doomed. However, there are a few basic ways to keep the departure of a key person from becoming a catastrophe:

➤ Keep the key person happy in the first place. Listen. Be aware of problems in advance. Most people don't just walk out—it takes time for them to become disgruntled. If there is a reason for the dissatisfaction, try to find it and fix it.

➤ Cross-train people as work proceeds on the project. This training can minimize the impact of losing a key person on the team because others will be familiar with the project.

➤ Make sure the key person is also part of the team. Try to have someone work with this person to document his or her work. If the key person works in isolation, the impact of this person's absence could be disastrous. On the other hand, if the work is documented, you can usually hire someone else to take over where the other person left off.

Costs Spiral Out of Control

Budget and cost control problems occur for many reasons, including lack of skill or discipline in estimating costs in the original plan; inadequate detail in the plan, which results in vague or inaccurate budget allotments; schedule delays that cause more resources to be used than planned; unforeseen technical problems; changes in material or service costs that weren't anticipated; and changes in the scope of a project that are not reflected in the updates to the budgets—among a myriad of other "justifiable" events.

In spite of the excuses to the contrary, there is only one way to control costs: Keep on top of expenses through regular monitoring and appropriate accounting controls. There simply isn't any other solution.

Cost overruns don't just happen. Costs increase because of poor communications, lack of control, inaccurate reporting, or inadequate documentation of project changes. Through diligent monitoring of expenditures during the project, money problems can be dealt with when budget problems first appear—*before* the costs get out of control.

The Staff Has More Enthusiasm Than Talent

Unfortunately, the most likable people are not always the most competent. If you choose people for their personalities alone and not their skills, you can end up in a situation where a congenial team just doesn't get the work done.

What should you do when you have a great group of fun people working on the project, but they just don't seem to deliver what you need? Here are some guidelines to help you decide:

➤ Develop an objective skills appraisal system to select team members at the beginning of the project. This can help keep friendly but unskilled people off the team. (We covered ways to do this in Chapter 8.)

➤ Watch the team to see if too much time is being spent in social activities. Sometimes the problem isn't a lack of competence at all; instead, the schedule suffers because of too much socializing during work hours. Usually, a simple meeting to reemphasize the priorities of the project can solve this problem.

➤ If a congenial but unskilled person (or group) is willing to be trained and that person has potential, additional education is sometimes a solution. However, getting people up to speed is only an option if the schedule can absorb the time required for training.

➤ If competence is the root of the problem, a consultant or outside vendor can sometimes make up the difference in skills, allowing the friendly person in question to remain on your team in a lesser capacity.

Ultimately, you may need to tell your "friends" that they aren't making the grade. Give people every opportunity to do the job, but if everything else fails, you'll have to find someone else for the team. When this is necessary, cut the ties earlier, rather than later. Getting rid of dead wood on the team is one task that most managers dread and put off. In business, if the goals for the project are important, the project must take priority—no matter how much you like the person (or the group).

The Impossible Remains Impossible

In an attempt to look good, novice project managers often commit to more work than is possible. Even worse, they commit to projects that are impossible from the start. The budget and schedule may be so unrealistic that there is no possibility for completing the work as specified.

It is difficult for project mangers to admit defeat, but often the best solution is to realize that some things just won't happen as planned. Like walking on water, some projects are outside the realm of possibility for ordinary people.

The best way to avoid an impossible project is to never start it in the first place. Document the risks before the project is approved. Let everyone know in advance that the project may be impossible. If you still find yourself caught in an impossible situation, in spite of your realistic communications, the best way to get out is as quickly as possible. As soon as you know the project is impossible, try to convince the powers that be to stop it and quit spending the money. Prolonging the agony makes the problem worse and has brought many a company (and project manager) down in the process.

Politics, Politics, and More Politics

Project Lingo
Political situation— Two people in a room trying to get something done.

Politics in human endeavors are unavoidable because people always have different opinions and motivations. If the political attitudes are annoying but they don't affect the end results of your project, ignore them. It's only when political agendas start undermining project goals that they pose a problem. When this happens, treat the politics as any other conflict and resolve the situation by following the conflict resolution options covered in Chapter 22.

Dopey Fads Mandated by the Boss

Senior management may push one of many ineffectively concocted-over-cocktails ideas on your team. Gently agree to consider the idea no matter how stupid or insufferably dopey the book or seminar where the idea came from. Then, if forced into management-by-fad, put the process into practice but complement it with the basics of good project management, inspired leadership, and common sense to make sure you actually get things done.

Basic work and organizational concepts, like the scientific method, have been honed and refined and repaired since the dawn of time. Proof of their timeless truth are the many large projects, such as the Golden Gate Bridge (1937), that *have* worked thanks to astute project management and good planning. Imagine if The Watermelon Workplace or another equally shallow fad had been used instead. We'd still be taking the ferry from San Francisco to Sausalito and points north.

A Parable of Last Resort

As project manager, you'll be faced with pressure from both above and below in the organization. Things often seem impossible when you have too many roles and too much to do. When you feel that way, consider the following story, which according to a computer industry wag, probably originated at IBM. The story goes something like this:

A new project manager proudly walks into her new office. She arrives just as her predecessor is walking out the door in disgrace. The departing manager tells her that he has left three envelopes numbered 1 through 3 in the top desk drawer. The departing manager instructs the new manager to open an envelope and follow the instructions only when an impossible-to-rectify problem occurs.

Several weeks go by and the project problems seem overwhelming to the new project manager. Everything is behind schedule and the new manager must explain the failures to the executive committee in a review meeting. Not knowing what to do, the project manager decides to open the first envelope before going to the meeting. The note inside instructs, "Blame it on the last manager." The new manager decides this is a way off the hook. In the meeting she points her finger to the last manager's inept handling of the project. The committee agrees and reluctantly approves more time and money to complete the project.

Time goes by and the project once again becomes mired in the murk. Stalled and without a clue on how to handle the problems, the manager must approach the executive committee for more project moola. Opening envelope number two, she is advised to blame the problem on the inept project team. Again, this tactic proves successful and the grumbling committee caves in and offers the project more time and more money. On leaving the meeting, the committee admonishes the project manager with, "This better not happen again!"

Six months fly by with winter changing to spring. Again overwhelmed with problems, the project manager feels trapped and helpless. The project is late again, way over budget, and probably doomed to failure. She pauses, takes a deep breath and then opens the third and final envelope. The instructions are simple: "Prepare three envelopes…"

You should remember this story when faced with the fatalism that infects some projects. Before you give in and write your envelopes, remember that almost anything *can* be fixed—but not if you blame the wrong source for the problems. You, as leader, must use what you know about project management to pull the rabbit out of the hat that others are assuming won't appear. If you do your work to plan and scope the project at the beginning and keep tracking things as they go along while always keeping the communications open, you'll probably never need the three envelopes. Yes, you'll have problems—but they will probably be solvable—or at least not fatal.

A Bag of Tricks

At this point, you have a bag of tricks for dealing with project problems. With these strategies and the reports and processes we cover in the rest of the book, you should be able to guide your project to a successful conclusion. In the next chapter, we'll explain how a project should be brought into the final project management phase. The closing phase is a time to wrap things up, but it's also a time to acknowledge your team's accomplishment of finishing the project on time and within budget. It's time to pop that champagne!

The Least You Need to Know

➤ Ask questions, listen, observe, and communicate with candor and clarity. If you do these four things, you'll reduce the impact of almost every project problem.

➤ Remember that problems and change go hand in hand. Change may cause new problems, but change handled well can often be the best solution to keeping a project on track.

➤ Always be honest (not brutal) in your assessment of project problems and make sure to support your honest appraisals with documentation.

➤ Tell your boss or customer as soon as you know something is wrong. Waiting will only delay the inevitable and make the problem worse.

Part 6
The Closing Phase

Whether it's a summer vacation or a visit to the smiling Dr. Kevorkian, there comes a time when all things good (or bad) must come to an end. The swan song. The last breath. Finish. Fin. That's all, folks! Likewise, your project must *undergo the closing phase so you can wrap up the details, pay the bills, and move on to the next project with a sense of satisfaction—or at least without regret. That's what this short section is all about—the steps to bring a project to a proper conclusion so life can go on.*

Chapter 26

Will the Last One Out Please Turn Off the Lights...

In This Chapter

➤ The steps for closing a project

➤ Moving team members from the project into other roles

➤ Projects that have taken on a life of their own

➤ Can you fix a project or should you end it now?

If you've successfully completed your project, the closing phase is a time of celebration and accomplishment. But not all projects end gracefully. Without a proper closing, some projects ramble on forever like a rickety truck on a bumpy road.

In this chapter, you'll learn how to close down any project, including those that finish successfully, those that must die a natural death, and the more annoying ones in which team members never seem to leave. Closure is important because it is the point at which, wiping your sweaty brow with relief, you say to yourself, "It's over." (And regardless of the outcomes, break out the chilled champagne! You deserve it.)

Is There Life After Project Termination?

When the end is near, project members get nervous. What will their next assignment consist of? Will there be a next assignment at all? Unfortunately, this morale problem occurs with the worst possible timing—when a project is almost complete. The problem runs deeper than just the risk of unemployment or a new assignment in Siberia. It means the end of budding friendships, interesting after-hours nights at the tavern playing poker for pennies, and the other good times that accompany a well-run project. Your people will miss it. You will too...really.

Why Is a Closing Phase Necessary?

People need to be acknowledged for goals that are achieved and to feel like the work is complete. Because project managers need to evolve their skills for managing projects, the techniques, processes, and procedures used on one project should be analyzed so they can be adapted and improved in the future. These are the most fundamental and underlying reasons to formally terminate a project. In addition, the following tasks are part of the termination process for most projects and are necessary to bring one to final closure:

➤ **Meet with stakeholders** to get their final approval of the project. They are the reason for the project existing in the first place. Their approval signals the project's completion.

➤ **Finalize all contractual commitments** to vendors, suppliers, and customers. This may include reports or final payments. It may also include letters thanking vendors for a job well done, when appropriate.

➤ **Transfer responsibilities** to other people, if required. For example, the end results of some projects are inputs for new projects to be managed by other people. Consider a project to design a new product, for example. Once the product is designed, the responsibility for it is transferred to the manufacturing department, where the product will be produced and distributed. The development of the on-going production system for the product becomes another project. In order to make this transfer, there are reports, drawings, and documentation that must be completed before manufacturing can begin. These activities are all part of the final termination of the product design project.

➤ **Reassign people** in the project and redirect efforts to other priorities or projects. People may be returned to their functional areas or assigned new projects, or both.

➤ **Release resources,** such as equipment and materials, so they can be disposed of or used for other work. Some construction and manufacturing projects also require clean-up tasks to prepare the facilities for new activities.

➤ **Complete the final accounting** of the project. This includes totaling the costs, paying all the bills, and closing the books on the project.

➤ **Document the results** of the project and make recommendations for the future. There is more information on the final reports and documentation required for a project later in this chapter. The amount and detail of final documentation will vary, based on the size, importance, and issues associated with each project.

Like a living entity, projects grow, mature, and finally become memories after the work is complete. And like the Energizer Bunny, some projects just won't quit.

Projects that aren't closed formally may continue to consume resources required elsewhere. Most projects should end as soon as either the goals have been achieved or you recognize that there's no hope for success.

Closing a Small Project

In small projects, the formal closing (also called a termination by some project managers) can be a simple matter of having a meeting with the team and the stakeholders to acknowledge attainment of the project goals and writing a brief final report on the project. The closing meeting should focus only on the accomplishments of the completed project, so people feel satisfied with the work performed.

Closing a Large Project

For large projects, the closing phase can be a time of stress and anxiety. Team members may have friendships and a sense of family. Some team members will be going their separate ways, adding to the anxiety. Termination of a long project with a close-knit team is always difficult, and it can be complicated. However, the frustration can be reduced if the team members are acknowledged for their current accomplishments and then given new assignments and challenges as soon as possible.

Because some people fear leaving the security of an established project team or changing roles after the project is complete, it is often difficult to get the final details of a large project completed. People may continue to work on insignificant tasks related to the project.

As a project manager, it is your responsibility to see that the project ends. The project manager should help the people involved with the project move forward into new challenges and opportunities. To reduce the stress associated with project termination, remind your team members of the overall goals that have been achieved and that the stakeholders consider the project completed. Emphasize the importance of the project to the business and their contribution in meeting the project objectives. Then remind them of the new goals and objectives they have yet to achieve on other projects and assignments.

In addition to having a formal meeting, or even a party, to acknowledge project completion, many projects involve other formal termination tasks, some of which we mentioned earlier, including reassigning personnel; auditing the final expenses and closing the books on the project; archiving any drawings or other project materials; passing the end results of the project on to another organization (for example, setting up a product for manufacturing or installing the final product at a customer's site); informing other departments, including purchasing, finance, manufacturing, or whoever needs to know, that the project is done; and completing other miscellaneous documentation of the project. And, of course, there will be an extensive final report.

The closing tasks for a large project are not always clear-cut. When such a project is almost complete, there may be some small details that need to resolved. The project manager must decide when a project is "finished" so it can move into the termination phase. Don't drag the close-out phase and clean-up details to keep the project alive. This is a common problem in large projects. Get on with it, because there are always more projects—and the next one will offer new relationships and new challenges.

When major goals for a project are complete, begin the closing phase of the project. Because of loose ends, the termination of a large project may be a mini-project in its own right, demanding schedules, priorities, and budgets. Identify the major steps in the project close-out and implement them as quickly as possible. Follow all the steps and methods for managing any other project.

For many projects, large or small, a checklist is useful in determining the requirements for termination. An example of a termination checklist for a complex product development project is provided to demonstrate the kinds of tasks that might be required to terminate a large project. Of course, the checklist may include entirely different elements for other kinds of projects, but our example should give you the basic idea of what to consider.

Under the Microscope, Again...

Closure is also the point at which management evaluates your success in meeting the goals and your skills as a project manager. Not all projects glide to success like a 747 touching down softly—some come to a crashing halt like the ill-fated *Hindenburg*. Termination replaces closure for such a monster, but the steps to closure are the same as for any project. Big success? Dismal failure? The termination process is essentially identical except that the smiles may be replaced with frowns.

Project Shutdown

The cleanest closure of a project comes when all work is done and team members already have other work or a return to their permanent jobs in place. The easiest project to close down is the small one in which tangible (visible) results demonstrate completion to one and all. For example, closing down a newsletter development project is relatively easy. Once it reaches print and is distributed, everyone can hold the tangible results in their hands. At least until the next issue!

On the other hand, closing down the project to build the twin World Trade Center towers in New York is much more complex, because not only are there multiple subplans, but for the uninitiated project manager, reaching the state of completion may seem impossible. Yes, the steel skeleton is in place, but what about electrical wiring, plumbing, elevators, and interior walls? In addition, some work may linger on. After completion, repairs may be on the project manager's shoulders as necessary. In a sense, the project continues rather than winding down in a planned and predictable process. While 99.8 percent of the work is complete, that other .2 percent must be addressed by the remnants of the team. Or outsiders must be hired at higher rates if former team members are no longer available.

The most frustrating kind of shutdown is rightfully called "project murder" (yes, that's the real term used to describe the cancellation of a project). You won't read about such murders in the newspaper (usually), but it does materially affect the lives of the project team and their leader. In this kind of termination, work may be suddenly halted even though the project is proceeding on schedule and within its allocated budget. Then we can only watch dumbstruck as the guillotine blade softly falls...

To shut down a project, steps are taken toward an orderly closure. Not all of these procedures will be popular with team members (or you) when a windfall paycheck suddenly disappears like teardrops in the rain. In a large project, shutdown may occur in phases, as one major component of the project is completed earlier than others as projected in the project plan. Shutdown of each facet should be treated similarly to the termination of the entire project. After all, each of these facets amounts to a project unto itself and deserves the celebration that accompanies completion of any project. The steps to project termination are as follows:

Project Lingo
Project murder may sound like the plot from an Agatha Christie novel, but it's really the sudden termination of a project for reasons that range from rational to absurd. An attempt on a project's life may take place during economic downturns, acquisition of the parent organization, or the unexpected death of a company's visionary founder.

Time Is Money
The formal ending of a project takes you off the hook for the budget, so everyone concerned must be fully aware that the deed is done. Otherwise, miscellaneous charges may pop up assigned to your now-closed project accounts. Should bills be unavailable upon termination of a project, ask whomever handles finances to build separate accounts for each one with your review before payment.

1. **Decision to terminate.** Careful scrutiny of the project tasks disclose that the project is (or should be) complete. Visual inspection must accompany this conclusion. It's always possible that a loose end remains or a part of the team has been feeding you overly optimistic information of their progress. (See "Use MBWA (Management by Walking Around)" in Chapter 17.)

The steps for an orderly closing phase for your project.

The Project Closing Process

Identify Final Tasks that require Completion

⬇

Reassign Staff if Required

⬇

Release Equipment and Materials for Other Projects

⬇

Final Accounting and Close Books

⬇

Final Report and Final Meeting

⬇

2. **Task list.** Make a list of small tasks that need to be accomplished and get them taken care of. For example, if the project requires user documentation and it's not fully "user ready," this must be done NOW!

3. **Consensus.** You, the team, and management agree that the project has satisfactorily met its goals. If termination is for other reasons, such as failure or budget depletion, consensus is limited to an agreement to shut down the project before more money is tossed over the cliff.

4. **Meetings.** Hold individual meetings with team members and team managers who reported to you. Thank them for their contribution, even if they did a lousy job. (They're someone else's problem now.) Make notes on what they thought of the project highlights and "lowlights," your leadership (take a deep breath first), and what they would like to do in the future if you don't already know their intentions.

5. **Communication.** All team personnel must be instructed in writing when the project will end. This puts pressure on the stragglers who need a little more time to complete their role. If you suspect that more time is needed, set the end date several weeks into the future with weekly reminders of the drop-dead date. For real problem people, visit them daily to assess their progress and remind them of the date.

6. **More communication.** Outside suppliers and vendors must be notified that the project will cease to exist in "X" number of days, weeks, or months. Since the project is ending, bills not received within 30 days of the termination date will not be accepted. (Be flexible on this one. It's really a tactic to get the bills coming in the door from vendors with tardy billing practices.) It also saves you interest charges, and really prompt payment may knock a percentage off the bill. If possible, check purchase orders to see what's outstanding.

Checklist for Closing a Large Project					
DESCRIPTION	NEEDED? YES	NO	REQUIRED DATE	RESPONSIBLE PERSON	NOTES
Identify Remaining Work	☐	☐			
Closing/Termination Plan	☐	☐			
Personal Evaluations	☐	☐			
Close-Out Work Orders	☐	☐			
Audit Final Changes	☐	☐			
Pay All Vendors	☐	☐			
Close-Out Books/Audit	☐	☐			
Final Delivery Instructions	☐	☐			
Customer Training	☐	☐			
Notify Purchasing of Completion	☐	☐			
Equipment Redeployed	☐	☐			
Materials Returned to Inventory	☐	☐			
Staff Reassigned	☐	☐			
Close-Down Procedures	☐	☐			
Engineering Documentation	☐	☐			
Final Staff Meeting(s)	☐	☐			
Final Report and Review Meeting	☐	☐			

A checklist for terminating a project.

7. **Even more communication.** Let managers of "borrowed" employees, temporary agencies, and contractors know—in writing—that the project's termination date is near. This provides the managers time to find other opportunities for their people or move them back into their usual job responsibilities.

8. **The books are closed.** Assuming that you are working with a finance department, once a project is complete, finance *must* close the books so that wayward bills aren't charged against a nonexistent budget. Most companies assign accounts for projects with code numbers. Assuming your project receives one or more codes, have finance render the codes invalid. That way you can review any invoices that pop up for legitimacy prior to payment or rejection.

9. **The celebration.** Once a project is (successfully) completed, a beer-and-pizza type event should be held. Awards may be in order for team members who performed above and beyond the line of duty. This event is not only fun, but it marks the official end of the project in everyone's mind. If the project was a flop, but not because of team failure, such an event should still be held, even if the occasion is somewhat more subdued. If you or the team failed, save the pizza money.

THIS WAY

Along the Critical Path

There is evidence, albeit limited, that something besides blueprints was used to build some of Egypt's most important monuments. It's unlikely computerized PERT technology was at work since even the Apple II was two millennia away, but several surviving documents and carvings appear to be a list of steps to be taken, the responsible party (probably a slave overseer), and some kind of obscure timing/dating system. Or, it could have been misinterpreted by archeologists. Maybe it's an order for take-out lunch from the local deli.

10. **Dispersal of resources.** An inventory is taken of current supplies and equipment. Borrowed and rented equipment is returned, unused supplies sent back for credit where possible, and unrecyclable trash hauled off to the landfill. If the project was large and ends up owning a lot of surplus equipment, an auction can be the ticket to parting with 12 table saws or a bank of 48 slightly dated computers. Money from such an event can go into the organization's general fund, be distributed to team members in the form of profit sharing, or donated.

11. **The new kids.** The transition team is brought in and trained. These are the people who will staff your project if it's one of that nature.

12. **Handing over the keys.** A transfer of responsibilities takes place if new staff must be brought in to man the completed project. (The people who built the Aswan High Dam probably aren't the same ones who manage its power generation and flood-gates. Instead, a new, specially trained crew was employed for this task to replace those whose expertise focused on pouring concrete.) You'll learn more about final reports later in this chapter.

Three Ways to Deep-Six a Workforce

Al Capone's mob might have other ideas, but there are three ways to terminate a project that are standard in the project management biz: inclusion, integration, or extinction.

You need to choose the right method for your project or you'll have lots of unhappy campers with nowhere to go.

Inclusion

Inclusion is a happy ending of sorts. Your project proved successful and upon nearing completion, it was absorbed into the organization. Again, it may become a part of the company or be run as a separate organization. In the happiest scenario, many of the original team members keep their jobs and continue to contribute. However, it may be that all staff are replaced because they are deemed unsuitable for the post-completion phase of the project. Some team members may choose to leave anyway, because while they found the project phase exciting, the thought of running day-to-day operations makes them yawn. You may find yourself the head of a hot new company, or updating your résumé and looking for another project.

Integration

Integration is the most common technique for dissolving a project workforce. Team members are reintegrated into the organization from which they were borrowed. On a long project, integration becomes complex, because management may have been forced to fill slots held by the team members. A new position must be found for the returning team member satisfactory to the employee and the headcount. Often new skills acquired by the project member open the door to new job responsibilities.

Extinction

The dinosaur route—outright extinction of a project and everything related to it—is an all too common route to unload personnel. Once a project is closed down, the people are simply let go. (There's a theory that a large meteorite striking the earth off the Yucatan invented this kind of staff reduction.)

Give It Up!

At the end of a project, especially a major one that has absorbed six or more months of your life (some take decades), there's a come-down period you should be ready for. It's like postpartum blues. You've spent nine months devoting your energies to a specific project (goal: a baby). You've been so focused on that one goal that once it is successfully achieved, you feel lost, directionless, sad. And you feel these emotions even though you know what your next project will be (raising the baby). Think how much more difficult it would be to cope if you didn't have the prospect of a new project and had to adjust to your former everyday routine.

Time Is Money
Leave good documentation for your successors. When you consider the project to bring the water from upstate New York to the Big Apple, you'll understand why this is a good idea. Scheduled completion is around 2007. Given current job tenure across the nation, chances are at least three people will run the project over the next ten years.

High Water! Changing from a role in a fast-paced project to the drudgery of answering piles of monotonous memos and megabytes of energy-sapping e-mail takes time. Most people adjust within a few days, but if feelings of anxiety persist for more than a few weeks, consider seeing your Doc about an evaluation. Or maybe you just need a long-deserved vacation.

Suddenly, you are no longer be the head honcho of a project with team members constantly seeking your advice and decisions. Instead, you return to civilian life with your normal job duties and responsibilities. There may be a period of let-down, in which the project stays on your mind and you keep thinking of improved ways to accomplish some tasks, or ideas come to you that might have better met the project's goals. Your "symptoms" may indeed be real. But if it's your skill and desire, freelance project managers do well and make good incomes, depending on their experience and success. This could be you! And be encouraged: There's always another project to manage somewhere.

Right now you should have a celebration. Your project is done (except for the final report, which you'll learn how to write in the next chapter. You didn't think you'd get away without another report, did you?).

Get your team together. Revel in your accomplishments. Then get on to the next project.

The Least You Need to Know

➤ Dissolving a project takes time and deliberate effort on your part.

➤ All projects *must* come to a end. Period.

➤ Closing down a project is a process that follows a predetermined series of steps.

➤ You need to find a place for the displaced workers if they came from within your organization.

➤ A journal and final report will help others learn from your successes and mistakes. Update the journal each day before you forget things.

Chapter 27

The Final Evaluation: The Short and Long of It

In This Chapter

➤ Why a final evaluation is a good idea

➤ Why do some projects succeed and others don't?

➤ Understanding your successes and shortcomings

➤ Talking back: The final report

➤ Team member performance appraisals

Now that your project is shut down, you may think you're finally done. But there's one more important step: The final project evaluation. The purpose of this step is to appraise your actions: What you did well and what you could have done better. Only through a final project evaluation will you learn how to better manage the next project.

The best project manager builds his or her skills over time with experience gleaned from multiple projects—even those that turn out to be fiascoes. Through an effective post-mortem, lessons learned from the project can be effectively applied to the next project. The final evaluation should be held after the project's completion. It should happen whether the project achieved its goals or evolved into a dismal failure.

Small leftover tasks, such as installing the built-in office coffeemaker or screwing in light bulbs, shouldn't delay the final evaluation from going forward. However, large leftover tasks indicate a project that's incomplete, making it too early to analyze results—even if the scheduled completion date has come and gone.

There are three components to the final evaluation: project assessment, a final written report, and team member performance reviews. A final meeting of the core team is often in order as well, as this will assist you in evaluating the project and producing input for the report. The team's technical expertise and experiences may provide data which you hadn't previously considered.

Understanding Why Some Projects Succeed and Others Flop

It may seem at this point that project management is a lot of work without a lot of guaranteed benefits. The chance that a project succeeds or fails varies according to the nature of the industry, project complexity, personalities involved, and the culture of the company. A fast-moving project that would fly through an aggressive start-up company might stumble quickly on the bureaucracy of a large public utility, stuffy corporation, or other sluggish organization.

In Chapter 1, we listed several general factors that contribute to the success of projects and project managers alike. That list probably makes more sense now that you have gone through the entire process and methodology on your own.

As you consider your own project experiences, remember these factors and determine if your project and your skills as a project manager measure up.

Words from the Wise

Those who cannot remember the past are condemned to repeat it.

—George Santayana, *A Life of Reason* (1905–06)

Projects that don't meet the majority of their objectives should be studied closely to understand what went wrong. But successful projects also deserve inspection and evaluation. There are lessons to be learned from every project.

By the way, a project that is terminated for unforeseen changes in the environment is not a failed project, it is just a project that was not brought to fruition. Projects that fail due to unforeseen circumstances or changes in the organization's requirements, culture, or direction are not true project failure either, although you may have trouble convincing the person paying the bills otherwise. Projects that are extremely late, come in over budget, use too many resources, or leave participants and clients unhappy are projects that were not properly managed. Depending on how much the problems impacted the budget and schedule, give yourself credit for completing the beast. At least it got done.

Why Projects Don't Meet Their Goals

There are several basic reasons why projects fail to meet their goals relating to cost, performance, and schedules. Predictably, these reasons are opposite of the reasons why projects succeed. Here are some common reasons why projects don't live up to expectations:

➤ Your plan is too simple, too complex, or unrealistic.

➤ Major conflicts are not ironed out and waste time and resources.

➤ Your leadership or that of managers under you is unskilled or inappropriate in style.

➤ The initial goals and objectives were not completely agreed upon and no resolution was forthcoming.

➤ Inadequate monitoring and controls keep problems from being anticipated or dealt with immediately upon their recognition.

➤ Staffing is inappropriate or insufficient.

➤ Tasks and resources required are overlooked and must be forced into the project later, if that's even possible.

➤ Weak communication between team members, the project manager, and senior management slows decision making.

➤ The wheel is reinvented. Rather than study other, similar projects and their fate, an inexperienced project manager jumps in headfirst taking his or her team down the primrose path.

Why Projects Succeed

The whole reason you read this book is to learn how to make projects succeed, and if you follow the processes presented here, we bet you'll have a better chance than most. We believe that projects succeed for the following reasons:

➤ A realistic plan has been built and agreed upon with stakeholders through careful analysis of the requirements involved.

➤ Conflict is quickly accelerated to the project manager's office for resolution.

➤ You as project manager are a strong leader and click both with team members and senior management.

➤ Goals and objectives are clear and concise. Team members fully understand them.

➤ Careful reporting and monitoring are in place for tracking the project from start to finish.

➤ The right people in the right number are available at the right time to handle each and every task.

➤ 98 percent of task and resource requirements were successfully identified and budgeted for before the project start date.

➤ The manager participates routinely with team members to help out, listen to their problems, and see firsthand what needs be done to address them.

➤ Similar projects are studied to learn what problems to expect and how to handle them.

Your Evaluation of the Project

Before you formally evaluate your completed or closed-down project, you need input from your core team. Ask for a brief written report or provide them with a simple questionnaire to complete. Then schedule an informal meeting with key players and ask them their opinions about the project and what they would do better next time. Take notes so you remember comments and confirm that you value their input.

The first question when evaluating a project is whether the desired results were accomplished. Then consider the stages from start to finish to understand what worked and what didn't. Look closely at problems and how you and your team coped with them. Picking up the pieces and successfully gluing them back together is an art. Consider when you did this well and when you could have done better.

Sit Down with Pen in Hand

There are no hard-and-fast rules for project evaluation. Essentially you match your achievements to the project's goals. If what you produce lines up clearly with well-defined goals, chances are you've succeeded. If you have met the goals only part way, your project may be considered a success by some and a failure by others. The toughest evaluation is one in which the goals were fuzzy to begin with.

To evaluate your project's success (or lack of success), make a list of the project's accomplishments and place it next to the goals page(s). Study each list, checking off goals as you consider your list of accomplishments. This is the best way to evaluate your project.

It's a Wrap! Time Now for the Final Report

With the exception of the smallest projects (and sometimes even those), a final report is mandated by management at the close of the project. The final report for a megaproject is more formal, and obviously longer than for a small, simple project. As we mentioned earlier, reports are necessary for both successfully completed projects and for those that are canceled. On a successful project, the final report may precipitate bonuses for the team members and their mentor (that's you). If the project went belly-up, the report serves to document the problems and help others avoid the quicksand you and your team slipped into. The report can also document why a project problem wasn't your fault. (To learn more, read "The Political Impact of Final Reports" later in this chapter.)

The Final Report

The final report is both a history of the project and a final evaluation of performance. Where the final report for a small project may be no more than a two-page memo, the report for a large project may be 10 or 20 pages in length. If you kept a project diary (remember back in Chapter 19?), producing the final report is relatively easy.

All of the topics covered in the project report for a simple project should be included in the final report for a large project, but they are covered in more detail. The main things to have in the final report include:

➤ Overview of the project including revisions to the original project plan

➤ Summary of major accomplishments

➤ Analysis of achievements compared to original goals for the project

➤ Final financial accounting and explanation of variances from the budget

➤ Evaluation of administrative and management performance

➤ Team performance (this section should be confidential when it applies to specific individuals and their performance)

➤ Issues or tasks that require further investigation

➤ Recommendations for future projects of this type

➤ Special acknowledgments to team members

In addition, the following elements are appropriate to include in the final reports for more complex projects:

➤ A summary of performance issues, conflicts, and resolutions

➤ Results of each phase of the project, including actual versus forecast dates and the budget versus actual expenses (budget use, additions, and so on, require thorough documentation)

➤ Description of ongoing project-related activities that will require further team member participation (if any)

➤ Recommendations for changes to future projects so that they will run more smoothly and be more compatible with the sponsoring organization

➤ In-depth analysis of reporting procedures and recommendations for improvements

➤ Analysis of the project management process as a whole

In each section of a final report on a project, the procedures used in the project should be analyzed. Things that worked should be acknowledged. Things that didn't work should be explained. Recommendations for improvements in future implementations of the project methodology should be made, with clear examples and rationales for the changes. All key team members should either contribute to the report or review its contents for accuracy before the report is finalized. You can have others write and submit their relevant portions of the final report, and then after editing, add your own two cents' worth as an overview to cement the document.

Packaging Options for the Report

Your final report should be reviewed by everyone involved in the project, your management, project stakeholders, and the administrative assistant that makes the copies. You may want to break it into five sections, as outlined in the following sections.

The Executive Summary

This one-to-two-page document summarizes the report's content for those who need a quick briefing and don't have time or are unable to digest the entire document.

The Report, Part A

This section contains information that can be disseminated to all team members, managers, and other interested parties. It includes a detailed review of the project and a goal-by-goal assessment of the project's success in meeting each one.

The Report, Part B

This section includes information that may be for management only or confidential in nature. (See "Confidential Reports," below.) It can contain information not appropriate for team members' eyes, such as salaries, team-member performance, and recommendations for using the results of the project. It can also include the financial reports for the project.

The Project Plan

The project's overall plan should be included along with copies of the goals information. If it fits and makes you look good, include the original plan and the final plan so readers can see how you met the scheduled dates.

Miscellaneous Components

If tangible proof of a project's success is possible, for example, the opening of a new store or discovery of life on another planet, photos can be included in this section and referenced from report Parts A and B.

Confidential Reports

Confidential reports are the most difficult to manage. Consisting of anything from a new product kept away from competitors to government and military material, it may be that your own boss isn't authorized to read it. All such documents must be kept under lock and key, be it a locking desk drawer or a sealed document repository much like a large bank vault. In James Bond terms, a portion of a report may be "for your eyes only," with the rest available for distribution. If you find yourself in the awkward situation of not knowing what to release, get advice from someone who can help you make that decision and is privy to the report's contents anyway.

The Political Impact of Final Reports

In a politically sensitive organization, a negative report can cause problems. Before you state emphatically that old so-and-so was the major roadblock to successfully completing the project, you had better be in line for another job or an unemployment check.

As was strongly (if wrongly) suspected on the Warren report on the slaying of President Kennedy, for political reasons there were two versions of the report: one for the public, and another for high-level government officials and operatives. You may want to consider this tactic to present complete information to your managers, while in a second brief report, withholding proprietary or personal information from rank-and-file team members.

In the building of the atomic bomb for World War II, a few senior government officials knew what was being developed. But thousands of project team members learned only about the part, system, or explosive components they were personally responsible for designing and building. It wasn't until months after the surrender of Japan that some of these people put the pieces together, so to speak.

> **Time Is Money**
> For a lesson on writing useful but inoffensive reports, study those of your predecessors who still work for the company and haven't been assigned to janitorial duties. If you're not a strong writer, leave controversy out of the report or keep it brief. Avoid sarcasm and wit. Your words may be misconstrued. Some comments are better made to management verbally than going on the record.

Who Accomplished What and How Well?

If your project involved people, you'll likely be called on to evaluate the performance of each team member. This may be limited to core team members, or it may apply to all team members, and even outside vendors, consultants, and suppliers. The evaluations can be used for anything ranging from promotions to new assignments to layoffs. In a project in which a team member's contribution is made before the project terminates, a review is held when the team member departs rather than waiting for project closure. Why? Because on a really large project, completion and the review might be years away.

Many companies have standard evaluation procedures that must be followed and the personnel department will insert itself into the evaluation process. Chances are personnel will provide standard evaluation forms for both you and the employee to fill out. In a matrixed project organization (see Chapter 18), other managers who work with the team member may contribute to the written evaluations as well.

The basic criteria for appraising team member performance include the following:

➤ Quality of work

➤ Timeliness

➤ Administrative performance

➤ Attitude

➤ Technical ability

➤ Consistency in meeting deadlines

➤ Cost consciousness

➤ Creativity

➤ Ability to work as part of team

➤ Communication Skills

➤ Recommendations for improvement

When giving a performance review in person, try for a relaxed atmosphere away from other team members. For stellar performers, this is a good time to hand out any bonus checks, with the agreement that the team member will keep it quiet so as not to make other members unhappy.

The Bottom Line and You

Besides the formal review of a project, every project manager needs to do some personal soul-searching to understand why a particular project went well or why it went poorly. After the project has been completed for a while and the emotion is gone, stand back and look at the project and your own management skills as objectively and dispassionately as possible. What did you do well? What could you have done better? What do you still need to learn? These are the observations, if acted on and taken seriously, that will help you prosper, develop, and improve as a project manager.

At this point, you have been exposed to the complete process of project management. You have learned how to complete project management calculations and develop diagrams, reports, and communications that will help you plan, monitor, and control your project to a successful conclusion. Congratulations—and good luck in your role as project manager!

The Least You Need to Know

> ➤ Each project is a learning experience.
> ➤ Once a project ends, take stock of what went right and what went wrong.
> ➤ On most projects, a final report is required to inform all participants and stakeholders of the project's results.
> ➤ Your daily project log or diary can be a useful tool in looking for problems and assembling the final report.
> ➤ Not all report information should be available to team members and outsiders.
> ➤ Performance should be formally or informally (depending on the organization) reviewed when team members depart the project or when the project is completed.

Part 7
The Final Chapter

You can do most things in project management in person or by hand, but why waste the effort if you can automate the processes to save time? In the next and final chapter of this adventure in project management, you'll learn about the options and benefits in using project management software to help you implement the administrative aspects of project management with less effort and more consistency. You will learn that there are easy ways to develop the schedules, reports, and changes in your project plan by choosing the right kind of computerized project management software for your business.

Software for All Projects Great and Small

Creating a detailed project plan and keeping it up to date for most non-trivial projects can be a very time-consuming process if completed manually. The complexity of figuring in vacations, holidays, weekends, early-starts, and other factors can be overwhelming to someone inexperienced in project management techniques or short on pencils. The details involved in producing networks and work breakdown structures seem daunting, and assembling a budget can be tedious.

Just producing the plan is a lot of work for a project. And, as you've hopefully concluded by now, project management entails more than just creating a good plan. Producing the reports, updating the charts, and incorporating changes to a project plan along the way adds complexity and more paperwork. Of course, if you need to manage multiple projects at the same time, the calculations, graphs, and reports can seem impossible.

In this chapter you'll learn about software that can help you keep it all straight. And, because the programs are easy to use, you won't have any excuses for not keeping your plans up-to-date.

Software that Simplifies the Details

All the graphing, changing, and reporting in project management can drive you crazy. Some naive managers simply reject project management methods because of the reports involved. Instead, they choose to manage projects with intuition and guesswork. (And much of the time they guess wrong.) But the benefits of the methods are too important to be ignored because the charts and graphs take time to produce. Today, thanks to the rise of the personal computer, there is a solution so everyone can benefit from using project management methods. There are easy-to-use project management programs such as Microsoft Project that anyone can master in a few hours.

With the right project management program, you can concentrate on the management of the project, with more time for thinking and planning, and let the computer provide tactical support in the form of charts, graphs, schedules, and resource allocations.

This chapter covers the basics of selecting and using computerized project management programs, so you won't give up on project management before you get started.

What Can Project Management Programs Do?

Project management programs range in capabilities from simple scheduling programs that produce Gantt charts to prodigious mainframe applications that are integrated with the corporation's budgeting, marketing, manufacturing, personnel, and other management information systems. We'll concentrate on the types you run on PCs.

The underlying methods supported by most project management programs are similar to those presented in this book. Depending on the capabilities of the program, you enter task sequences, resources, dates, and costs, just as described in the last nine chapters—and the computer calculates or modifies the schedules, budget, or resource utilization for you. Most programs even draw the networks or can convert one network format into another.

In addition to helping you calculate schedules and costs, project management programs produce a wide variety of reports, from simple to comprehensive. If you have a special project management requirement, such as a custom report or chart, there is probably a program out there with the capability to produce the output you need.

Not even the most sophisticated software package is a substitute for competent leadership and skilled decision making, and by itself it can't correct any task-related problems or human-centered conflicts. But project management software can be a terrific boon to the project manager tracking interrelated variables, schedules, resources, costs, and tasks that come into play. Although not all programs do all of the following things, most of them can help you do these things:

How project man-agement software works.

➤ Graph costs, schedules, and resource utilization using Gantt charts, histograms, line diagrams, and a variety of other charts.

➤ Create standard and custom reports, including standard accounting and tracking. Some programs will even produce special report formats required by government agencies, such as the Department of Defense (DOD).

➤ Maintain resource and project calendars that record the availability of staff and equipment. These internal program calendars are used to create optimum schedules. This feature allows the project manager to establish workweeks based on actual workdays and specify non-work periods such as weekends, holidays, and vacations. The project calendar can be printed out in detail or in a summary format.

➤ Make schedule changes based on a variety of resource leveling parameters (for example, no overtime!) and priority scheduling attributes.

➤ Maintain skills inventories that match resources to task requirements.

➤ Track and schedule multiple projects at the same time. Some packages feature a single, comprehensive database that enables cross-project analysis and reporting. Cost and schedule modules share common data files that allow integration among projects and minimize problems of schedule inconsistencies and redundancies.

➤ Allow multiple people to access, input, and report on project data at the same time.

➤ Collapse the view of projects by work breakdown structure or organization structure, subproject or milestone.

➤ Calculate and display the critical path for a network.

➤ Display alternative schedules, task assignments, and cost criteria, so the immediate impact of schedule, sequence, and resource changes can be evaluated.

➤ Assign early-warning parameters that let the program inform you of potential trouble, including schedule problems, resource conflicts with other projects, and cost overruns.

➤ Integrate with material management, purchasing, and accounting systems to assist in ordering materials, supplies, equipment, and contractor services.

➤ Produce presentation-quality graphics for making reports to management and customers on the plans and status of a project.

➤ Display actual and planned data simultaneously.

➤ Summarize data in a variety of ways, including expenditures, timing, and activity data.

➤ Complete cost analyses, cost accounting, and variance analyses.

➤ Create free-format reports with an integrated word processor or other report generator for incorporating personalized project annotations.

So What's in It for Me?

One of the most powerful benefits of using software to assist in the implementation of project management methodology is the *what-if analysis* capabilities facilitated by interactive software products. Changes to the time estimates of individual tasks can be made and a new schedule is immediately displayed for review. The sequence in tasks can be changed and then put back the way they were, almost instantaneously. The same thing can be done with costs and resources. Imagine trying to do that with pencil and eraser. It would take hours. With a computer, it takes seconds!

To facilitate what-if analyses, many programs establish a separate, duplicate project database before changes are entered. The software then performs a comparative analysis and displays the new against the old project plan in tabular or graphical form. This makes it fast and easy for managers to review the impact of changes and come to better, more-informed conclusions.

Simple Versus Complex Projects and the Software They Need

If you manage your projects using manual techniques, you will probably limit yourself to Gantt charts and simple precedence or PERT networks. Early project management programs were also limited to these simple displays, because they used "character-based" graphics. The imprecise resolution of character-based project management graphics makes it hard to build projects and more difficult to view results.

For a project management software program to be considered for general business use today, it must facilitate interactive changes and support high-quality graphics.

Traditionally, project-driven organizations preferred mainframe software. Many of these mainframe programs offer desktop versions that can be integrated into a corporate-level project management system. Organizations that were less project-driven looked for less expensive, personal-computer software that was either networked or not, depending on the size and consistency desired in project management procedures.

The Types of Project Management

For purposes of easy classification, project management software products can be divided into four categories based on the functions and features they provide. These include *scheduling programs, single-project programs, corporate-level programs*, and *megaproject programs*. Let's take a closer look at each of these.

Scheduling Programs

Scheduling programs are relatively simple software products, typically designed for people who manage small projects with only a few team members. These programs usually produce Gantt charts and work in a fashion similar to spreadsheet programs like Microsoft Excel. There are a large number of these programs available for most common personal computers. They typically cost less than $200 and offer little, if any, ability to report on resources or budgets. These programs are usually limited to producing a small number of charts and reports. Some of the programs allow you to enter actual data to be displayed simultaneously with planned data, others do not.

Choose a scheduling program if your projects are very schedule-intensive but require minimal control of costs and resources. If your reporting requirements are simple and your projects are small, one of these programs can be very useful. The good ones are easy to learn, provide color display capabilities, and offer a variety of Gantt-charting symbols.

Single-Project Programs

A step up in sophistication from scheduling programs are full-featured software packages designed for managing single projects. These products are still relatively simple and easy to use, and their output is easy to understand. Most of them provide the ability to produce Gantt charts in a variety of formats, network diagrams (either PERT or precedence), and a number of standard reports. These programs sometimes offer simple resource management and cost control capabilities.

Single-project programs are best for projects with less than two hundred tasks. They provide only a limited analysis of the data, and since programs at this level often fail to provide automatic rescheduling based on specific resource changes, they are not useful for projects that require extensive staffing changes and what-if analyses. Programs in this category cost as little as $200, and are almost always less than $500.

Corporate-Level Programs

There are many programs in this category. Some of them are produced by well-known personal computer software companies like Microsoft, Computer Associates, Software

Publishing, and Symantec. Others are produced by companies that specialize in project management programs like Time Line, SMG, and Scitor. (Some companies and their products are listed in Appendix B; contact them for information.)

These corporate-level programs extend the features already discussed for the other two categories of software and many run on personal computers. Others run on minicomputers or graphics workstations, and their manufacturers often provide a personal-computer version for smaller projects. These programs typically allow sophisticated cost accounting, resource leveling, charting, and what-if analyses. The specific features vary considerably—as do their ease-of-use, flexibility, and reporting capabilities.

If you intend to regularly manage projects with one hundred or more tasks, or coordinate multiple projects, you need to start looking at software in this category. Some corporate-level programs offer a beginner's and an expert's mode that allow you to start out simple and add functions and capabilities as your project management skills develop.

Corporate-level programs range in price from $400 to over $3,000 for a single user. Network, multi-user, or minicomputer versions, when available, can be considerably more expensive. The most sophisticated programs in this category may offer add-on modules for contract control or specialized reporting functions that rival the capabilities of the megaproject programs designed for mainframes.

Megaproject Programs

Megaproject programs, which may or may not have more features than the most sophisticated desktop computer programs, are typically designed for minicomputers and mainframes. There may be a personal-computer version available that can share data with the mainframe program, but these PC-based versions are often difficult to use and lack the graphics sophistication of programs designed specifically for a personal computer. Some of the mainframe programs also lack the flexibility and interactive features of personal computer-based programs.

Megaproject programs can handle thousands of tasks and hundreds of resources. They almost always have sophisticated cost-accounting modules and resource-leveling functions. They are sometimes difficult to use and certainly difficult to install, but they offer advantages in processing speed and information exchange that are not available yet on personal computer networks. Most importantly, their success depends on a commitment from management to standardize on the program and use it consistently across projects.

Mainframe packages (with sophisticated accounting and cost analysis modules) are priced from $50,000 to $150,000—and that doesn't count the equipment, training, and other implementation costs for a complex system.

If your project management requirements include the management of thousands of tasks or complex multiple projects with shared resources, adherence to government contract specifications, and integration with corporate accounting and information systems, then these programs may be necessary. Such systems are designed for experienced project managers, and are not recommended unless they are absolutely required.

Choices and More Choices

As features and functions continue to be added to the less-sophisticated programs over time, the division between the types of programs is not as clear-cut as presented here. And with more than 200 different software packages available for project management, the evaluation and selection of software can become a tedious process. Use the following requirements checklist to identify the kind of features you must have in a project management program. This will help you narrow the choices down to a specific category of software.

For a more detailed report on project management software, write to the Project Management Institute, 130 South State Road, Upper Darby, PA 19082, tel. 610/734-3330, fax 610/734-3266; or visit their Web site at **http://www.pmi.org**. This organization produces a report that is updated regularly. You might want to join PMI at the same time, so you can continue to learn about new project management techniques, conferences, and facilities. The organization is geared toward professional, full-time project managers, but there are many members who join for the general contacts and ideas the institute provides.

Another source of information of project management programs are computer magazines. *MacWorld*, *MacUser*, *PC World*, *ComputerWorld*, and many others, available in bookstores and on newsstands, frequently run reviews of popular project management programs.

If you are looking for a mainframe or minicomputer program, or need a sophisticated corporate-level program for your division or company, you should look in your telephone book for consultants that specialize in project management systems. There are many consulting firms that can advise you in the selection of a program, help you install it, and train people after it is purchased.

How Do You Choose?

After you determine the category of software you need for your project management efforts, there are several critical factors for evaluating software you should consider before you make a purchase decision. Complete the following worksheet, then consider the factors in the following sections.

Cost/Feature Analysis

Prices for project management software vary greatly. Depending on the kinds of projects you intend to manage, study the features of products under consideration to match your requirements. The most expensive products are not always the most capable. On the other hand, unless your budget is heavily constrained, rule out programs that skimp on features just to save a few dollars. A product that lacks basic functionality results in frustration, because it won't do what you need it to. After a couple of poorly managed projects, you'll once again be out shopping for software.

Requirements Checklist for Project Management Software

Scheduling Programs

- [ ] Schedules
- [ ] Gantt Charts
- [ ] Presentation

Single-Projects Programs

- [ ] Network Diagrams
- [ ] Simple Resource Tracking
- [ ] Actual versus Planned Reports

Corporate-Level Programs

- [ ] Tracks Multiple Projects
- [ ] Internet/World Wide Web Publishing
- [ ] When-If Analysis
- [ ] Task Splitting
- [ ] Sub-Project Tracking
- [ ] Variance Reports
- [ ] More then 200 Tasks per Project
- [ ] More then 50 Resources per Project
- [ ] Multiple Operating Systems

- [ ] Email/Group/Network Communications
- [ ] Multiple Budget Types
- [ ] Reporting by Resource
- [ ] Reporting by Milestone
- [ ] Multiple Calenders
- [ ] PERT-Least to Most Likely Projections
- [ ] Integration with General Applications
- [ ] Resource Leveling
- [ ] Audit Trails

Mega-Project Programs

- [ ] Integration with Corporate Mainframe Programs
- [ ] Over 2,000 Tasks to Be Coordinated
- [ ] Government Requirements for a specific Program or Report
- [ ] Advanced Cost and resource Accounting

If you check boxes at more than one level, choose a product in the highest category checked.

As you evaluate different products, add features to your requirements list that you hadn't considered before studying the software options. Don't make the mistake of selecting a package simply because it has more features at its price than any other package. Consider the other factors we discuss later in this section—but do make sure there are enough features for your current needs and those in the foreseeable future.

If you have the opportunity to evaluate products before purchase (either at a dealer's showroom or through a demo disk or the company's Web site), try using the package to assemble the plan for a small project. That way you can test the package's reliability and see how it performs. Also check the program's speed when saving to disk, recalculating after new tasks are added, and printing efficiency. A program with a strong features set that takes all day to print a network diagram is probably not the one for you.

Once you select what appears to be the right product, try to purchase it from a source that allows you a 30-day money-back guarantee. That way, if the product performs poorly or ultimately doesn't fill the bill, you can return it and try something else. If you purchase software through mail order, use a credit card. You'll have more leverage returning the product because your credit card company may take your side.

```
┌─────────────────────────────────────────────────────┐
│  Project Management Software Selection Worksheet      │
│                                                       │
│  Product Name _____ Date _____ │
│                                                       │
│  Price: List Price $_____   Street Price $_____     │
│                                                       │
│  Dealer Name and Address _____ │
│ ┌───────────────────────────────────────────────────┐│
│ │ Rate each product from 1 to ten with 10 being the  ││
│ │ highest rating:                                     ││
│ │                                                     ││
│ │  Features  [    ]   Ease of Use [    ]  Flexibility [    ] ││
│ │                                                     ││
│ │  Compatibility [    ]   Documentation [    ]        ││
│ │                                                     ││
│ │  Reputation of the Manufacturer   [    ]            ││
│ │                                                     ││
│ │  Experience of Others with the Product  [    ]      ││
│ │                                                     ││
│ │  Technical Support [    ]  Training Availability [    ] ││
│ │  _____   ││
│ │  Overall Rating [    ]                              ││
│ └───────────────────────────────────────────────────┘│
│  Comments: _____  │
│            _____  │
│            _____  │
│            _____  │
│            _____  │
│            _____  │
└─────────────────────────────────────────────────────┘
```

Use this project management software selection worksheet to compare products and make the best choice for your needs.

When considering the cost of the software, don't forget the other system configuration requirements. Will the program work on your existing computer or do you need to buy new hardware? What about printers—is the software compatible with the types and models you plan to use? Do you need to add memory to your personal computer or a new monitor to take advantage of the features? If you need to upgrade your system or buy a new one, add these costs together and put them on the evaluation sheet.

Ease of Use and Consistency of the Interface

One of the most important aspects of choosing software for managing projects is to select a package that's easy to use and responds consistently throughout its interface. The easier the product is to use, the more likely you'll keep using it.

For example, if you choose the most feature-laden package, you may get a product with a number of menus, commands, dialog boxes, and cryptic functions that not only get in your way, but actively interfere with laying out and managing projects. While these are important functions for the professional project manager, unless you have four months to learn the package, it may get shelved and never used. Such a package forces you into overmanaging even comparatively simple projects, thereby negating its usefulness.

Flexibility to Adapt to Various Projects

Because projects in business vary from small to large and from simple to complex, you want a package that's flexible in how it adapts to various project requirements.

Compatibility with Other Programs

In many cases, you will want to take network diagrams and other project-oriented charts and combine them in other documents such as reports and presentation materials. If this is important to you, look for a package that can save or export images in a format compatible with the word processing, page layout, or presentation software you own or plan to acquire.

Documentation and Support for the Program

Your first point of reference when looking for a solution to a problem of learning how to use a product is the manual (whether online or printed in a book). Check the documentation and help menus carefully before purchase.

Study the documentation carefully. The information should be well organized, have a detailed index, and plenty of screen shots showing how the product works. A lengthy troubleshooting section doesn't hurt, either. Keyboard templates, quick reference cards, and disk-based sample projects are also useful. Complex products with skimpy manuals should be avoided at all costs.

The detailed Gantt charts produced by modern project management software let you see how your whole project unfolds. You can also change dates and let the computer do the hard scheduling calculations for you.

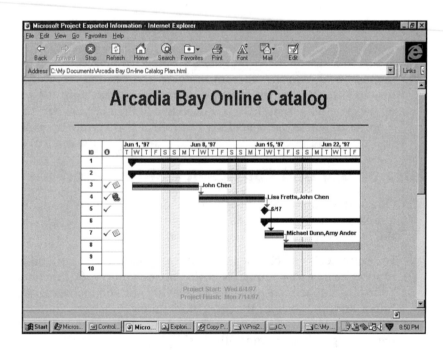

Reputation of the Product Manufacturer

If you are purchasing an expensive product that will get considerable day-to-day use, check up on the company that designed the product. If the company discontinues the product or closes its doors, you'll be on your own with the software. Look for a stable company with a strong track record of designing useful software and providing regular updates and bug fixes. Once a product becomes incompatible with the current version of your computer's operating system, project plans that could have been revamped for future use become unavailable if the software is not updated.

Word of Mouth Experiences

Talk to other users of a particular package to get feedback on how well the product performs with real-world projects. The users you query should use the package for projects similar in scope to the ones you plan to carry out. If calling references provided by the manufacturer, take anything less than a glowing tribute to mean that the product performs less adequately than expected.

Technical Support

When considering any software product, evaluate the technical support provided by the manufacturer. Find out if it's free or if you must pay an annual fee after 90 days or a per-use fee after a certain number of calls. Do they provide a toll-free number, or must you listen to an automatic telephone system recite a long list of options before connecting you to a technician at your expense? Dial the number and see what happens. Check out the technical support information on their Web site. If you're fortunate enough to have other users to ask for recommendations, query them on the quality of technical support.

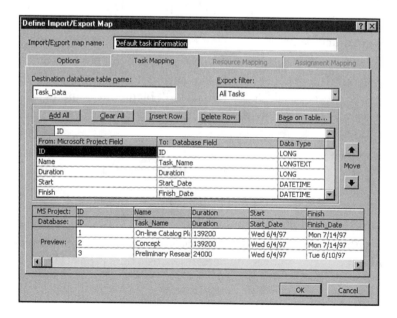

Software makes creating network diagrams a breeze. And you can easily update precedence and task relationships as the project proceeds.

Software makes creating network diagrams a breeze. And you can easily update precedence and task relationships as the project proceeds.

So, which computerized tool is best for you? The one that meets your feature requirements, with the most flexibility, with an acceptable learning curve, from a reliable and supportive vendor, at a price you can afford. (This is pretty much the standard formula for choosing any software or computer product, not just project management software.)

Things Project Management Software Can't Do

As powerful and efficient as project management programs are, many aspects of the project management process are not within the computer's realm. Using computer-assisted project management streamlines administration, reporting, and analysis, but the following are things the computer can't and shouldn't be allowed to do:

➤ *Project management software can't gather data.* You'll have to decide how much and what type of information you need to manage the project. You or members of your team will still need to gather data regarding the project status, as described in Chapter 21. The computer only helps compute and display the information after it is gathered and entered.

➤ *Project management software can't make decisions.* The computer can make it easier and faster to look at alternatives, but it is ultimately you and your project team who will have to make the choice between the alternatives and take responsibility for the decisions.

➤ *Project management software can't solve problems that require subjective judgments.* Sometimes human intuition is the most important ingredient in project management, especially when dealing with people. People require understanding. Software is programmed and not intuitive. It only reports back what you put into it. You still have to manage the conflicts, solve the problems, and use your own judgment.

➤ *Project management software can't find the errors in your input.* If you put biased, incomplete, or erroneous data into the project management program, it will output biased, incomplete, and erroneous project reports. Don't blame the computer for human error. The best way to eliminate this problem is to check the reports and entries a couple of times before they are distributed.

➤ *Project management software can't do your communication for you.* Software is great at producing reports that look good and contain a wealth of detailed information, but there is more to reporting on a project than sending out the report. You still need to communicate with people face to face, build interfaces between people and departments, and listen to what is going on around you.

➤ *Project management software won't save money by reducing the need for project personnel.* Automation almost never really reduces the personnel costs on a project. The software can make you more efficient and make decision-making more effective because the information is better, but project management software will not significantly reduce the need for project management people.

Go Get Yourself Some!

Now you have been introduced to the features for selecting project management software for your needs. Start talking to store personnel, reading computer magazines, and asking friends and colleagues about the programs they use. Then go out, select a program, and get started in computer-assisted project management. Follow the step-by-step guidelines for implementing the project management process you have read about. As your projects come in on time and within budget, you will have achieved membership in the league of successful project managers—and the opportunities available to you and your company will take on new perspective. With each success, you will contribute to the business, the economy, and your own career—no mean feat for just learning a few project management skills. Go for it!

The Least You Need to Know

➤ There are project management programs for projects of all sizes and complexities that run on most common personal computers.

➤ To get the most benefit from its features, choose your project management software carefully.

➤ No software program can replace the communication, negotiating, assessment, and other management skills required to manage a project.

Project Lingo—A Glossary of Project Terms

action plan   A plan that describes what needs to be done and when it needs to be completed. Project plans are action plans.

activity   A specific project task that requires resources and time to complete.

activity-on-arc (AOA) or **activity-on-node (AON)**   The two ways of documenting and drawing a network: placing the activities on the arcs or on the nodes.

answer-back diagram   If a process is highly technical, involves creative effort, or is large or complex in scale, an answer-back diagram can help. In an answer-back diagram, the vendor takes your specs and builds a simple model that demonstrates (or doesn't) a clear understanding of your project specifications.

arc   The line connecting two nodes or representing precedence in a PERT or CPM network.

audit   A formal and detailed examination of the progress, costs, operations, results, or some other aspect of a project or system.

baseline plan   The initial approved plan to which deviations will be compared as the project proceeds.

bill of materials   The formal documentation of the complete set of physical elements required to build a product, which is used by the project manager or purchasing department to order any material or supplies that are required.

budget decrement   A reduction in the amount of money available for a project task or activity.

buying the job   When a vendor bids at a loss to blow away the competition and get the work, it's called buying the job. An unusually low quote amidst a pile of higher but nearly identical quotes is either a "bought" job or the effort of a vendor who doesn't know what he's doing. Before you accept the low bid, make sure you know which it is.

champion   A person who takes on personal responsibility (though not usually day-to-day management) for the successful completion of a "visionary project" or creative change in an organization. It may involve a product launch, an innovation in process, or any type of project.

confidence level   A level of confidence, stated as a percentage, for a budget or schedule estimate. The higher the confidence level, the lower the risk.

conflict   Sounding like something worked out via fisticuffs, a project conflict is one in which people, priorities, or problems (the three "Ps") begin to interfere with completing a project on time and within budget.

consultant   Here's the old joke that defines consultants (more true than it should be): A consultant is an unemployed person who has a watch and a briefcase. Make sure the consultants on your project have better credentials than this.

contingency plan   An alternative for action if things don't go as planned or if an expected result fails to materialize. See *padding*.

control   A process for assuring that reality or actual performance meets expectations or plans. Control often involves the process of keeping actions within limits by making adjustments to a plan to assure that certain outcomes will happen.

cost-benefit analysis   An analysis, often stated as a ratio, used to evaluate a proposed course of action.

crash   Conducting a task at an abnormally accelerated pace to meet a deadline. Crashing is completed at a greater cost than a normally paced task or project.

critical activity   An activity or event that, if delayed, will delay some other important event, commonly the completion of a project or a major milestone in a project.

critical path   The sequence of tasks that determine the minimum schedule for a project. If one task on the critical path is delayed, the schedule will be late.

Critical Path Method (CPM)   One of the two most common forms of networking systems. CPM uses a one-time estimate for creating a project schedule. See *Project Evaluation and Review Technique (PERT)*.

critical ratio   A ratio that measures an important characteristic. This ration is often plotted or tracked in some way to determine priorities among items or events.

cross-check   One of the best tests of completion, be it doors in an airliner or the workability of a project plan, is to cross-check it. To cross-check a plan, one person lists a procedure and another verifies it. With two independent bodies carefully verifying the plan, chances for error are much smaller.

Decision Support System (DSS)   A sophisticated computer program to assist managers in making decisions. It may include simulation programs, mathematical programming routines, and decision rules.

deliverables   The clearly defined results, goods, or services produced during the project or at its outcome. Deliverables and goals are often synonymous. Deliverables, like goals, may include organizational attributes, reports, and plans, as well as physical products or objects.

dependency diagram   Another name for a network or precedence diagram that shows the dependencies (precedence) among tasks.

duration   The period of time over which a task takes place, in contrast to effort, which is the amount of labor hours a task requires. Duration establishes the schedule for a project. Effort establishes the labor costs. Each task in a project has a duration, usually specified in work days or portions of work days, that may or may not be different than the amount of effort (or labor) required to complete the task.

early warning system   A monitoring system that provides advance notification or indication of potential problems in a project. Many computerized project management systems incorporate early warning functions.

effectiveness   A measure of the quality of attainment in meeting objectives; to be distinguished from efficiency, which is measured by the volume of output achieved for the input used.

effort   The amount of work or labor (in hours or work days) required to complete a task. Effort is used to establish the labor costs associated with a project. Effort is in contrast to duration, which is the span of time over which the effort takes place. (See *duration* for more information.)

element   See *subtask*.

evaluate   To appraise or determine the value of information, resources, or options being provided to you as a project manager.

event   In CPM and PERT networks, the end state for one or more activities that occurs at a specific point in time.

extinction   The end of all activity on a project, usually before meeting its state objectives. The end results of a project terminated by extinction are neither terminated by inclusion nor integration.

facilitator   A person who makes it easier for other people to accomplish objectives by offering advice and assistance in solving problems, either with technical issues or with other people. Project managers are often referred to as facilitators.

float   The amount of time for a task to be freely scheduled without affecting other tasks in a project. Also, the difference between the duration available for a task and the duration required to complete it. Float is also known as slack or slack time.

functional management   The standard departments of a business organization that represent individual disciplines such as engineering, marketing, purchasing, and accounting.

Gantt chart   A chart that uses timelines and other symbols to illustrate multiple, time-based activities or projects on a horizontal time scale.

go/no-go indicator   A level of measurement that quickly tells a reviewer if an object's dimension is within certain limits. In the case of project management, this can be any monitoring or observation that allows a manager to decide whether to change, terminate, or continue an activity or a project.

hierarchical planning   A planning approach where each managerial level breaks planning tasks down into the activities that must be done at that level. Typically, upper-level planning establishes the objectives for the next lower-level manager's planning.

inclusion   A way of terminating a project by incorporating the project operations and team into the organization as an ongoing entity. The project work still exists, but the project is no longer separate from the business operations.

integration   A way of terminating a project by bringing project team members back into the organization and distributing project results and outcomes among existing functions. The project as an entity no longer exists after integration.

interface management   Managing the problems that often occur between people, departments, and disciplines, rather than within the project team itself.

interfaces   The formal and informal boundaries and relationships between people, departments, organizations, or functions.

lag   The amount of time after one task is started or finished before the next task can be started or finished.

lateral communication   When information exchange occurs across lines of equivalent authority or between managers at the same level in an organization's hierarchy.

lead   The amount of time that precedes the start of work on another task.

Material Requirements Planning (MRP)   An approach for material planning and ordering based on known or forecast demand requirements, lead times for obtaining each item, and existing inventories of all items.

matrix organization   An organizational structure that uses functional supervisors as well as project supervisors to manage the same people, depending on the assignment. A strong matrix is similar to a pure project organization, while a weak matrix operates more like a functional organization.

milestone   A clearly identifiable point in a project that summarizes the completion of a related or important set of tasks. Milestones are commonly used to summarize the important events in a project for managers and stakeholders who don't want or need to see the details in a project plan.

mixed organization   This organizational structure includes both functional groups, pure project groups, and perhaps a matrixed group in its hierarchy. It is similar to a matrix organization.

model   A way of looking at reality, usually for the purpose of abstracting and simplifying it to make it understandable in a particular context. A plan is a type of model used to describe how a project will be completed.

network diagram   The logical representation of tasks that defines the sequence of work in a project. Networks are usually drawn from left to right, with lines drawn between tasks to indicate the precedences among tasks. On a large project, several network diagrams may exist: one for the overall project based on the project milestones, and one each for each subproject that represents the completion of a milestone.

one-on-ones   Meetings (often scheduled and formal) between two people involved in a project. These meetings are used to discuss priorities, resolve issues, and communicate overall responsibilities and statuses on a project.

padding   A standard project management tactic used to add a little extra time or money to estimates to cover for the uncertainty and risk in trying to see into the future. Also a type of contingency planning. Too much padding can get you into trouble. Padding of 15 to 25 percent is probably the most you should ever use. If you need more than this to feel comfortable with your plan, you need help with the estimates from experts or more experienced managers.

path   A sequence of lines and nodes in a project network.

Project Evaluation and Review Technique (PERT)   One of the two most common forms of networking systems. PERT uses three time estimates to determine the most probable project completion time. See *Critical Path Method (CPM)*.

Project Management Institute (PMI)   A professional organization that studies and promotes project management techniques. If you want to join PMI to learn more about project management, contact information is provided in Appendix B.

political situation   Two or more people in a room trying to get something done. This means projects always have a political dimension.

portfolio   A group of projects or other items that are being worked on at the same time or that have been completed and are used as an indicator of ability.

precedence   When one task must be completed before another task can be started, the first task is said to have precedence over the other.

pro forma   Projected or anticipated, usually applied to financial data such as balance sheets and income statements.

project   A project is a sequence of tasks with a beginning and an end that uses time and resources to produce specific results. A project has a specific, desired outcome, a deadline or target date when the project must be done, and a budget that limits the amount of people, supplies, and money that can be used to complete the project.

project duration   The time it takes to complete the entire project, from starting the first task to finishing the last task.

project management   The combination of systems, techniques, and people required to successfully complete a project on time and within budget.

Project Management Information System (PMIS)   A system used to chart activities and data and to track progress and information flow in a project that is most frequently computerized, but not always.

project management process   The five phases of initiation, planning, executing, controlling, and closing that can help people bring projects in on time and within budget.

project manager   Any person who takes overall responsibility for coordinating a project, regardless of size, to make sure the desired end result comes in on time and within budget.

project murder   The sudden termination of a project for reasons that range from rational to absurd. An attempt on a project's life may take place during economic downturns, acquisition of the parent organization, or something entirely unexpected—in the case of a well-known computer map-making program, the unexpected death of its visionary founder sunk a hot new project the next day. A knife in a project's back may lead to not only angry team members, but possible lawsuits.

resource leveling   The process of shifting the use of resources to even out the workload of team members and equipment. If, in your ideal plan, Joe is required to work 86 hours a week on the project, you'll need to find other resources that can take on part of Joe's workload and adjust the schedule accordingly. Computer programs can help do this for you. Be aware, however—that resource leveling will likely cause changes in the network diagram, budget, or timing of a project.

resource loading   The time individual resources (people, vendors, and so on) have committed to a project. A team member or other resource who has a large block of time committed to the project can't work on other projects. If the load exceeds his or her work week, you'll have to pay overtime or add resources.

risk analysis   An evaluation of the feasibility or probability that the outcome of a project or policy will be the desired one. Usually conducted to compare two or more alternative scenarios, action plans, or policies.

rush charges   Charges that are applied by outside vendors when you, well, rush them. If at all possible, avoid incurring rush charges through the techniques described in this book.

scope   The magnitude of the effort required to complete a project. As you would rightly assume, the project scope for bringing a new toy airplane to market is much smaller than a project for designing a new attack jet.

situational management   The approach of matching management style to the specific needs of a situation. Project managers must effectively apply the best management style for the job—whether task-oriented, employee-oriented, or reward-oriented leadership—to meet the needs of individual team members.

slack   See *float.*

split   Dividing a task into two or more tasks.

stakeholders   People who have a personal or enterprise interest in the end results of a project. Not all stakeholders are involved in completing the actual work on a project. Common stakeholders include customers, managers, corporate executives, and representatives of government agencies.

standard task unit   An agreed-upon description and amount of effort for a common task that is used in multiple projects.

Statement Of Work (SOW)   An integrated set of task descriptions, goal descriptions, risks, and assumptions that accompany the evolving master project plan during its development. When completed, the SOW will detail the work to be completed on a project and the contingencies for dealing with known risk factors.

subcontract   Delegating tasks or subprojects to contractors or to other organizations.

suboptimization   The optimization of one component of a system or project, such as task sequence or schedule, often to the detriment of the overall plan or project.

subproject   A portion of the whole project that can be viewed as a project in its own right. An example would be building the new Trip to Jupiter ride (a subproject) within the project to build a new Disneyland theme park in Africa.

subtask   A portion of the complete task. For example, the task might be to write the articles for a newsletter, while a subtask might be to write the lead article for the newsletter.

systems approach   A wide-ranging method for addressing problems that considers multiple and interacting relationships. This approach is often contrasted with the analytic approach. Project management is a systems approach to managing projects.

task   A cohesive unit of work on a project—one that's not too big or too small to be tracked. A task may include several steps (or subtasks) that are conceptually related.

task description   A description that defines all the work required to accomplish a project activity, including inputs, outputs, and quality specifications.

termination team   A project team responsible for wrapping up the administrative details of a project.

trade-off   Allowing one aspect to change, usually for the worse, in return for another aspect of a project getting better.

win-win negotiation   When both parties are better off after a negotiation has been completed.

Work Breakdown Structure (WBS)   A basic project diagram or listing that documents and describes all the work that must be done to complete the project. The WBS forms the basis for costing, scheduling, network diagramming, and work assignments.

Resources for Project Managers

The following companies sell or distribute project management software. This is by no means a comprehensive list. There are many other companies and products out there, with more being added every day. The companies listed here have either products that we have worked with or that have been recently reviewed in computer literature. A listing in this book should not be considered a testimonial for the functionality or suitability of any of these products—it is only provided to get you started in your search for project management software. Most, but not all, of the products listed are corporate-level programs or above. Note that all product and company names are trademarks and registered trademarks of the respective companies.

Company	Project Management Products
Ballantine & Company, Inc. P.O. Box 805 Carlisle, MA 01741 Telephone: (508) 369-1772 Fax: (508) 369-9179 Web site: www.ballantine-inc.com	QuickGantt
Claris Corporation P.O. Box 526 Santa Clara, CA 95052 Telephone: (408) 727-8227 Web site: www.claris.com	MacProject (purchase through retail stores)
Microsoft Corporation One Microsoft Way Redmond, WA 98052-6399 Telephone: (206) 882-8080 Web site: www.microsoft.com	Microsoft Project, Microsoft Schedule (purchase through retail stores)

Company	Project Management Products
Scitor Corporation Business Solutions Group 333 Middlefield Rd., flr. 2 Menlo Park, CA 94025 Telephone: (650) 462-4200 Fax: (650) 462-4201 Web site: www.scitor.com	Project Scheduler and others
Time Line Solutions Corporation 7200 Redwood Blvd., Suite 300 Novato, CA 94945 Telephone: (800) 222-TLSC or (415) 898-1919 Fax: (415) 898-0177 Web site: www.tlsolutions.com	On Target, Time Line, and others

Company	Management Training Tool
Strategic Management Group, Inc. (SMG) 3624 Market St. University City Science Center Philadelphia, PA 19104 Telephone: (800) 582-4060 or (215) 387-4000 Fax: (215) 387-3653 Web site: www.smginc.com	Understanding Project Management (CD-ROM)

Project Mangement Institute
130 South State Road
Upper Darby, PA 19082
Web site: www.pmi.org

Project Management Institute (PMI) is a non-profit organization dedicated to the advancement of project management methodology and the training of project managers. The quarterly *Project Mangement Journal*, published by PMI, includes timely articles about project mangement procedures, experiences, and techniques. The institute holds regular seminars and meetings for members. As of this writing, the membership fee is $80 per year. A subscription to *Project Management Journal* and *PM Network* is included as part of the membership fee.

Index

Q-R